PRO TOOLS® 101:

AN INTRODUCTION TO PRO TOOLS 10

Frank D. Cook

Course Technology PTR

A part of Cengage Learning

COURSE TECHNOLOGY
CENGAGE Learning®

Australia, Brazil, Japan, Korea, Mexico, Singapore, Spain, United Kingdom, United States

COURSE TECHNOLOGY
CENGAGE Learning®

Pro Tools® 101:
An Introduction to Pro Tools 10
Frank D. Cook

Publisher and General Manager,
Course Technology PTR:
Stacy L. Hiquet

Associate Director of Marketing:
Sarah Panella

Manager of Editorial Services:
Heather Talbot

Marketing Manager:
Mark Hughes

Acquisitions Editor:
Orren Merton

Project and Copy Editor:
Cathleen D. Small

Interior Layout:
Shawn Morningstar

Cover Designer:
Avid Technology, Mike Tanamachi

DVD-ROM Producer:
Avid Technology, Brandon Penticuff

Indexer:
Larry Sweazy

Proofreader:
Mike Beady

For product information and technology assistance, contact us at
Cengage Learning Customer & Sales Support, 1-800-354-9706

For permission to use material from this text or product,
submit all requests online at **cengage.com/permissions**
Further permissions questions can be emailed to
permissionrequest@cengage.com

Digidesign, M-Audio, Pro Tools, VENUE, Sibelius, and all related product names and logos are registered trademarks of Avid Technology, Inc. in the United States and/or other countries. Glad® is a registered trademark of The Glad Products Company. Used with permission. The Glad® image is ©2009 The Glad Products Company. Reprinted with permission.

All other trademarks are the property of their respective owners. All images ©Avid Technology, Inc. unless otherwise noted. The media provided with this book, and accompanying course material, is to be used only to complete the exercises contained herein. Rights are not granted to use the footage/sound materials in any commercial or non-commercial production or video. All product features and specifications are subject to change without notice.

PT101, Version 10.0
PN: 9900-65037-00
Library of Congress Control Number: 2011940778
ISBN-13: 978-1-133-77655-0
ISBN-10: 1-133-77655-8

Course Technology, a part of Cengage Learning
20 Channel Center Street
Boston, MA 02210 USA

Cengage Learning is a leading provider of customized learning solutions with office locations around the globe, including Singapore, the United Kingdom, Australia, Mexico, Brazil, and Japan. Locate your local office at:
international.cengage.com/region

Cengage Learning products are represented in Canada by Nelson Education, Ltd.

For your lifelong learning solutions, visit **courseptr.com.**

Visit our corporate Web site at **cengage.com.**

Printed in China
5 6 7 13

This book is dedicated to musicians, sound designers, audio editors, mixing engineers, and Pro Tools enthusiasts everywhere—industry leaders of the future.

Acknowledgments

The following individuals have provided critical assistance, input, information, and material for this book and its many editions over the years.

Avid/Digidesign (current and former): Alex Steinhart, Andy Cook, Andy Hagerman, Anthony Gordon, Chandra Lynn, Cheryl Panepinto, Chris Now, Christopher Woodland, Dave Lebolt, Don Falcone, Eric Kuehnl, Greg Robles, Jim Metzendorf, John Given, Ken Johnson, Mark Altin, Mark Jeffery, Paul Foeckler, Rachelle McKenzie, Scott Church, Simon Sherbourne, Tim Carroll, Tim Mynett, Tom Dambly

Amanda Goodroe, DDB San Francisco

Frank Brooks, DDB San Francisco

Joe Kay, Independent Pro Tools Consultant

Joel Krantz, Independent Pro Tools Consultant

Rob Campbell at Encompass Audio

Special Thanks

Special thanks to Cathleen Small for diligently editing the manuscript and to Shawn Morningstar for updating the layout.

Extra-Special Thanks

Kudos and extra-special thanks to all Avid Learning Partners and certified instructors, who have tirelessly worked with us to help shape this program and who have generously provided their valuable feedback for our courseware.

About the Author

The courseware for this book was developed by **Frank D. Cook**, with contributions from numerous Avid staff and independent contractors. The book is published through an ongoing partnership between Insource Writing Solutions and Avid Technology, Inc.

Frank is a bass guitarist and longtime Pro Tools user. The owner of Insource Writing Solutions and NextPoint Training, Frank has worked in the technical publications and education industries for more than 15 years. As a writer, editor, technical publications manager, and business owner, Frank has authored and contributed to hundreds of guides, manuals, reports, textbooks, and other publications for clients in a wide variety of industries. His writing and consulting company, Insource Writing Solutions, specializes in documentation for the digital audio industry. His training venture, NextPoint Training, focuses on advanced training in Pro Tools, VENUE, digital media, and related products and technologies.

Frank has been a consultant for Digidesign/Avid for the past six years, helping to define the strategy and to develop curriculum for Avid's official training and certification programs. Frank also teaches Pro Tools courses as an adjunct professor at American River College in Sacramento, California, and is an Avid Master Instructor.

Contents

Exercise 1   Pro Tools Hardware   32

Lesson 2
Getting Inside Pro Tools   35

Exercise 2   The Software Interface   75

PART II
Working with Sessions   81

Lesson 3
Creating Your First Session   83

Exercise 3   Creating a Session   102

Lesson 4
Making Your First Audio Recording   107

Lesson 5
Importing and Working with Media in a Session 125

Exercise 4   Importing Audio 140

Lesson 6
Making Your First MIDI Recording 143

Lesson 7
Selecting and Navigating   175

Exercise 5   Configuring the Session and Adding Memory Locations   201

Lesson 8   Basic Editing Techniques   205

Exercise 6   Editing Audio   237

Lesson 9
Basic Mixing Techniques   241

PART III
Hands-On Projects   291

Overview
Project Introduction and Setup   293

Project 1
Music Hands-On Project   297

Project 2
Post Hands-On Project   333

PART IV
Course Completion Information and Appendixes   363

Information for Course Completion   365

Appendix A
Avid Pro Tools Plug-Ins   369

Appendix B
Creative Collection Plug-Ins   373

Index   375

Introduction

Welcome to Pro Tools 101

Congratulations on entering the official Avid training program. This book represents the first step on your journey toward mastery of your Pro Tools system. The information, exercises, and projects you will find here apply to all Pro Tools 10 systems. Whether you are interested only in self study or you would like to pursue formal certification through an Avid Learning Partner, this book will develop your core skills and introduce you to the awesome power of Pro Tools. Avid's award-winning Pro Tools technology is embraced by audio production professionals around the world. Get ready to join their ranks as you unleash the creative power and technology of Pro Tools!

About This Book

This book is designed for the audio enthusiast with relatively little Pro Tools experience. While *Pro Tools 101* can be completed through self study, Avid recommends obtaining hands-on experience through an instructor-led class offered by one of our authorized training partners. For more information on the classes offered through the Avid Learning Partner program, visit www.avid.com, click on Support & Services, and then click on a Training link, or go directly to www.avid.com/training.

Pro Tools 10.0 Edition

This edition of *Pro Tools 101* has been updated and improved for Pro Tools 10.0. The material is focused to cover the basic principles you need to understand to complete a Pro Tools project, from initial setup to final mixdown. Whether your project involves recording live instruments, preparing MIDI sequences for virtual instruments, looping and beat-matching audio files, or editing notation and preparing scores, *Pro Tools 101* will teach you the steps required to succeed.

The DVD at the Back of the Book

Included at the back of this book is a DVD-ROM containing media files for the *Pro Tools 101* exercises and hands-on projects. The DVD also contains various Pro Tools videos and video tutorials.

Supplemental Exercises

The Exercise Media folder on the DVD provides audio files for the eight exercises included in Parts I and II of this book. The Completed Exercises folder provides session files of each completed exercise for reference.

Hands-On Projects

The Hands-On Projects folder on the DVD provides content for two projects included in Part III of this book. The Music Hands-On Project folder includes a session template file and associated media for Project 1, and the Post Hands-On Project folder includes a session template file and associated media for Project 2. These project folders can be copied to your hard drive for use with Pro Tools.

Projects for Older Systems

The Projects for Older Systems folder on the DVD provides media and session templates compatible with older systems (Pro Tools 7–9) for readers who have not yet upgraded to Pro Tools 10. It also includes PDF files of instructions for completing the Hands-On Projects on a Pro Tools 9 system.

Video Extras

The Video Extras folder on the DVD includes various Pro Tools video files that provide an introduction to some of the new features in Pro Tools 10.

Also included in this folder are collections of older tutorial videos covering popular virtual instruments, Elastic Audio features, and production techniques.

These video files are provided in a high-resolution format (1280×720). For best playback results, you should copy the files to a local hard drive prior to viewing them.

Course Prerequisites

Most Pro Tools enthusiasts today have at least a passing familiarity with operating a computer. If you consider yourself a computer novice, however, you should review some basics before beginning this course. You will need to know how to complete such tasks as:

- Starting up the computer
- Using the mouse, standard menus, and keyboard commands for standard operating system commands
- Locating, moving, and renaming files and folders
- Opening, saving, and closing files

This course focuses on using Pro Tools in a digital audio recording and production environment. The work requires a basic understanding of recording techniques, processes, and equipment, such as the following:

- Miking techniques
- Mixer signal flow
- Audio monitoring equipment
- MIDI devices

If you are a beginner in the field of audio production, you can supplement this text with independently available literature or courses on audio recording tools and techniques. Visit your local bookstore, library, or community college to research available study materials and courses.

Course Organization and Sequence

This course has been designed to familiarize you with the practices and processes you will use to complete a recording project. The material is organized into four parts. Part I provides background information that will help you understand the material that is presented later and put it into context. Part II presents specific processes and techniques that you would use to complete a project, from creating a new session to completing a final mixdown. Part III provides tutorial-style walk-throughs of various tasks required to complete two hands-on projects using the media included on the enclosed DVD. Part IV, to be completed at any Avid Learning Partner location, includes information on additional projects and course completion options.

Part I: Background Information

Part I focuses primarily on background information relevant to Pro Tools and audio production. This part builds a foundation for using Pro Tools by introducing concepts of digital audio, Pro Tools hardware configurations, Pro Tools session file structures, and the Pro Tools user interface and tool set.

Part II: Working with Sessions

Part II provides information and instructions for working with Pro Tools sessions to accomplish common audio production tasks. This part discusses creating sessions, creating audio and MIDI recordings, navigating within audio and MIDI recordings, and editing and mixing using Pro Tools.

Part III: Hands-On Projects

Part III is designed to provide you with experience applying the concepts of Part II. Two projects have been selected to represent typical scenarios and workflows encountered in music and post-production environments. The project instructions follow roughly the same progression as the chapters in Part II. The instructions are written to allow students to complete the projects without having first completed Part II, enabling a hands-on learning experience that draws on Part II as a reference.

Part IV: Course Completion

Part IV of the Pro Tools 101 course can be completed in an instructor-led environment at an authorized Pro Tools training center. In this part of the course, students have the opportunity to work on additional projects using a variety of Pro Tools hardware and software components.

Conventions and Symbols Used in This Book

Following are some of the conventions and symbols we use in this book. We've tried to use familiar conventions and symbols whose meanings are self-evident.

Menu choices and keyboard commands are typically capitalized. Hierarchy is shown using the greater than symbol (>), keystroke combinations are indicated using the plus sign (+), and mouse-click operations are indicated by hyphenated strings, where needed. Brackets ([ ]) are used to indicate key presses on the numeric keypad.

Convention	Action
File > Save Session	Choose Save Session from the File menu.
Ctrl+N	Hold down the Ctrl key and press the N key.
Command-click (Mac)	Hold down the Command key and click the mouse button.
Right-click	Click with the right mouse button.
Press [1]	Press 1 on the numeric keypad.

The Avid Learning Partner Program

Pro Tools 101 has been written as a textbook for teaching and learning Pro Tools. In addition to being an off-the-shelf guide for consumers, this book is also the official text for the first course in Avid's Pro Tools certification program. By completing the coursework in this text, you are taking an important step toward certification. And consider this: Having a certification from Avid just might help you land that next gig, find others with similar skills and interests, or even obtain your dream job in the industry.

To become certified in Pro Tools, you must enroll in a program at an Avid Learning Partner location, where you can complete additional Pro Tools coursework and take one of Avid's Certification Exams. Detailed information on current requirements is available at avid.com/training.

Curriculum and Certification Levels

Avid offers three levels of certification associated with Pro Tools Training: Pro Tools User, Pro Tools Operator, and Pro Tools Expert. The 100-, 200-, and 300-level Pro Tools courses are designed to prepare candidates for each of these certification levels, respectively.

User Certification

The User certification program prepares individuals to operate a Pro Tools system in an independent production environment. Courses associated with User certification include Pro Tools 101, *Introduction to Pro Tools*, and Pro Tools 110, *Pro Tools Production I*. These core courses can be complemented with Pro Tools 130, *Pro Tools for Game Audio*.

Operator Certification

The Operator certification program prepares engineers and editors to competently operate a Pro Tools system in a professional environment. Candidates can specialize in Music Production, Post-Production, or both.

Courses associated with Operator certification include Pro Tools 201, *Pro Tools Production II*, Pro Tools 210M, *Music Production Techniques*, and Pro Tools 210P, *Post Production Techniques*. Control surface certification options and a live sound certification option are also available at the Operator level.

Expert Certification

The Expert curriculum offers professionals the highest level of proficiency with individual or networked Pro Tools systems operating in a professional, fast-paced environment. Candidates can specialize in Music Production, Post-Production, and/or ICON worksurface techniques.

Courses associated with Expert certification include Pro Tools 310M, *Advanced Music Production Techniques*, Pro Tools 310P, *Advanced Post Production Techniques*, and Pro Tools 310I, *Advanced ICON Techniques*.

Courses Offered in the Training Program

Avid Learning Partners offer three levels of coursework to help you become proficient using Pro Tools: 100-level, 200-level, and 300-level.

- 100-level Pro Tools courses provide the foundational skills needed to learn and function within the Pro Tools environment at a basic level. The goal of the courses at this level is to help individuals start working on their own projects in Pro Tools.

  The 100-level VENUE coursework covers essential skills for operating a VENUE system in a live sound environment.

- 200-level courses build the fundamental skills needed to competently operate a Pro Tools HD system, control surface, or VENUE system in a professional environment. Pro Tools coursework at this level involves a study of production essentials and post-production, music production, or control surface techniques.

  VENUE coursework at the 200-level involves comprehensive hands-on training on a VENUE system, including system hardware and software configuration.

- 300-level courses focus on advanced operation of Pro Tools systems for music or post-production. Coursework involves working in real-world scenarios through example exercises from advanced music production projects (Music Production track), TV and film production projects (Post-Production track), or direct hands-on worksurface techniques (ICON Worksurface track).

Avid Course Configuration

The coursework for the Avid Learning Partner program has evolved and expanded over the years. Avid uses a version-specific approach to course design, enabling authorized training partners to teach classes based on products and software versions that meet their particular needs and training environments.

Audio Curriculum

Avid's audio coursework includes programs supporting certification in dedicated focus areas, including Pro Tools, Worksurface Operation, and Live Sound.

Available Pro Tools certification paths are illustrated below. Course components are designed to be completed individually and in sequence. However, individual training partners may offer the same content through slightly different class configurations.

Descriptions of each of the courses offered through the Avid Learning Partner Program are available on the Avid website. (Go to www.avid.com/US/support/training/curriculum.)

Figure FM.1
Avid audio certification options

Pro Tools User Certification

Pro Tools 101 is the first course of study in the training curriculum targeting User certification. The User certification training materials (100-level coursework) prepare students to operate a Pro Tools system in an independent production environment. Following completion of the User certification coursework and certification exam, students can proceed to the 200-level courses to pursue Operator certification.

How Can I Learn More?

If you want to learn more about Avid training, please check out the official online resource by going to www.avid.com/training. There you will find information about training partners, specifics on the various certification options available, and detailed course descriptions for each course offered through the program.

DVD-ROM Downloads

If you purchased an ebook version of this book, and the book had a companion DVD-ROM, you may download the contents from www.courseptr.com/downloads. Please note that you will be redirected to the Cengage Learning site.

If your book has a DVD-ROM, please check our website for any updates or errata files. You may download files from www.courseptr.com/downloads. Please note that you will be redirected to the Cengage Learning site.

Background Information

OVERVIEW

Part I focuses on background information relevant to Pro Tools and audio production. Lesson 1 builds a foundation for using Pro Tools by introducing Pro Tools' capabilities in audio, MIDI, notation, mixing, and video post-production; providing a brief history of Pro Tools systems; introducing concepts of digital audio; and providing an overview of available Pro Tools configurations. Lesson 2 introduces basic Pro Tools operations and functions, reviews the Pro Tools session file structure, and provides an overview of the Pro Tools user interface, tool set, and modes of operation.

COMPONENTS

Getting to Know Pro Tools

This lesson introduces you to Pro Tools' capabilities in audio, MIDI, mixing, and video post-production. You will learn about the evolution of Pro Tools technology and get an introduction to factors that affect digital audio and analog-to-digital conversion. You will also get a glimpse of what's new in Pro Tools 10.0 and learn about the different Pro Tools configurations available today.

Duration: 90 Minutes

GOALS

- Identify the advantages of recording and editing in the digital realm
- Recognize the contributions of historical developments in sampling and sound editing, MIDI technology, computer I/O, and recording technology to today's digital audio workstation
- Describe the relationship between sample rate and frequency response in digital audio
- Describe the relationship between bit depth and dynamic range in digital audio
- Recognize components and features of various Pro Tools systems

What Is Pro Tools?

Pro Tools is the most widely used application for music and post-production (sound for film, video, and multimedia) in the world today, integrating capabilities in audio and MIDI recording, composition, editing, and mixing, as well as support for desktop video. As such, Pro Tools software empowers both music and post-production professionals to easily achieve all of their production tasks within one easy-to-use interface.

At its core, Pro Tools is a multi-track software-based digital recording and editing system. It uses the power of the personal computer to combine hard-disk audio recording, graphical audio editing, MIDI sequencing, digital signal processing (DSP), and mixing into an integrated system. With the ability to incorporate QuickTime and Avid video files, Pro Tools has also established itself as an industry choice for post-production video editing and mixing to picture.

Audio

Pro Tools works with audio that is stored electronically in digital format. The software records audio and stores it as files on your hard drive. Like a digital camera that stores a photograph as a collection of discrete pixels, Pro Tools stores recorded audio as a collection of discrete samples. Pro Tools 10 supports audio formats with resolutions up to 32-bit floating point and sample rates up to 192 kHz.

Just as you can use an image editor to modify, enhance, and otherwise alter your digital photographs in creative ways, so too can you use Pro Tools to take your digital audio in new directions. Working in the digital realm makes it easy to copy, paste, move, delete, modify, and otherwise manipulate your recordings. Pro Tools lets you trim waveforms, reprocess sections of audio, pitch-correct a compromised performance, replace drum sounds, rearrange song sections, and more. With Elastic Audio, you have the power to manipulate the speed of your audio clips in real time, allowing you to freely experiment with tempo. You can even quantize audio for quick rhythmic fixes or creative exploration.

MIDI

Using built-in sequencing technology, Pro Tools also enables you to record and edit MIDI data in the same work environment as your audio recordings. MIDI recordings differ from their digital counterparts in that they capture performance event data rather than sound samples. You can record MIDI signals from a keyboard or other device through a MIDI or USB interface and then edit the data using Pro Tools' intuitive graphical display. The Pro Tools MIDI Editor windows provide a platform for detailed MIDI editing on one track or on multiple superimposed tracks.

A Pro Tools session can have up to 512 MIDI tracks in addition to its Audio tracks. Available features include MIDI Time Stamping, Groove Quantize, Restore Performance, native ReWire support, tick-based and sample-based timelines, and a growing array of plug-in virtual instruments. Pro Tools also includes several great-sounding virtual instrument plug-ins from Avid's Advanced Instrument Research group.

Notation

Pro Tools supports standard music notation display for MIDI notes. MIDI Editor windows provide a Notation view, in which each MIDI and Instrument track is represented on a separate staff. Additionally, Pro Tools includes a dedicated Score Editor window, allowing you to view, edit, arrange, and print MIDI data from your session as music notation.

The notation features and Editor windows in Pro Tools provide productivity and workflow enhancements for composers, songwriters, and others. With a focus on speed and usability, the Notation view and Score Editor window provide additional ways to display and work with your music, utilizing Sibelius-quality music notation and printing capabilities.

Mixing

Beyond recording, editing, and arranging, Pro Tools offers a software-based mixing environment that provides control over signal routing, effects processing, signal levels, panning, and more. The mixing operations in Pro Tools can be automated and stored with your session, enabling you to recall, edit, and refine your mixes over time. When you save a session, all routing, automation, mixing, and effects settings remain exactly as you've left them.

Additionally, Pro Tools software can be combined with Avid and third-party hardware in various configurations to provide multiple channels of simultaneous input and output for your Pro Tools sessions. Massive sessions including up to 768 simultaneous Audio tracks can be managed without audio degradation. Pro Tools systems can range from very simple to extremely advanced and powerful.

Post-Production

Pro Tools also provides a powerful platform for audio post-production tasks. You can import QuickTime movies, Avid video files, or Windows Media (VC-1 AP) clips (Windows systems only) and use Pro Tools' fast, random-access visual reference as you "sweeten" the audio by adding and modifying sound effects, music, Foley, and dialog. With support for QuickTime HD, multiple Video tracks, and video editing, you can perform non-destructive editing and arranging of video files and scenes like never before. When completed, your finished movie file can be exported with the final audio mix embedded.

The Story of Pro Tools

The art of manipulating digital audio has evolved with, and been dramatically influenced by, the evolution of Pro Tools. Introduced in 1991 by Digidesign, Pro Tools helped pioneer the concept of multi-track digital audio recording and is recognized for having revolutionized the audio recording industry. While the Pro Tools 10 release introduces enhanced capabilities across the platform, the core functionality of Pro Tools traces its roots to humble beginnings and the experimental work of the company's founders, Peter Gotcher and Evan Brooks.

In the Beginning

In the early 1980s, Peter Gotcher and Evan Brooks were college band-mates searching for a new sound. In their quest, the two devised a process for recording drum and percussion sounds onto computer EPROM chips.

Recognizing a growing market in electronic music, Peter and Evan began offering their chips for retail. Soon they were producing multiple chip sets, including Rock Drums, Electronic Drums, Latin Percussion, Sound Effects, and more.

Figure 1.1
Early drum-sound chip sets

In 1984, Peter and Evan formed Digidrums and found themselves selling their drum chips by the tens of thousands. With this success, they forged ahead into other types of software and hardware design.

Among their software projects was a product named Sound Designer, which enabled users to edit sounds captured by a sampling keyboard. Sound Designer was the first commercial product to combine waveform editing with a front panel emulation/editor.

Figure 1.2
The original Sound Designer package

Evolving into Digidesign

In 1985, the company changed its name to Digidesign. Over the next few years, Digidesign began developing products for working with MIDI and synthesis on Macintosh computers.

By 1987, Digidesign began prototyping a mono sample playback card for digital audio, and the following year, the company released Sound Accelerator, a CD-quality two-channel output card for the Mac II. This proved to be the first step toward enabling computer systems to provide professional-quality audio output.

Digidesign continued to develop software products for sampling and synthesis. At the same time, the company began work on products designed for digital recording. In 1989, Digidesign released Sound Tools, a two-track hard-disk recorder. Billed as the world's first "tapeless recording studio," Sound Tools consisted of Sound Designer II software, a Sound Accelerator card, and a hardware box called the AD-In that provided two analog-to-digital converters.

Figure 1.3
Components of the Sound Tools system

In 1990, the first AudioMedia card was created and marketed toward musicians, consumers, and independent studios. Its low cost helped drive the "democratization" of music and the recording industry, making hard-disk audio recording accessible to the masses.

The Birth of Pro Tools

The first-generation Pro Tools system was released in 1991, supporting four tracks of audio. Eventually, using additional cards and interfaces, these Pro Tools systems expanded to support up to 16 tracks of simultaneous recording and playback.

Figure 1.4
Early Pro Tools system

In 1992, Session 8 was released as the first Windows-based version of Pro Tools. Two years later, Digidesign introduced Pro Tools TDM, opening the door for real-time effects plug-ins as we now know them.

Figure 1.5
The Session 8 system for Windows NT

The Pro Tools TDM system utilized Time Division Multiplexing (TDM) technology to reliably route multiple streams of digital audio data between system components. TDM technology paved the way for rapid expansion among third-party applications and plug-in developers.

By March 1995, Pro Tools was recognized as having dramatically changed the economics of the recording industry, providing the same capabilities found in million-dollar studios at prices that small studios could afford. That year, Digidesign merged with its biggest customer, Avid Technology.

Pro Tools Matures

In 1997, Pro Tools|24 was released, offering 24-bit audio capabilities. These systems included the 888|24 I/O audio interface, new cards called DSP Farms, an increased number of inputs and outputs, and higher track counts than ever before.

The first Pro Tools TDM system for Windows was released in 1998. The following year, Pro Tools LE was introduced, providing host-based audio processing.

As Pro Tools systems evolved, so did the need for compatible mixing consoles and control surfaces. Operating as a division of Avid, Digidesign soon began offering a line of dedicated control surfaces for Pro Tools, starting with the ProControl console in 1998 and followed by Control|24 in 2001. These consoles provided touch-sensitive control of mixing, automation, and plug-in parameters.

Figure 1.6

ProControl integrated control surface for Pro Tools TDM systems

Figure 1.7
The Control|24 integrated front end
for Pro Tools LE and TDM systems

The influence of Pro Tools continued to spread, and in 2001, Digidesign received a Technical GRAMMY® Award from the National Academy of Recording Arts and Sciences®, for "breaking the boundaries of digital recording and revolutionizing the way music is produced."

In 2002, Pro Tools|HD systems were unveiled as successors to Pro Tools TDM and Pro Tools|24. These systems provided support for higher sample rates and very large mixing topologies, addressing the needs of high-end music and post-production studios.

On the opposite side of the spectrum, the first Mbox was introduced as a portable "studio in a box" for the hobbyist and small project studio markets. The Digi 002 and Digi 002 Rack audio interface options followed, extending the capabilities of Pro Tools LE.

Growth of Avid Audio

In August 2004, Avid acquired M-Audio, a leading provider of computer audio peripherals, keyboard controllers, and related music and recording gear. The subsequent release of Pro Tools M-Powered software provided compatibility with a vast array of existing M-Audio devices and interfaces.

One year later, Avid acquired Wizoo Sound Design, a pioneering developer of virtual instruments, sample libraries, and real-time effects. The Wizoo R&D team formed what is now Avid's Advanced Instrument Research (A.I.R.) group. The A.I.R. group has since developed a host of innovative plug-ins for Pro Tools, including all of the virtual instruments and effects in the Creative Collection (included with Pro Tools), as well as the Hybrid, Strike, Velvet, Structure, and Transfuser virtual instruments for Pro Tools.

In 2006, Sibelius Software Ltd. joined the Avid Audio family. Under Avid, Sibelius continues to develop and market its own line of software, including its well-known professional music notation package. Today, Pro Tools incorporates notation capabilities directly and can export MIDI data as a score for Sibelius software.

ICON Integrated Console Environment

The ICON integrated console environment debuted in 2004. ICON systems feature either the flagship D-Control worksurface or the medium-format D-Command worksurface. Both ICON options employ a modular architecture, allowing facilities to scale their system as needs dictate.

Expandable to 80 physical faders, D-Control provides a central mixing environment for facilities with larger rooms. D-Control includes a comprehensive array of touch-sensitive controls and provides operators with extensive hands-on control over their Pro Tools projects.

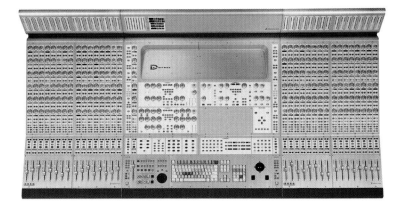

Figure 1.8
ICON D-Control worksurface with 32 faders (expandable to 80 faders)

The more compact D-Command worksurface is expandable up to 40 physical faders, providing a similar feature set configured for single-operator facilities. D-Command offers hands-on control of Pro Tools in a smaller package.

Figure 1.9
ICON D-Command ES worksurface with 24 faders (expandable to 40 faders)

VENUE Live Sound Environment

Digidesign introduced VENUE in 2005 as a purpose-built solution for live sound. VENUE is a state-of-the-art live sound mixing and production environment. VENUE systems seamlessly integrate with Pro Tools for direct recording and playback of multi-track live performances.

A VENUE system is built around one of three consoles: the flagship VENUE D-Show mixing console, the smaller VENUE Profile, or the compact and fully integrated VENUE SC48.

Figure 1.10
The VENUE D-Show mixing console (expandable to 56 faders)

Figure 1.11
VENUE Profile (24 bankable input faders)

Figure 1.12
VENUE SC48 (16 bankable input faders)

Euphonix Acquisition

In April 2010, Avid acquired Euphonix, a leader in digital audio consoles, media controllers, and peripherals. The Euphonix product line, including their Artist Series controllers (Artist Control, Artist Mix, Artist Transport, Artist Color) and Pro Series consoles and controllers (MC Pro, System 5, System 5-MC, System 5-B, S5 Fusion, Max Air), continue development under the Avid brand. Additionally, Avid has extended the EUCON high-speed Ethernet control protocol to offer fully integrated control of Pro Tools from Artist and Pro Series control surfaces.

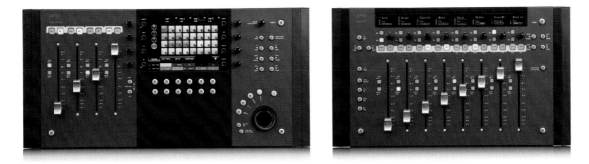

Figure 1.13
Artist Series controllers: Artist Control (left) and Artist Mix (right)

Figure 1.14
Pro Series controllers: MC Pro (left) and System 5-MC (right)

Where We Are Today

Throughout 2010, Avid worked to consolidate operations and unite its various products under the Avid brand. Today, Avid continues to develop audio hardware and software alongside its video editing, broadcast, and newsroom systems. Avid audio systems address all segments of the music creation, live sound, broadcast, and video post-production markets, from home recording enthusiasts to large-scale motion picture sound designers and mixers.

In late 2010, Avid released the third-generation Pro Tools Mbox family of audio interfaces, new HD-series interfaces, the HD-Native platform, and Pro Tools 9 software, providing a single, unified installer for all versions of Pro Tools. With the Pro Tools 9 release, standard Pro Tools software (known simply as *Pro Tools*) replaced the former Pro Tools M-Powered and Pro Tools LE platforms and introduced compatibility with third-party Core Audio or ASIO audio interfaces. For the first time ever, Pro Tools software could run with third-party hardware, providing a wealth of new I/O choices for Pro Tools users. Additionally, the Aggregate I/O option for using the built-in audio on a Mac allowed the software to run with *no* connected interface, recording and playing back through the computer's onboard audio ports.

The Pro Tools 10 release brings improvements for all Pro Tools systems, including support for 32-bit floating-point audio files, support for real-time fades, and the introduction of clip-based gain features. The Edit window has been updated to include Sync, Solo, and Mute status indicators for the session, as well as a new Automation Follows Edit button/indicator in the Edit window toolbar. Plug-in options have been enhanced with the introduction of the new AAX real-time format and the addition of the Avid Channel Strip, Mod Delay III, and Down Mixer plug-ins. AudioSuite plug-ins have also been updated and now allow multiple AudioSuite windows to remain open simultaneously. Other AudioSuite features include the ability to preserve fades and metadata after an AudioSuite render and the ability to provide handles of processed audio in the underlying audio (outside of the clip boundaries).

Other Pro Tools 10 enhancements include the following:

- Support for interleaved audio files
- Support for the RF64 (WAVE Extensible) audio file format
- Pro Tools in-application web browser for easy access to online resources and the Avid Store to purchase plug-ins, manage your Avid account, search the Knowledge Base and online forums, etc.
- Improved import and export features, including the ability to export selected tracks as a new session and add bounced files to your iTunes library or SoundCloud account
- Disk cache enhancements
- Support for network-attached storage and Avid shared storage optimizations
- Increased Automatic Delay Compensation up to 16,383 samples (increase not supported on Pro Tools|HD hardware)

In addition, the maximum Audio track count has been increased for Pro Tools HD software (up to 768 tracks), and the maximum internal mix bus count has been increased for all systems (up to 512). The Complete Production Toolkit option continues to provide expandability for standard Pro Tools systems, including surround mixing capabilities, increased track counts, and a variety of advanced features otherwise available only with Pro Tools HD software.

Pro Tools 10 also introduces some important changes to Pro Tools terminology, functionality, and session file format.

- Several changes have been incorporated to Pro Tools file and path names, including changing the application and plug-in file paths from …/Digidesign/ Pro Tools/ and …/Digidesign/DAE/Plug-ins/ (Pro Tools 9 and earlier) to …/Avid/Pro Tools/ and …/Avid/Audio/Plug-ins/ (Pro Tools 10 and later).

- The term *region* has been replaced throughout the Pro Tools user interface with the term *clip*, to provide consistency with Avid Media Composer software.

- The *Trimmer* tool has been renamed as the *Trim* tool for consistency with Avid Media Composer software.

- The software supports mixed bit-depth files within a single session (16-bit, 24-bit, and 32-bit floating point), as well as both interleaved and split-stereo (multi-mono) files.

- The software allows changing the session bit depth, audio file format, and/or stereo file format (interleaved vs. multi-mono) at any time, through the Session Setup window.

- Pro Tools 10 uses a new session file format with the suffix .ptx; consequently, Pro Tools 10 sessions cannot be opened directly in earlier versions of the Pro Tools software.

Many of the above changes are discussed in more detail in later lessons in this book.

To make the most of your experience with Pro Tools 10 and to optimize your results using the platform, it is helpful to understand some of the technology behind Pro Tools and to familiarize yourself with the available configuration options. The remainder of this lesson focuses on these topics.

Basics of Digital Audio

Today's Pro Tools systems give you the power to capture the subtlest details of a sound or performance and to work on digital audio with absolute precision. The sample rates and bit depths supported by Pro Tools provide the frequency response and dynamic range required for truly professional results. Becoming acquainted with the fundamentals of sound and digital audio will help you to maximize the power of Pro Tools and the capabilities of your system. This section describes some of the factors that affect sound and influence the accuracy of digital audio.

Tip: The following information provides an overview of the concepts of digital
      audio theory. Although you do not need to be an expert in this material,
      gaining exposure to these principles now will enrich your understanding
      of many of the processes discussed later in the book.

Basic Parameters of Sound: Waveform, Frequency, and Amplitude

To work effectively with sound, it is helpful to understand a bit about what sound
actually is and what gives a sound its character. When we hear a sound, what we
actually experience is a variation in the air pressure around us. This variation results
from vibrations in material objects—whether a tabletop, a car engine, or a guitar
string. When a vibrating object moves through one complete back-and-forth
motion (one cycle), the variation in air pressure that it produces becomes an audi-
tory event. If the object is vibrating at a frequency that falls within the range of
human hearing, we perceive it as a sound. The nature of the sound we hear is
determined by the waveform, frequency, and amplitude of the vibration.

Tip: The range of human hearing is between 20 and 20,000 cycles per second.

Waveform

The waveform of the sound pressure variations that reaches our ears creates our
perception of the sound's source, be it a knock on a table, a running car engine,
or a plucked guitar string. The waveform is the "shape" of the sound—or, more
accurately, the shape of the vibration that produced the sound. As a vibrating
object moves through its back-and-forth motions, its path is not smooth and
continuous. Instead, the cycles of vibration are typically complex and jagged, influenced by factors such as the physical material that the object is composed of and
the resonance induced by the object's surroundings. Each object vibrates differently; the waveform of the vibration gives the sound its unique character and tone.

Frequency

The frequency of the sound pressure variations that reaches our ears creates our
perception of the pitch of the sound. We measure this frequency in *cycles per second*
(CPS), also commonly denoted as *Hertz* (Hz). These two terms are synonymous—
15,000 CPS is the same as 15,000 Hz. Multiples of 1,000 Hz are often denoted
as kilohertz (kHz). Therefore, 15,000 Hz is also written as 15 kHz.

As the frequency of vibration increases, the pitch of the sound goes up—numerically higher frequencies produce higher pitches, while numerically lower frequencies produce lower pitches. Each time the frequency doubles, the pitch raises by

one octave. By way of example, the A string on a guitar vibrates at 110 Hz in standard tuning. Playing the A note on the 12th fret produces vibrations at 220 Hz (one octave higher).

Amplitude

The intensity or amplitude of the sound pressure variations that reaches our ears creates our perception of the loudness of the sound. We measure amplitude in *decibels* (dB). The decibel scale is defined by the dynamic range of human hearing, with the threshold of hearing defined as 0 dB and the threshold of sensation or pain reached at approximately 120 dB. The dB is a logarithmic unit that is used to describe a ratio of sound pressure; as such, it does not have a linear relation to our perception of loudness.

As the amplitude of pressure variations increases, the sound becomes louder. Doubling the intensity of sound-pressure variations creates a gain of 3 dB; however, we do not perceive this change as doubling the sound's loudness. An increase of approximately 10 dB is required to produce a perceived doubling of loudness. By way of example, the amplitude of ordinary conversation is around 60 dB. Increasing the amplitude to 70 dB would essentially double the loudness; increasing amplitude to 80 dB would double it again, quadrupling the original loudness.

Recording and Playing Back Analog Audio

The task of a recording microphone is to respond to changes in air pressure—the waveforms, frequencies, and amplitudes that make up a sound—and translate them into an electronic output that can be captured or recorded. The continuous electrical signal produced by a microphone is an alternating current with a waveform, frequency, and amplitude that directly corresponds to, or is analogous to, the original acoustic information. Hence the term *analog audio*.

If this continuous analog signal is captured on traditional recording media, such as magnetic tape, it can be played back by directly translating the electrical waveform, frequency, and amplitude back into analogous variations in air pressure through the means of an amplifier and loudspeaker.

Analog-to-Digital Conversion

Before you can record or edit with Pro Tools, the analog audio signals relayed by a microphone, guitar pickup, or other input device must be digitized, or translated into digital (binary) numerical information that can be stored, read, and subsequently manipulated by a computer. This process is referred to as *analog-to-digital conversion*, commonly abbreviated as *A/D conversion*. Two essential factors affect the A/D process: *sample rate* and *bit depth*.

How Sample Rate Affects Frequency Resolution

Sampling is the process of taking discrete readings of a signal at various moments in time. Each reading, or sample, is a digital "snapshot" of the signal at that particular instant. Played back in succession, these samples approximate the original signal, much like a series of photographs played back in succession approximates movement in a film or video.

The sample rate is the frequency with which these digital snapshots are collected. The sample rate required for digital audio is driven by a fundamental law of analog-to-digital conversion, referred to as the *Sampling theorem* or the *Nyquist theorem*.

The Nyquist theorem states that in order to produce an accurate representation of a given frequency of sound, each cycle of the sound's vibration must be sampled a minimum of two times. If the sample rate is any lower, the system will read the incoming frequencies inaccurately and produce the wrong tones. (In concept, this is much like the effect seen in early motion pictures, where a wagon wheel will appear to rotate backward due to the low frame rates being used.) In digital audio, the false tones produced by this type of frequency distortion are known as *alias tones*.

Because the range of human hearing is generally accepted to be 20 Hz to 20 kHz, this law indicates that a sampling rate of at least 40 kHz (twice the upper range of human hearing) is required to capture full-frequency audio. Most professional digital recording devices today offer sampling rates of 44.1 kHz and 48 kHz or higher. The digital information on an audio CD is stored at a standard sample rate of 44.1 kHz.

How Bit Depth Affects Amplitude Resolution

The useful dynamic range of speech and music is generally considered to be from 40 to 105 dB. To capture this range, an A/D converter must be able to accurately represent differences in amplitude of at least 65 dB; stated another way, it must have a minimum 65-dB dynamic range. The relative amplitude (or loudness) of a sample is captured through a process known as *quantization*. This simply means that each sample is quantified (assigned) to the closest available amplitude value.

Computers use binary digits called *bits* (0s or 1s) to quantify each sample that is taken. The number of bits used to define a value is referred to as the *binary word length*. The range of values represented by a binary word is defined by the binary word length and is equal to 2 to the nth power (2^n), where n is the number of bits in the binary word.

Tip: The binary word length is also commonly referred to as the *bit depth*.

A 4-bit binary word is able to represent 16 different numeric values (2^4); used by an A/D converter to capture amplitude, this 4-bit binary word would record the amplitude continuum using 16 discrete amplitude levels. By contrast, a 16-bit digital word could define 65,536 discrete amplitude levels (2^{16}), and a 24-bit digital word could define 16,777,216 discrete amplitude levels (2^{24}).

As such, larger binary words are able to quantify variations in amplitude with much greater accuracy. Therefore, a 24-bit audio file will always more accurately reflect the dynamic range of the original sound than its 16-bit counterpart.

Tip: **32-bit floating-point files use only 23 bits to represent discrete amplitude levels, with one bit reserved for the sign (the same as 24-bit files). The 8 additional bits provide exponent biasing and allow for headroom above full-scale 24-bit audio.**

A very general rule of thumb can be used to calculate the dynamic range capability of an A/D system. By multiplying the word size by six, you can estimate the useful dynamic range of a fixed-point system. For example, a system with an 8-bit binary word (or 8-bit quantization) would produce a dynamic range of about 48 dB, while a 16-bit system would accommodate a 96-dB dynamic range. A 24-bit system would have a theoretical dynamic range of 144 dB.

Tip: **In theoretical terms, the dynamic range (or signal-to-quantization noise ratio) increases by approximately 6 dB for each bit added to the binary word length.**

A consequence of files with greater bit depth is the higher storage capacity required to record them. Each minute of 16-bit/48-kHz stereo audio occupies about 11.4 MB of hard-drive storage space. In contrast, each minute of 24-bit/48-kHz stereo audio occupies about 17 MB of hard-drive storage space, while the same audio in a 32-bit float file at 48 kHz will require about 22.8 MB of hard-drive space per minute.

Recording in Digital Format

When you are recording into Pro Tools using audio that is already in a digital form (on DAT or CD, for example), you don't need to translate the audio before bringing it into the system. The process of converting from digital to analog and back to digital can introduce distortion and degrade the original signal. Therefore, unnecessary conversions should be avoided. If the audio information remains in the digital domain while being transferred between machines, it will retain its sonic integrity with no discernible signal degradation.

On the rear panel of many Pro Tools audio interfaces are two types of connections for accomplishing digital transfers. One is labeled *S/PDIF*, which has RCA jacks (sometimes called *coaxial jacks*), and the other is *AES/EBU*, which uses XLR-type connectors. S/PDIF is the *Sony/Philips Digital Interface* standard, a consumer format, and AES/EBU is the *Audio Engineering Society/European Broadcast Union* digital interface standard, a professional format. Although both formats are nearly identical in audio quality (it's virtually impossible to hear the difference), if given the choice, you should always use the AES/EBU format over the S/PDIF format because the professional format is technically more stable and filters out any copy protection encoded in the digital audio stream. Almost all digital recording or storage devices will support one or both of these formats.

Pro Tools System Configurations

The requirements for your digital audio recording projects will determine the type of Pro Tools system that you will need to use. Pro Tools 10 is supported in three types of systems: Pro Tools, Pro Tools Core Audio/ASIO, and Pro Tools HD. All three options are available for both Mac OS X (Snow Leopard and Lion) and Windows 7 operating systems, and all deliver the same core technology. The primary difference between the options is the hardware that each Pro Tools software option works with.

Pro Tools systems are host-based, meaning they use the processing power of the host computer to carry out real-time routing, mixing, and processing of audio signals. These systems use Pro Tools software with an audio interface from the 003 or Digi 002 family, the Eleven Rack interface, a Pro Tools Mbox or Digidesign Mbox 2 family audio interface, or M-Audio hardware to provide input and output (I/O) to the Pro Tools software.

Pro Tools Core Audio/ASIO systems are also host-based and use Pro Tools software with third-party audio interfaces with supported Core Audio (Mac) or ASIO (Windows) drivers, including the built-in audio available on Mac computers (Core Audio).

Pro Tools HD software is supported with Pro Tools|HD Native hardware, Pro Tools|HD hardware, and the forthcoming Pro Tools|HDX hardware. Pro Tools|HD Native uses one or more Pro Tools HD-series interfaces combined with a Pro Tools|HD Native PCIe card and host-based processing. By contrast, Pro Tools|HD systems use one or more HD-series interfaces combined with one or more HD-series PCI/PCIe cards, providing dedicated digital signal processing (DSP) power for mixing and real-time processing operations. Similarly, Pro Tools systems with Pro Tools|HDX hardware will use one or more HD-series interfaces combined with one or more Pro Tools|HDX PCIe cards, providing superior DSP power for mixing and real-time processing.

Pro Tools vs. Pro Tools HD

Throughout this book, we use the term *Pro Tools* to refer to standard Pro Tools software running on any supported hardware configuration. We use the term *Pro Tools HD* to refer to *Pro Tools HD* software running on a supported system. The terms *Pro Tools|HD*, *Pro Tools|HD Native*, and *Pro Tools|HDX* are used to refer to specific card-based hardware options.

All Pro Tools options use the same software installer, which also installs a variety of included software plug-ins, providing additional functionality. All systems share the same file format, with full cross-compatibility between Macs and PCs, providing seamless interchange between Pro Tools systems.

Pro Tools 10.0 Software

Pro Tools 10.0 provides sampling rates of up to 192 kHz, with bit depths up to 32-bit floating point. It will power up to 96 simultaneous mono or stereo Audio tracks (up to 128 total voiceable tracks) and up to 512 simultaneous MIDI tracks.

Tip: The Complete Production Toolkit increases the Pro Tools track count, providing up to 192 simultaneous voices, with up to 512 total voiceable tracks. See the "Complete Production Toolkit" section later in this lesson for more details.

A variety of PCI, FireWire, and USB peripherals are available, providing a multitude of interface options, for up to 32 channels of I/O to the system. Many of these peripherals can be powered by the computer's FireWire or USB bus, enabling laptop systems to function as completely portable Pro Tools workstations.

Supported M-Audio peripherals include FireWire family interfaces, such as the ProFire 2626; USB interfaces, such as the Fast Track series and the ultra-compact Transit; PCI audio interfaces, such as the Audiophile and Delta series; and keyboard/synthesizer based systems, such as the KeyStudio 49i and ProKeys series and the Venom synthesizer.

Figure 1.15
M-Audio ProFire 2626 audio interface

Figure 1.16
M-Audio Transit audio interface

Figure 1.17
M-Audio Delta 44 audio interface

Figure 1.18
M-Audio ProKeys Sono 61 keyboard-based audio interface

Figure 1.19
M-Audio Venom synthesizer-based audio interface

All current Pro Tools audio interfaces also work with Pro Tools 10.0, including the Pro Tools Mbox (third generation) and Digidesign Mbox 2 (second generation) family audio interfaces, Eleven Rack, and the 003 and Digi 002 family audio interfaces.

IMPORTANT: The original Mbox hardware (first generation) is no longer supported. Support for this product ended with Pro Tools 8.0.3.

The Pro Tools Mbox Family

The third-generation Pro Tools Mbox family includes the high-performance Mbox personal studio, the compact Mbox Mini, and the high-definition Mbox Pro desktop studio. The Mbox family interfaces are designed to provide ease of use and portability while maintaining professional sound quality at an affordable price.

The Mbox and Mbox Mini feature powered USB connectivity. The Mbox Mini supports up to 24-bit/48-kHz audio resolution. It includes a single XLR mic/line combo input and 2×2 simultaneous channels of I/O. The larger Mbox supports up to 24 bits at sample rates up to 96 kHz and features two XLR mic/line combo inputs, 4×4 simultaneous channels of I/O, and MIDI connectivity.

The Mbox Pro is a FireWire-powered interface that provides high-definition audio and MIDI in a portable package. It features support for audio resolutions up to 24 bits at sample rates up to 192 kHz. The Mbox Pro includes four XLR mic inputs, four ¼-inch TRS line inputs, six ¼-inch TRS balanced line outputs, two channels of S/PDIF digital I/O, and MIDI input and output.

Figure 1.20
Pro Tools Mbox and Mbox Mini audio interfaces

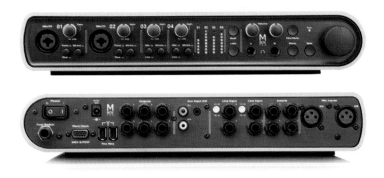

Figure 1.21
Pro Tools Mbox Pro audio interface

Eleven Rack

Eleven Rack is a guitar recording and effects processing system designed to serve as an audio interface for Pro Tools as well as a standalone amp tone and effects signal processor for guitar. When used as a Pro Tools interface, Eleven Rack provides up to eight simultaneous channels of recording at bit depths of up to 24 bits and sample rates up to 96 kHz. The unit provides stereo balanced XLR outputs as well as dedicated ¼-inch outputs. Also included are a mic input, two ¼-inch line-level inputs, AES/EBU and S/PDIF digital I/O, and MIDI I/O. Eleven Rack communicates with Pro Tools via a high-speed USB 2.0 connection.

Figure 1.22
Eleven Rack audio interface

The 003 Family

The 003 family consists of the 003, the 003 Rack, and the 003 Rack+ FireWire-enabled interfaces. All three units provide up to 18 channels of simultaneous I/O. The 003 provides I/O by way of an integrated control surface with eight motor-ized, touch-sensitive faders in a portable 8×4×2 digital mixer. The 003 Rack and 003 Rack+ each provide the same I/O functionality in a rack-mounted unit, with the 003 Rack+ providing additional mic preamps built into the interface. All units provide 24-bit, 96-kHz audio and include the following I/O features:

- Eight analog inputs

- Eight ¼-inch analog outputs

- Professional mic preamps (four on the 003 and 003 Rack; eight on the 003 Rack+) with gain controls and high-pass filter switches

- Stereo ¼-inch TRS monitor outputs with level control
- Eight channels of 24-bit ADAT optical I/O
- Two channels of 24-bit S/PDIF digital I/O
- MIDI input and output ports
- Dual headphone outputs with individual level controls

Figure 1.23
003 audio interface

Figure 1.24
003 Rack+ audio
interface

Pro Tools HD Software

A Pro Tools HD authorization lets you run Pro Tools HD on a supported Mac or Windows computer with Pro Tools|HD, Pro Tools|HD Native, or Pro Tools|HDX hardware (once available). A Pro Tools HD authorization also authorizes Pro Tools with Complete Production Toolkit functionality on supported Mac or Windows systems without HD hardware (Pro Tools version 9.0 and later). This allows Pro Tools HD users to run a Pro Tools laptop system with Complete Production Toolkit when away from the studio, for on-the-go editing and mixing using the same authorization.

Pro Tools HD-series audio interfaces provide sampling rates of up to 192 kHz, with bit depths up to 24 bits. Pro Tools|HD Native hardware provides up to 64 channels of I/O, while Pro Tools|HD hardware provides up to 160 channels of I/O. Pro Tools|HDX systems will provide the most robust Pro Tools option, utilizing superior DSP hardware and technology to carry out real-time routing, mixing, and processing of audio signals and support for extremely large mixing configurations. Pro Tools HD 10 software with Pro Tools|HDX hardware will support up to 768 simultaneous Audio tracks (record and playback), up to 512 simultaneous MIDI tracks, and up to 192 channels of I/O.

Pro Tools HD software requires at least one HD-series interface to be connected in order to run. All Pro Tools HD-series interfaces can be used for Pro Tools systems with Pro Tools|HD, Pro Tools|HD Native, and Pro Tools|HDX hardware.

HD OMNI

HD OMNI provides two premium mic/DI inputs with built-in preamps, four line inputs, and eight line outputs in a compact, single space rack-mountable chassis. It also provides digital I/O, including eight channels of ADAT I/O with S/MUX II and IV support, 2×8 channels of AES/EBU I/O, and two channels of S/PDIF I/O.

Figure 1.25
Avid HD OMNI audio interface

HD I/O

HD I/O is available in one of three configurations, providing differing analog and digital I/O options. The standard 8×8×8 configuration provides eight analog inputs, eight analog outputs, and eight channels of AES/EBU digital I/O, in addition to two channels of AES/EBU digital I/O provided on the chassis in all configurations. The 16×16 analog configuration provides 16 channels of analog input along with 16 channels of analog output, plus the two channels of AES/EBU digital I/O on the chassis. Similarly, the 16×16 digital configuration provides 16 channels of digital input and 16 channels of digital output, plus the two channels of AES/EBU digital I/O on the chassis.

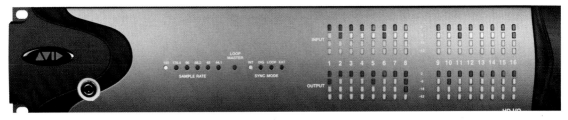

Figure 1.26
Avid HD I/O audio interface

HD MADI

HD MADI is a 64-channel MADI interface for Pro Tools HD. This single rack space unit provides coaxial and optical connectors for sending and receiving digital audio streams between Pro Tools and other MADI devices. The MADI protocol enables up to 32 channels of digital audio to be transmitted across distances of up to 2 kilometers via a single connection. The HD MADI interface provides bidirectional sample-rate conversion on both inputs and outputs, enabling easy integration into complex mixed sample-rate environments.

Figure 1.27
Avid HD MADI audio interface

Included Plug-Ins and Extras

Plug-ins are special-purpose software components that provide additional signal processing and other functionality to Pro Tools. Pro Tools plug-ins come in three varieties: Native plug-ins, which process audio in real time using the host computer's processing power; DSP plug-ins (Pro Tools|HD and HDX systems only), which utilize card-based DSP chips for real-time processing; and AudioSuite plug-ins, which provide non-real-time, file-based processing.

Pro Tools 10 includes a number of Native, DSP, and AudioSuite plug-ins that are installed with the Pro Tools software. Plug-ins installed with Pro Tools include the DigiRack plug-in collection, the TL Utilities plug-ins, and the Pro Tools Creative Collection suite of instruments and effects.

DigiRack Plug-Ins

The DigiRack collection is comprised of plug-ins that are installed with Pro Tools. DigiRack plug-ins provide digital signal processing effects, such as EQ, dynamics, delay, and more. More than 30 separate plug-ins are included in the DigiRack collection, many in Native, DSP, and AudioSuite formats. The plug-ins included in the DigiRack collection are listed in Appendix A, "Avid Pro Tools Plug-Ins."

TL Utilities

The TL Utilities plug-ins provide professional metering, metronome, and instrument tuning for Pro Tools. TL Utilities include the following plug-ins:

- **TL Metro.** A versatile metronome used for quickly and easily creating a click track.

- **TL InTune.** A professional tuner providing the performance of a rack-mounted digital tuner in a convenient plug-in format.

- **TL MasterMeter.** The first oversampling meter for Pro Tools, designed for critical mixing and mastering applications.

Pro Tools Creative Collection

Pro Tools Creative Collection is a set of Native effects and instrument plug-ins included with all Pro Tools systems. The Creative Collection includes 20 A.I.R. effects plug-ins and six A.I.R. virtual instruments. These plug-ins are all installed automatically with Pro Tools 10. A list of the Creative Collection plug-ins is provided in Appendix B, "Creative Collection Plug-Ins."

Complete Production Toolkit

The Complete Production Toolkit for Pro Tools 10.0 enables numerous Pro Tools feature enhancements for non-HD systems. This software add-on provides full surround mixing in Pro Tools 10 and enables up to 512 voiceable tracks for greater session interchange with systems running Pro Tools HD software. The Complete Production Toolkit provides multi-channel surround tracks; QuickPunch, TrackPunch, and Destructive Punch support; up to 512 Auxiliary Input tracks; and up to 128 Instrument tracks. It also provides VCA tracks, AutoFades, advanced automation features, advanced video features and video editing capabilities, and other functions that are otherwise available only with Pro Tools HD software.

Mixing and Automation Features

The Complete Production Toolkit provides numerous mixing and automation enhancements, including the following:

- TrackInput functionality for input monitoring on individual tracks
- Surround mixing up to 7.1 with a compatible audio interface
- Snapshot automation for writing or trimming automation data
- Glide Automation commands
- Trim Automation modes

Video Features

The Complete Production Toolkit provides the following advanced features for working with digital video:

- Multiple Video tracks in the Timeline (only one can be played back at a time)
- Multiple QuickTime movies on an individual Video track
- Multiple playlists for Video tracks
- Ability to store video files in the Clip List
- General video editing capabilities, including non-destructive editing; multiple undos; selecting and editing across multiple tracks; capturing, separating, and healing clips; clip looping; and more
- Video clip groups

Cross-Platform Issues

Pro Tools configurations are available for both Mac and Windows systems. Most Pro Tools controls, tools, procedures, and menus are similar on both systems. There are, however, some differences in keyboard commands and file-naming conventions that can impact your work when moving between different platforms.

Keyboard Commands

Many keyboard commands in Pro Tools use *modifier keys*, which are keys pressed in combination with other keys or with a mouse action. In addition, other equivalent keys have different names on each platform. The following table summarizes equivalent keys on Mac and Windows:

Keyboard Shortcuts

Mac	Windows
Command key (⌘)	Ctrl (Control) key
Option key	Alt key
Control key	Start (Win) key
Return key	Enter key on main (not numeric) keypad
Delete key	Backspace key

File-Naming Conventions

A few differences exist in the way files are named and recognized by Mac and Windows.

File Name Extensions

For cross-platform compatibility, all Pro Tools files in a session must have a three-letter file extension added to the file name. Pro Tools 10 session files use the *.ptx* extension. Pro Tools 7.0 through 9.x session files use the extension *.ptf*. Sessions created in versions of Pro Tools older than 7.0 may use the extension *.pts* or *.pt5*. WAV files have the *.wav* file extension, and AIFF files have the *.aif* file extension.

Incompatible ASCII Characters

Pro Tools file names cannot use ASCII characters that are incompatible with a supported operating system. The following characters should be avoided in order to maintain cross-platform compatibility:

/ (slash)	" (quotation marks)
\ (backslash)	' (apostrophe)
: (colon)	< (less-than symbol)
* (asterisk)	> (greater-than symbol)
? (question mark)	| (vertical line or pipe)

You should also avoid any character typed with the Command key on the Macintosh.

Review/Discussion Questions

1. Name and describe five types of production tasks that Pro Tools can be used for. (See pages 4 and 5.)

2. When was the first Mbox audio interface introduced? Was this before or after Avid acquired M-Audio? (See page 10.)

3. After being acquired by Avid, Wizoo Sound Design became Avid's Advanced Instrument Research (A.I.R.) group. What types of products does the A.I.R group specialize in? Give some examples. (See page 10.)

4. What is the frequency range of human hearing? (See page 16.)

5. What does the frequency of a sound wave affect in terms of how we perceive the sound? How is frequency measured? (See page 16.)

6. What does the amplitude of the sound wave affect? How is amplitude measured? (See page 17.)

7. How does the sample rate of a system relate to the frequency of audio it can capture? What is the name of the law that specifies the relationship between sample rate and audio frequency? (See page 18.)

8. How does the bit depth of a system relate to the dynamic range of audio it can capture? How can you estimate the dynamic range of a system? (See page 19.)

9. Give two examples of connections, commonly found on audio interfaces, that are used for making digital transfers. What type of jacks does each use? (See page 20.)

10. Name three audio interfaces that are compatible with Pro Tools HD software. (See pages 26 and 27.)

11. Describe some of the features of the Complete Production Toolkit. (See pages 28 and 29.)

Pro Tools Hardware

In this exercise worksheet, you will identify various audio interfaces available for use with Pro Tools and identify the software platform that is compatible with each. This exercise reviews the material covered in Lesson 1.

Duration: 10 Minutes　　　**Media: None Required**

Audio Interfaces

Refer to Figures EX1.1 through EX1.5 when answering the questions below. See the section on "Pro Tools System Configurations" in Lesson 1 for assistance.

Questions 1 and 2 refer to Figure EX1.1.

1. The audio interface shown in Figure EX1.1 is called the

   _____.

2. This interface is compatible with (select all that apply):

   ❏ Standard Pro Tools software

   ❏ Pro Tools|HD Native hardware

   ❏ Pro Tools|HD hardware

Figure EX1.1
An M-Audio interface for Pro Tools

Questions 3 and 4 refer to Figure EX1.2.

3. The audio interface shown in Figure EX1.2 is called the

   _____.

4. This interface is compatible with (select all that apply):
   - ❏ Standard Pro Tools software
   - ❏ Pro Tools|HD Native hardware
   - ❏ Pro Tools|HD hardware

Figure EX1.2
A Pro Tools audio interface

Questions 5 and 6 refer to Figure EX1.3.

5. The audio interface shown in Figure EX1.3 is called the

   _____.

6. This interface is compatible with (select all that apply):
   - ❏ Standard Pro Tools software
   - ❏ Pro Tools|HD Native hardware
   - ❏ Pro Tools|HD hardware

Figure EX1.3
An audio interface for guitar

Questions 7 and 8 refer to Figure EX1.4.

7. The audio interface shown in Figure EX1.4 is called the

   _____.

8. This interface is compatible with (select all that apply):

   ❑ Standard Pro Tools software

   ❑ Pro Tools|HD Native hardware

   ❑ Pro Tools|HD hardware

Figure EX1.4
A single-space rack-mountable audio interface for Pro Tools

Questions 9 and 10 refer to Figure EX1.5.

9. The audio interface shown in Figure EX1.5 is called the

   _____.

10. This interface is compatible with (select all that apply):

   ❑ Standard Pro Tools software

   ❑ Pro Tools|HD Native hardware

   ❑ Pro Tools|HD hardware

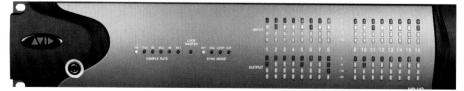

Figure EX1.5
A double-space rack-mountable audio interface for Pro Tools

Getting Inside Pro Tools

This lesson covers basic Pro Tools operations and functions. It introduces the user interface as well as common tools and modes of operation.

Duration: 120 Minutes

GOALS

- Recognize the basic Pro Tools session file structure
- Power up a Pro Tools system
- Navigate the Pro Tools menu system to locate common commands
- Recognize and work in the main Pro Tools windows
- Understand the Edit tools and Edit modes
- Work with Time Scales, Timebase Rulers, and MIDI controls

This lesson presents an overview of basic Pro Tools operations and functions. You will be introduced to the filing structure that Pro Tools uses for its sessions and backups, the steps required to start up a Pro Tools system, the primary elements of the Pro Tools interface, and some of the common tools and modes you will use to work in Pro Tools.

Target Systems

Although most of the concepts discussed in this book are applicable to all Pro Tools systems, the book is specifically written for Pro Tools 10 software. While Pro Tools 10 can be used with various Pro Tools, M-Audio, and third-party audio interfaces, certain menus, commands, and functions may differ slightly from one configuration to another. Pro Tools HD users will also have access to additional features.

New features introduced in Pro Tools 10 are generally identified as such in the text. All descriptions are based on the user interface in Pro Tools 10 systems, unless otherwise noted. Screenshots represent Pro Tools version 10.0 running on Windows 7, unless otherwise noted.

Pro Tools File Structure

Before you create or edit a recording project, or *session*, in Pro Tools, it is helpful to understand how the software works with the various files that are related to a project. Rather than storing a session as a single file, Pro Tools stores various session components separately and maintains a roadmap to the files it uses in a session file. All of the files used for a project are grouped together in a *session folder*.

File Organization

When you create a Pro Tools session, the system sets up a standard hierarchy for the session and its associated files by automatically creating a top-level session folder containing the session file as well as subfolders for various types of supplemental files used for the session. When you record, convert on import, or edit material, specific files will appear in each of these subfolders.

Pro Tools keeps related files together in this hierarchy to facilitate backups of sessions and transfers between Pro Tools systems.

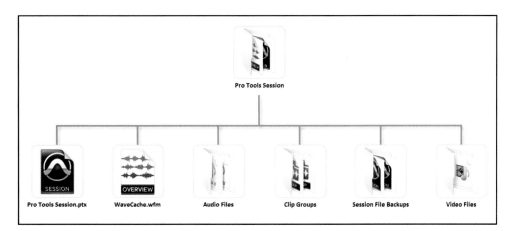

Figure 2.1
Pro Tools session file hierarchy

File Types

The types of files that Pro Tools generates and stores in each folder in the hierarchy are described in the following sections. Many of these files are created by Pro Tools automatically as you work on a project, although some are generated by export operations only.

Pro Tools Session File

A *session file* is the document that Pro Tools creates when you start a new project. Pro Tools creates this file (along with various subfolders) inside a session folder of the same name. Pro Tools 10 session files are recognizable by their *.ptx* extensions. (Earlier versions of Pro Tools use the *.ptf* extension.)

The session file contains a map of all the tracks, audio and video files, settings, and edits associated with your project. Session documents can be saved and reopened, recalling a given project with all of its edit information, input/output assignments, and links to the associated audio files. You can easily copy and rename session documents, allowing you to save alternate versions of a project without changing the source audio.

WaveCache File

Each Pro Tools session you create will also have an associated *WaveCache.wfm* file created inside the session folder. This file stores all of the waveform display data for any audio in the session and enables the session to open more quickly. The WaveCache file can be included whenever a session is transferred to another Pro Tools system.

Pro Tools also maintains a distinct WaveCache file inside the Avid Databases folder on the system drive, which retains waveform data for all files used on the system.

Tip: WaveCache files can be deleted without harming the session or your system. If the WaveCache is missing, Pro Tools will recalculate the session waveform data; however, the session may open more slowly.

Audio Files

When audio is recorded into a Pro Tools session, each take of the audio recording is stored as a separate file inside the corresponding session's Audio Files folder. Pro Tools natively supports audio files in either the WAV or AIFF format. However, for cross-compatibility purposes, WAV is the default file format for both Mac and Windows Pro Tools systems.

Note: Audio that you record in Pro Tools is saved *only* in the Audio Files folder; it is not saved in the session file. When transferring sessions between systems, be sure to copy over the entire top-level session folder in order to include all associated audio files and other material needed for the session.

Fade Files

With Pro Tools 10, all fades are calculated and played back in real time, eliminating the need to store rendered fade files. Earlier versions of Pro Tools included a Fade Files folder within the session folder, containing the fade files rendered by Pro Tools for volume fade-ins, fade-outs, and crossfades created while editing a session (EDIT > FADES > CREATE).

MIDI Files

MIDI data is normally stored within the Pro Tools session; as such, no MIDI files will exist outside the session document. However, MIDI files can be exported from Pro Tools using the EXPORT > MIDI command. Exported MIDI files can be recognized by their *.mid* extensions.

Sibelius Files

If you work with scores inside Pro Tools (WINDOW > SCORE EDITOR), you can use either the SEND TO SIBELIUS command or the EXPORT > SIBELIUS command to generate a score file that can be opened/edited with the full-featured Sibelius notation software. Exported Sibelius files can be recognized by their *.sib* extensions.

Clip Groups

The Clip Groups folder is the default directory that Pro Tools uses for any clip groups you export from your Pro Tools session. If you do not export any clip groups, this folder will remain empty and will be removed when you close the session; clip groups used in your session are not stored in this folder unless they've been exported.

Rendered Files

Whenever you use rendered Elastic Audio processing, Pro Tools creates temporary files for the audio on the affected tracks. These temporary files are kept in an auto-created Rendered Files folder in the session folder. If you commit Rendered Elastic Audio processing to a track, a new file is written to disk in the Audio Files folder, and the temporary rendered file is deleted from the Rendered Files folder.

If you do not use Rendered Elastic Audio processing in your session, no Rendered Files folder will be created in the session folder.

Session File Backups

If you enable the AutoSave function in Pro Tools, the Session File Backups folder will be created automatically, and auto-saved session files will be stored in this location.

Video Files

The Video Files folder is used when you digitize a movie into Pro Tools using an Avid video peripheral, such as the Avid Mojo. When you import a movie that is already in digital form (such as a QuickTime or Avid video file), the session references that movie in its stored location and does not copy it into your current Pro Tools session folder.

Tip: For maximum session portability, you might want to create a Video Files folder, if it does not already exist, and copy existing movies into it prior to importing them into your session.

Starting Pro Tools

Because Pro Tools systems are typically composed of both hardware and software, preparing your system for use might involve more than simply turning on your computer and launching the Pro Tools application. The larger the system, the more important it becomes to follow a specific startup sequence.

Powering Up Your Hardware

When starting your Pro Tools hardware, it's important to power up the system components in the proper order. Starting components out of sequence could cause a component to not be recognized, prevent the software from launching, or cause unexpected behavior.

The recommended sequence for starting a Pro Tools system is as follows:

1. Make sure all your equipment (including your computer) is off.

2. Turn on any external hard drives that use external power and wait about 10 seconds for them to spin up to speed.

3. Turn on any MIDI interfaces and MIDI devices (including any MIDI control surfaces) and synchronization peripherals.

4. Turn on your audio interface. Wait at least 15 seconds for the audio interface to initialize.

5. Start your computer.

6. Turn on your audio monitoring system, if applicable.

Tip: Some audio interfaces, such as the Fast Track USB and the Pro Tools Mbox, get their power from the computer; these interfaces do not need to be powered up in advance.

Tip: Additional steps may be required to start up a Pro Tools system with HD-series interfaces and peripherals. Consult the Getting Started guide that came with your system for details.

Using the PACE iLok System

Pro Tools 10 software is protected with an iLok key, as are many other Avid third-party software products and plug-ins. Using an iLok key for Pro Tools enables you to use a single key for all of your plug-ins and software options.

The iLok is a USB smart key that contains licenses for your protected software products. Pro Tools 10 is compatible with the original iLok key as well as the newer, second-generation iLok key. The original iLok design stored more than 100 separate licenses from multiple software vendors on a single key; the new design will store up to 500 separate licenses. The iLok enables you to carry your software licenses with you wherever you go in a portable, convenient, and hassle-free key. Details and tools for managing your iLok keys and licenses are available at www.ilok.com.

Figure 2.2
The PACE iLok key (original design, left; new design, right)

Because your Pro Tools software requires iLok authorization, you'll need to insert your iLok key into an available USB port on your computer before launching Pro Tools 10.

Launching Pro Tools

Pro Tools software can be launched by double-clicking on the application icon on the system's internal drive or by double-clicking on a shortcut to the application. In Windows systems, the application is typically installed under C:\Program Files\Avid\Pro Tools, and a shortcut is placed on the desktop. In the Mac OS, the application is typically placed under Applications\Avid\Pro Tools.

Figure 2.3
The Pro Tools application icon

Tip: On Windows systems, Pro Tools may also be available from the Start menu at the lower-left corner of the display.

Tip: Mac users might want to create a shortcut to the Pro Tools application on the Dock. To do so, simply drag the application icon onto the Dock.

When you launch Pro Tools, the application starts with no session open. From this point, you can change settings that affect the application's overall performance, depending on your needs. (Note that you might have to dismiss the Quick Start dialog box first; see the "Quick Start Dialog Box" section in Lesson 3, "Creating Your First Session.")

Optimizing Host-Based Pro Tools Performance

Pro Tools systems (without DSP cards) utilize the computer's processing capacity (called *host-based processing*) to carry out operations such as recording, playback, mixing, and Native plug-in processing (effects and virtual instruments). Pro Tools|HD and Pro Tools|HDX systems use dedicated DSP cards for most of their audio processing power; however, they can also use host-based processing capacity for Native plug-in processing.

While the default system settings are adequate for most processing tasks, Pro Tools lets you adjust the performance of a system by changing settings that affect its host-based processing capacity (the Hardware Buffer Size and the CPU Usage Limit).

Hardware Buffer Size

The Hardware Buffer Size (H/W Buffer Size) controls the size of the hardware cache used to handle host-based tasks, such as Native plug-in processing.

- Lower Hardware Buffer Size settings reduce monitoring latency and are useful when you are recording live input.

- Higher Hardware Buffer Size settings allow for more audio processing and effects and are useful when you are mixing and using more Native plug-ins.

Tip: The H/W Buffer Size setting does not affect DSP processing, which is performed by dedicated cards on Pro Tools|HD and Pro Tools|HDX systems.

CPU Usage Limit

The CPU Usage Limit controls the percentage of the computer's processing power allocated to Pro Tools host processing tasks.

- Lower CPU Usage Limit settings limit the effect of Pro Tools processing on other processing-intensive tasks, such as screen redraws, and are useful when you are experiencing slow system response or when you are running other applications at the same time as Pro Tools.

- Higher CPU Usage Limit settings allocate more processing power to Pro Tools and are useful for playing back large sessions or using more Native plug-ins.

Modifying Hardware Buffer Size and/or CPU Usage Limit Settings

Adjustments to the Hardware Buffer Size and CPU Usage Limit can be made in the Playback Engine dialog box, as follows:

1. Choose SETUP > PLAYBACK ENGINE.

2. From the H/W Buffer Size pop-up menu, select the audio buffer size in samples—lower the setting to reduce latency; raise it to increase processing power for plug-ins.

3. From the CPU Usage Limit pop-up menu, select the percentage of CPU processing to allocate to Pro Tools—lower the setting to increase system response; raise it to increase processing power for Pro Tools.

4. Click **OK**.

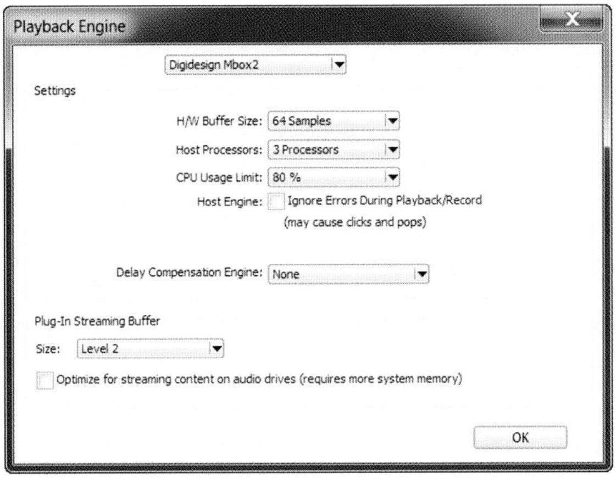

Figure 2.4
Pro Tools Playback Engine dialog box

▲▼ ▮▶
In the Avid Learning Series

Additional details on the Playback Engine dialog box are covered in the Pro Tools 110 course.

The Pro Tools Software Interface

Before beginning to work on a session, you should have some basic familiarity with the Pro Tools software interface. The software interface is displayed once you create or open a session by choosing FILE > NEW SESSION, FILE > OPEN SESSION, or FILE > OPEN RECENT. Details on creating and opening sessions are provided in Lesson 3.

This section introduces you to the menu structure and main windows in Pro Tools 10.

The Menu Structure

Among the first things you see upon launching Pro Tools is the menu system across the top of the screen. Learning how the menus are organized will save you a lot of time when you are trying to find a specific Pro Tools function. Following is a brief description of each menu.

File Menu

File menu commands let you create and maintain Pro Tools sessions. The File menu includes options for opening, creating, and saving sessions; bouncing tracks; and importing and exporting session components.

Edit Menu

Edit menu commands allow you to edit and manipulate the current selection and to affect data in the Timeline. The Edit menu includes options for copying and pasting; duplicating, repeating, and shifting selections; trimming, separating, and healing clips; and performing similar operations.

View Menu

View menu commands control how Pro Tools windows, tracks, and track data are displayed. Some View menu commands toggle the display of various component parts of Pro Tools windows. Select the command to display a component or view feature; deselect the command to hide it.

Tip: Though commonly confused, the View menu and the Window menu serve distinctly different functions. Commands in the View menu affect parts of a window or change how the elements within a window are displayed. By contrast, commands in the Window menu show or hide entire windows or arrange the windows on the screen.

Track Menu

Track menu commands let you set up and maintain tracks in a Pro Tools session. The Track menu includes track-based operations, such as options for creating, duplicating, grouping, deleting, and modifying tracks and track settings.

Clip Menu

Clip menu commands allow you to work with Pro Tools *clips*. Clips are essentially "pointers" to available audio or MIDI files or file segments. The Clip menu includes options for arranging, grouping, looping, quantizing, warping, and otherwise modifying clips and clip settings.

Tip: In Pro Tools HD software, certain Clip menu commands are also available for working with Video clips.

Tip: Clips in Pro Tools 10 were known as *regions* in earlier versions of the software.

Event Menu

The Event menu contains commands for modifying the time and tempo settings of your Pro Tools session, for working with MIDI and audio events and operations, and for adjusting various properties of MIDI recordings.

AudioSuite Menu

The AudioSuite menu allows you to access all AudioSuite plug-ins currently installed in your system's Plug-Ins folder. AudioSuite plug-ins apply non-real-time, file-based processing to selections in Pro Tools. AudioSuite processing applies a plug-in effect permanently, replacing a selection with a newly rendered audio file.

Options Menu

The Options menu commands let you select several editing, recording, monitoring, playback, and display options. From this menu, you can enable loop recording, turn on pre- and post-roll, engage Dynamic Transport mode, set scrolling options, and make other similar choices.

Tip: The Options menu displays independent functions that toggle on or off. Menu items with a check mark next to them are currently on, or enabled; items without a check mark are off, or disabled. Selecting an item toggles its state on/off.

Setup Menu

The Setup menu lets you configure various Pro Tools hardware and software parameters. It includes options for configuring your peripheral devices, such as audio interfaces; configuring host-based processing options; setting disk allocations; mapping I/O settings; configuring session and MIDI settings; configuring Click/Countoff behavior; and modifying your Pro Tools preferences.

Tip: All items under the Setup menu display a dialog box when selected. The choices in the Setup menu allow you to configure functions or operations that involve multiple settings.

Window Menu

Window menu commands allow you to display various Pro Tools windows and palettes. The Window menu includes commands for toggling the Edit, Mix, and Transport windows; the Pro Tools Task Manager; the Workspace and Project browsers; and the Window Configurations, Automation, Memory Locations, Video, Color Palette, Undo History, and other displays.

Store Menu

New to Pro Tools 10, the Store menu provides easy access to the online Avid Store, allowing you to log in to your Avid account and/or purchase plug-ins using an in-application web browser.

Help Menu

The Help menu provides links to important Pro Tools documentation and online resources, including the Pro Tools online help system, the Pro Tools Knowledge Base, Avid Audio Forums, the Customer Assist tool, the Audio Plug-Ins Guide, the Pro Tools Menus Guide, the Pro Tools Reference Guide, and Pro Tools Shortcuts documentation.

Main Pro Tools Windows

Pro Tools software provides a host of windows you can use to perform a variety of tasks and functions. The three primary windows that you will need to be familiar with to begin working with Pro Tools are the Edit window, the Mix window, and the Transport window. Pro Tools also includes two additional types of main windows: the MIDI Editor window and the Score Editor window.

Edit Window

The Edit window provides a timeline display of audio, MIDI data, video, and mixer automation for recording, editing, and arranging tracks. It displays waveforms for the audio in your session and is the main window that you will use to work directly with audio, MIDI, and video files in Pro Tools. Each Audio and MIDI track displayed in the Edit window has controls for Record Enable, Solo, Mute, and Automation Mode.

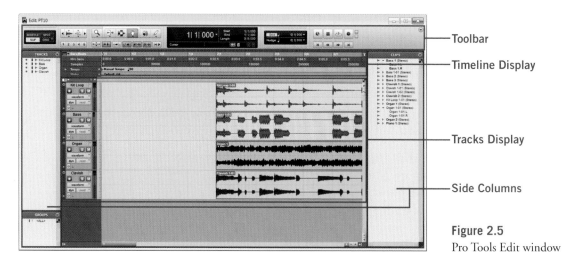

Figure 2.5
Pro Tools Edit window

Edit Tools

Pro Tools provides several Edit tools in the toolbar area at the top of the Edit window. The Edit tools are used to select, move, trim, and otherwise modify regions in Pro Tools. The functionality of each Edit tool is described in the "Edit Tool Functions" section later in this lesson.

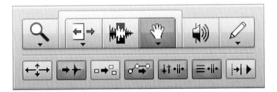

Figure 2.6
Edit tool buttons

Edit Modes

Pro Tools provides selector buttons in the toolbar area at the top of the Edit window for activating each of its four Edit modes. The Edit modes (Shuffle, Spot, Slip, and Grid) affect the movement and placement of audio and MIDI clips (and individual MIDI notes). The Edit modes also affect how commands such as Copy and Paste function and how the various Edit tools (Trim, Selector, Grabber, and Pencil) work. The Edit modes are described in the "Edit Mode Features" section later in this lesson.

Figure 2.7
Edit mode buttons

Edit Window Side Columns

The Edit window includes columns on the left and right sides that provide additional view and display options for your session data. Along the left side of the Edit window is a vertical column that contains the Track List and Edit Group List. The Track List is at the top of the column and contains a pop-up menu used to display and sort tracks. Directly beneath the Track List is the Edit Group List, where the track grouping status is displayed. (Track grouping is covered in the Pro Tools 110 course.) Both lists in the left-side column contain display areas and pop-up menus for their respective functions.

Along the right side of the Edit window is a separate vertical column that contains the Clip List. The Clip List includes a pop-up menu and display area for the audio and MIDI files and file segments (clips) that are currently available in the session. On systems running Pro Tools HD software, the Clip List will also display Video files and clips.

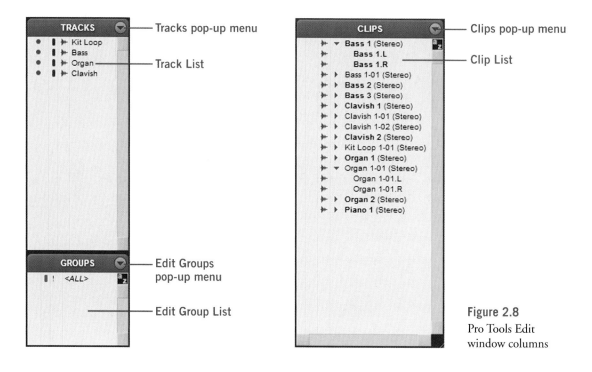

Figure 2.8
Pro Tools Edit window columns

Pro Tools lets you customize the display of Edit window side columns to accommodate your needs at any given point in your project. You can show and hide the left and right columns independently or adjust their display widths and heights as needed. By sizing or hiding these columns, you can control the amount of horizontal display area that is available for your track views in the Edit window, as well as simplify the Edit window view.

To show or hide either the left or right side column, do the following:

■ Click the arrow icon located in the bottom corner corresponding to the column you want to show or hide. The arrow icon will reverse to point in the opposite direction, and the column will slide into or out of view.

■ Click the corresponding arrow icon again to return to the previous view.

-Or-

■ Double-click with your pointer positioned over the column separator (where the cursor changes to a double-headed arrow). The column will slide into or out of view.

To adjust column width or height, follow these steps:

1. Position your pointer over the column separator where the cursor changes into a double-headed arrow.

2. Click and drag on the column separator to adjust its position as needed.

Ruler Views

Rulers are horizontal displays that appear in the Timeline display area of the Edit window, just above your tracks display. Pro Tools' Rulers provide measurement indicators to help you identify specific locations in your session's Timeline. You can display or hide any combination of the following Rulers in the Edit window:

■ **Bars|Beats.** This Ruler is useful for music editors, composers, and musicians.

■ **Min:Sec.** This Ruler is useful for radio or those who need to measure in absolute time.

■ **Samples.** This Ruler displays the system's smallest editing resolution.

■ **Time Code and Time Code 2.** These Rulers are primarily used for video and film post-production and some professional music applications.

■ **Feet+Frames.** This Ruler is also used for video and film post-production work.

■ **Tempo.** This Ruler allows you to specify changes in tempo within the session.

■ **Key Signature.** This Ruler allows you to specify key changes within the session.

■ **Chord Symbols.** This Ruler allows you to add chord symbols to the session to indicate chord changes.

■ **Meter.** This Ruler allows you to specify changes in meter within the session.

■ **Markers.** This Ruler allows you to create markers to identify and recall important track locations and view settings within the session.

Additional information on Rulers is provided in the "Time Scales and Rulers" section later in this lesson.

Figure 2.9
Pro Tools Ruler displays

Customizing the Toolbar

Pro Tools allows users to customize the toolbar in the Edit window using the Edit
Window Toolbar menu in the upper-right corner of the window. This menu lets
you show or hide various controls and displays in the toolbar. You can also move
toolbar controls and arrange them according to your preferences.

Tip: You can show and hide control and display elements in the MIDI Editor and
      Score Editor windows using the same methods.

To show or hide a control or display, click on the Edit Window Toolbar menu icon
(or right-click on the toolbar background) and select or deselect an item from the
menu.

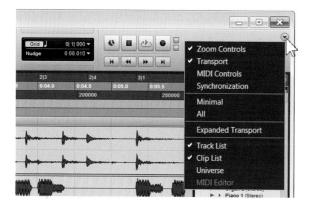

Figure 2.10
Using the Edit Window Toolbar menu
to show or hide parts of the window

The display elements available under the Edit Window Toolbar menu include the
following:

■ **Zoom controls.** When selected, the Zoom controls are displayed in the Edit
   window toolbar.

Figure 2.11
Zoom controls in the Edit window

■ **Transport.** When selected, the Transport controls are displayed in the Edit window toolbar.

Figure 2.12
Transport controls in the Edit window

■ **MIDI controls.** When selected, the MIDI controls are displayed in the Edit window toolbar.

Figure 2.13
MIDI controls in the Edit window

To move a set of controls in the toolbar, Ctrl-click (Windows) or Command-click (Mac) on a non-active part of the toolbar near the controls you wish to move and drag the set to a new area of the toolbar. For example, if you prefer the Zoom controls to be located to the right of the Edit tools in the toolbar, simply Ctrl-click (Windows) or Command-click (Mac) and drag them to that location.

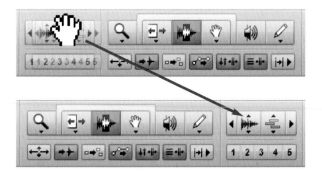

Figure 2.14
Moving controls in the Edit window toolbar

Mix Window

The Mix window provides a mixer-like environment for recording and mixing audio. In the Mix window, tracks appear as mixer strips (also called *channel strips*). Each track displayed in the Mix window has controls for inserts, sends, input and output assignments, Automation mode selection, panning, and volume. The channel strips also provide buttons for enabling record, toggling solo and mute on and off, and selecting voice assignments and mix groups.

Figure 2.15
Pro Tools Mix window

Signal Routing Controls

The top portion of each channel strip in the Mix window provides controls for routing signals into and out of the track. These controls include Insert selectors, Send selectors, Input selectors, and Output selectors. Insert selectors can be used to add real-time effects processing to a track using one of your loaded plug-ins. Send selectors can be used to route a track's signal to an available bus path or output path. The Input and Output selectors are used to route input and output signals from your audio interface for recording or playback.

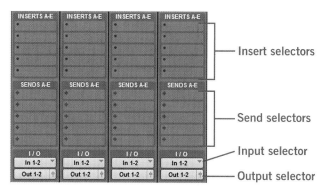

Figure 2.16
Signal routing controls

Record and Playback Controls

Immediately beneath the signal routing controls in the Mix window is a series of controls that are used to set record and playback options. These controls include the Automation Mode selector; the Pan controls; the Track Record Enable, Solo, and Mute buttons; and the Volume Fader for each track. The Automation Mode selector can be used to enable various options for Pro Tools' automatable parameters. The Pan controls can be used to position the output of a track within a stereo field (or output pair). The buttons for Track Record Enable, Solo, and Mute can be used to activate and deactivate each of these functions for a track during record and playback operations. The Volume Fader can be used to adjust the playback/monitoring level of a track.

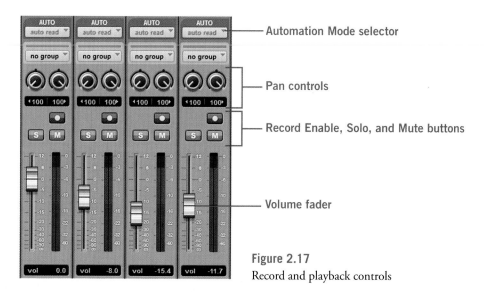

Figure 2.17
Record and playback controls

Tip: The Volume Fader in the Mix window does not affect the input gain (record level) of a signal being recorded. The signal level must be set appropriately at the source or adjusted using a preamp or gain-equipped audio interface.

Mix Window Side Column

The Mix window includes a single column located on the left side that provides additional view and display options for your session data. The Mix window side column contains the Track List and Mix Group List. The Track List is at the top of the column and is used to display and sort tracks. Directly beneath the Track List is the Mix Group List, where the track grouping status is displayed. (Track grouping is covered in the Pro Tools 110 course.) Both lists in the Mix window side column contain display areas and pop-up menus for their respective functions.

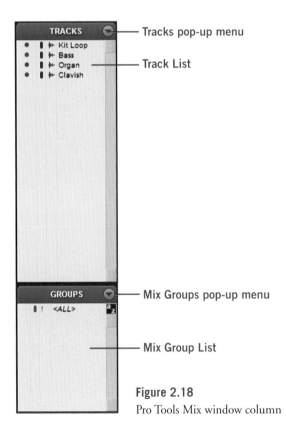

Figure 2.18
Pro Tools Mix window column

As with the Edit window side columns, Pro Tools lets you customize the display of the Mix window side column as needed. You can show and hide the side column, adjust the display width, and adjust the relative height of the lists in the same manner as the columns in the Edit window.

Transport Window

The Transport window provides buttons for various transport functions that operate similarly to the controls on a CD or DVD player. (These are the same Transport controls that can optionally be displayed in the Edit window toolbar.) The Transport window can also be set to display counters (Location Indicators) and MIDI controls. The Location Indicators in the Transport window mirror the Main and Sub Counters at the top of the Edit window in normal operation.

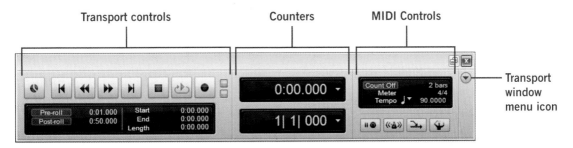

Figure 2.19
The Transport window, showing Transport controls, counters, and MIDI controls in Expanded Transport display

Tip: Controls and display elements in the Transport window can be shown/hidden using options under the main View > Transport menu or the Transport window menu.

Counters

Enabling the counters in the Transport window will display the Location Indicators to the right of the Transport controls. The Location Indicators provide information for navigation and editing via a Main Location Indicator and a Sub Location Indicator. The Main and Sub Location Indicators can be set for different Time Scale formats (such as Samples, Bars|Beats, or Minutes:Seconds).

The Main Location Indicator in the Transport window provides a convenient way to navigate to a specific time location. To navigate with the Main Location Indicator, follow these steps:

1. Click in the **MAIN LOCATION INDICATOR**.

2. Type in a location.

3. Press **ENTER** (Windows) or **RETURN** (Mac). The Timeline insertion point will automatically move to the new location.

MIDI Controls

The Transport window includes a MIDI controls section, providing options for playing back your session and recording MIDI data. The MIDI controls let you set options for triggering MIDI recording, playing metronome clicks, overdubbing MIDI, using a tempo map, and setting the tempo and meter. The functions of the MIDI controls are described in more detail in the "MIDI Control Features" section later in this lesson.

Additional Editor Windows

Although the primary Edit window works well for general editing operations, Pro Tools provides two additional types of editor windows focused on specific editing and presentation tasks. These are the MIDI Editor window and the Score Editor window.

MIDI Editor Window

Pro Tools provides MIDI Editor windows for detailed MIDI composition and editing tasks. MIDI Editor windows can show MIDI data and automation data for Auxiliary Input, Instrument, and MIDI tracks. You can open several separate MIDI Editor windows simultaneously, each providing a different view of the MIDI data in your Pro Tools session. You can also display a "docked" MIDI Editor window (also known as the *MIDI Editor view*) at the bottom of the primary Edit window.

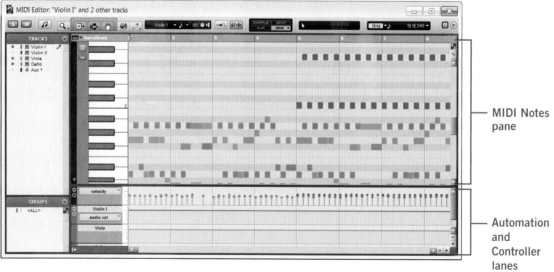

MIDI Notes pane

Automation and Controller lanes

Figure 2.20
MIDI Editor window

MIDI Editor windows display and let you edit MIDI data for one or more MIDI and Instrument tracks. When displaying multiple tracks, the MIDI Editor window superimposes the notes from each of the tracks in the MIDI Notes pane. The MIDI Editor window can also display automation and controller lanes for velocity stalks, volume automation playlists, and other continuous controller and automation data.

Tip: **Automation playlists are discussed in Lesson 9.**

Score Editor Window

The Score Editor window lets you view, edit, arrange, and print MIDI data from your session as music notation. The Score Editor transcribes MIDI notes in real time and provides tools for navigating and editing in Notation view. It also provides Notation Display Track settings to specify how individual MIDI and Instrument tracks appear in the Score Editor. You can set the page layout and staff spacing and specify the title and composer for the score using the Score Setup window.

Figure 2.21
Score Editor window

Window Management

The Pro Tools Window menu provides commands to tile or cascade all open windows. These commands do not affect floating windows or the Transport window, but all other windows will rearrange automatically according to the selected command.

The Tile command arranges open windows in a tiled pattern on the screen, resizing each window as needed to fit. Two other commands, Tile Vertical and Tile Horizontal, resize windows uniformly, creating evenly distributed patterns. The Tile Vertical command arranges windows as narrow vertical strips, side by side; whereas the Tile Horizontal command arranges windows as long horizontal strips, stacked top to bottom. These two commands are not available when too many windows are open to display at once.

The Cascade command arranges open windows in a cascading pattern on the screen. The windows are overlaid on top of one another and resized to near full-screen. Only the top and left edges of underlying windows remain visible behind the foreground window.

Help Menu Items and Tool Tips

The Help menu provides links to the Pro Tools Help system, online resources, and various other reference files that are installed with Pro Tools.

In addition to the Help menu, the Pro Tools user interface provides Tool Tips in all main windows to help you solve any question that you may come across in Pro Tools. When you park the cursor for a few seconds over an abbreviated name (such as a track name or an output assignment) or over an unlabeled icon or tool, Pro Tools will display the full name of the item or its function.

Tool Tips are an optional display element controlled via the Tool Tips Display options in the Display Preferences pane (SETUP > PREFERENCES, DISPLAY tab). Tool Tips settings provide two options: *Function* shows the basic function of the item, and *Details* shows the complete name of an abbreviated name or item. Tool Tips can be set to display either or both of these options, or they can be turned off altogether.

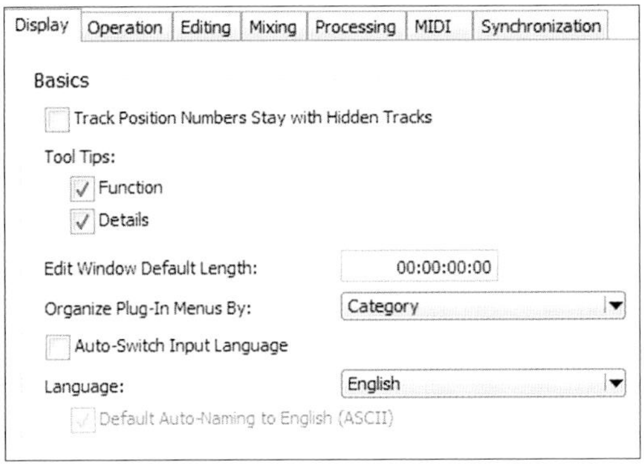

| Display | Operation | Editing | Mixing | Processing | MIDI | Synchronization |

Basics

☐ Track Position Numbers Stay with Hidden Tracks

Tool Tips:
    ☑ Function
    ☑ Details

Edit Window Default Length: `00:00:00:00`

Organize Plug-In Menus By: `Category ▼`

☐ Auto-Switch Input Language

Language: `English ▼`

    ☑ Default Auto-Naming to English (ASCII)

Figure 2.22

Basics section of the Display Preferences page showing selected Tool Tips options

Edit Tool Functions

The Edit tools located in the toolbar area at the top of the Edit window provide access to Pro Tools' powerful audio and MIDI editing functions. The Edit tools include the Zoomer tool, the Trim tool, the Selector tool, the Grabber tool, the Scrubber tool, the Pencil tool, and the Smart Tool.

Zoomer Tool

Use the Zoomer tool to zoom into and out of a particular area within a track. Zooming in is often helpful to examine a clip or waveform closely.

The Zoomer tool offers two modes: Normal and Single Zoom mode.

■ In Normal Zoom mode, the Zoomer tool remains selected after zooming.

■ In Single Zoom mode, the previously selected tool is automatically reselected after zooming.

Figure 2.23
Normal Zoom mode

Figure 2.24
Single Zoom mode

To use the Zoomer tool, select it and click on the desired point within the track onto which you want to zoom in. Each click zooms all tracks in by one level, and the Edit window is centered on the zoom point.

To zoom in on a particular area in the Edit window, drag with the Zoomer tool over the area you want to view. As you drag, a gray box will appear, indicating the range on which you will be zooming in. Release the mouse to fill the window with the selected portion of the waveform.

Tip: You can also use the Zoomer tool for Marquee Zooming, allowing you to
zoom in on a waveform both horizontally and vertically. To use Marquee
Zooming, Ctrl-drag (Windows) or Command-drag (Mac) with the Zoomer tool.

To zoom out, hold ALT (Windows) or OPTION (Mac) while clicking with the
ZOOMER tool.

Reverse an Operation with the Alt/Option Key

The Alt/Option modifier (Windows/Mac, respectively) provides several standard functions in
Pro Tools. Among these is the Reverse Operation function. By adding the Alt/Option modifier
to a keyboard or Edit tool action, you can cause Pro Tools to perform the reverse or opposite
action. Try adding this key with the Trim tool to reverse the trim direction or with the Pencil
tool when editing MIDI notes to use it as an eraser.

Shortcut: Double-click on the ZOOMER tool to get a full track view that fills the
Edit window with the longest visible track in the session.

Trim Tool

Use the Trim tool to trim excess audio, MIDI, or video content from the beginning or end of a continuous section of program material, or *clip*. The Trim tool
modifies clips non-destructively, leaving the underlying source audio or video files
unchanged. This tool allows you to quickly crop a clip or to adjust the cropping
on a clip to re-expose material up to the entire length of the underlying source
file. The first time you trim an uncropped clip, Pro Tools automatically adds a
new item to the Clip List corresponding to the newly created subset clip. The subset clip is given a new name to differentiate it from the original.

Figure 2.25
Standard Trim tool

Tip: The Trim tool button also provides access to the Time Compression/Expansion
(TCE) Trim tool, the Loop Trim tool, and the Scrub Trim tool (Pro Tools HD only).

*In the Avid
Learning Series*

Alternate Trim tools are covered in detail in the 200-level Pro
Tools courses.

Selector Tool

Use the Selector tool to position the playback cursor or to select an area in a track for playback or editing. To position the playback cursor, click with the **Selector** tool at the point where you want playback to begin. To select an area for playback or editing, drag with the **Selector** tool across any area on one or more tracks. To add to or remove from an existing selection, hold the Shift key and click (or click and drag) to the left or right.

Figure 2.26
Selector tool

The Selector tool selects horizontally and vertically, allowing selections across multiple tracks in a single operation. Selected areas appear highlighted in the Edit window. In addition, the selection is indicated by a dark overlay in the Timeline area at the top of the window.

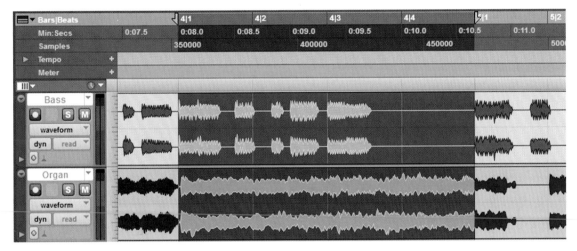

Figure 2.27
Selection across multiple tracks

You can use the Selector tool to quickly make a lengthy selection, as follows:

1. Click with the **Selector** tool to position the playback cursor where you want the selection to start.

2. Scroll to the desired endpoint using the scroll bar at the bottom of the Edit window.

3. Shift-click at the desired endpoint to complete the selection.

Grabber Tool

Use the Grabber tool to select an entire clip with a single mouse click, to move clips along the Timeline within their current tracks, and to move clips between tracks.

Figure 2.28
Grabber tool button

To select a clip, click anywhere on the clip in the Edit window using the **GRABBER** tool. To move a clip along the Timeline, click anywhere on the clip and drag to the left or right with the **GRABBER** tool. Dragging a clip vertically with the Grabber tool will move the clip to another track in your session.

The Grabber tool can be used to position clips in a variety of ways, depending on the Edit mode that is currently selected. Clips can be moved freely along the Timeline in Slip mode or can be positioned numerically via a dialog box using Spot mode. Clips can also be made to snap to other clips or to Timeline increments using Shuffle or Grid mode, respectively. An overview of the Edit modes is provided in the "Edit Mode Features" section later in this lesson.

Tip: The Grabber tool button also provides access to the Separation Grabber and Object Grabber tools.

In the Avid   Alternate Grabber tools are covered in the Pro Tools 201 course.
Learning Series

Scrubber Tool

Use the Scrubber tool to "scrub" slowly across Audio tracks in the Edit window to find a particular moment or audio event. Scrubbing originated in tape editing as a process of rocking the tape back and forth past the playhead to locate a precise position (usually for the sake of performing a splice). By scrubbing back and forth over an audio waveform in Pro Tools, you can listen closely and zero in on an exact edit point.

Figure 2.29
Scrubber tool

To scrub audio or MIDI in Pro Tools, click on a track in the Edit window with the **SCRUBBER** tool and drag left or right to begin playback at that point. Playback speed and direction vary with mouse movement. Scrubbing becomes smoother as you increase the magnification of the screen. For best results and more precise scrubbing, zoom in on the material you want to scrub.

Tip: Dragging the Scrubber tool between two adjacent mono or stereo Audio tracks allows you to scrub the two tracks together.

Pencil Tool

You can use the Pencil tool to destructively "redraw" waveform data. This feature is most commonly used to repair a pop or click in an audio file. A pop or click appears as a sudden sharp spike in a waveform. This tool becomes active only when the Edit window is zoomed in to the sample level.

Figure 2.30
Pencil tool

The Pencil tool is also useful for creating and editing MIDI data. The Pencil tool shapes (Freehand, Line, Triangle, Square, and Random) can be used to enter pitches with varying durations and velocities. The various Pencil tool shapes can be particularly useful for drawing and editing different types of automation or MIDI control data—common examples include using Line for volume, Triangle for pan, Freehand for pitch bend, and Square or Random for velocity.

Smart Tool

Use the Smart Tool to provide instant access to the Selector, Grabber, and Trim tools and to perform fades and crossfades. This tool is active when the Trim, Selector, and Grabber are all selected (highlighted in blue). To activate the Smart Tool, click on any one of the member tools and then Shift-click on any other member tool. When active, the position of the cursor in relation to a clip or note or within an automation playlist determines how the Smart Tool functions.

Figure 2.31
Smart Tool in the Edit window

To use the Smart Tool as a Selector, position the tool over the middle of an audio clip, in the upper half. To use it as a Grabber, position it in the lower half. For the Trim tool, position the Smart Tool near the clip's start or end point.

The Smart Tool can also be used to create fade-ins, fade-outs, and crossfades.

In the Avid Learning Series   **The functions of the Smart Tool are covered in detail in the Pro Tools 201 course.**

Edit Mode Features

Pro Tools has four Edit modes: Shuffle, Slip, Spot, and Grid. The Edit mode is selected by clicking the corresponding mode button on the left side of the toolbar area in the Edit window.

Figure 2.32
Edit mode buttons

Shortcut: You can also use function keys F1 (Shuffle), F2 (Slip), F3 (Spot), and
F4 (Grid) to set the Edit mode.

The Edit mode affects the movement and placement of audio clips, MIDI clips and notes, and video clips. It also affects how commands such as Copy and Paste function, as well as how the various Edit tools work (Trim, Selector, Grabber, and Pencil).

Shuffle Mode

In Shuffle mode, clip movement is constrained by other clips, and any changes you make affect the placement of subsequent clips on the track. When you move a clip in Shuffle mode, it will snap to the previous or next clip on the track. Additionally, when you perform an edit (trim, cut/delete, or paste material), all clips to the right will slide along the Timeline in train-car fashion to make space (when adding material) or to close a gap (when removing material).

Use Shuffle mode as a convenient way to make clips line up next to each other, without overlapping or leaving silence between them.

Slip Mode

In Slip mode, you can move, trim, cut, or paste clips freely within a track without affecting the placement of other clips on the track. In this mode, you can place a clip anywhere on a track, leaving space between it and other clips, if desired. It is also possible to move a clip so that it overlaps or completely covers another clip.

Use Slip mode when you want the Trim, Selector, Grabber, and Pencil tools to work without restrictions to placement in time.

Spot Mode

In Spot mode, you can move or place clips at precise locations by specifying the destination location in a dialog box. As in Slip mode, edit operations do not affect the placement of other clips on the track.

When Spot mode is enabled, Pro Tools prompts you with a dialog box when working with clips, allowing you to specify the start, end, duration, or other relevant parameters. Use Spot mode when you want to control the placement or duration of a clip using precise numerical values.

Grid Mode

In Grid mode, clips and MIDI notes that are moved, trimmed, or inserted will snap to the nearest time increment using the currently selected Time Scale and Grid size. Grid mode can be applied using either Absolute or Relative positioning options. (See Lesson 8 for details.)

Use Grid mode for making precise edits and aligning clips and selections using precise time intervals.

Time Scales and Rulers

Every Pro Tools session uses a Main Time Scale and a Sub Time Scale. The Main Time Scale is the time format used for Transport functions; selection Start, End, and Length fields; and Grid and Nudge values. The Sub Time Scale provides additional timing reference and can be displayed along with the Main Time Scale in the Counters areas of the Edit window and the Transport window.

Pro Tools also provides various Rulers to help you navigate along the Timeline. Rulers can be displayed for a variety of time formats, including, but not limited to, the time formats used for the Main Time Scale and Sub Time Scale. Rulers appear in the Timeline display area at the top of the Edit window.

Main Time Scale

When the Main Time Scale in a Pro Tools session is set to Min:Sec, Timeline locations are represented in minutes and seconds relative to the start point of the session. When set to Bars|Beats, Timeline locations are represented in bars, beats, and ticks relative to the start point of the session (Bar 1, Beat 1).

The Main Time Scale determines the timebase units used for the following:

■ The Main Counter in the Edit window

■ The Main Location Indicator in the Transport window

- Selection Start, End, and Length values

- Pre- and Post-Roll amounts

- Initial Grid and Nudge values

The Main Time Scale can be set to Bars|Beats, Minutes:Seconds, Time Code, Feet+Frames, or Samples. To set the Main Time Scale, do one of the following:

- Select the desired timebase using the VIEW > MAIN COUNTER menu.

Figure 2.33
Main Counter menu

- Select the desired timebase from the MAIN TIME SCALE pop-up menu for the Main Counter at the top of the Edit window.

Figure 2.34
Main Time Scale pop-up menu

■ If a Ruler is displayed for the desired timebase, click on its name so it becomes highlighted.

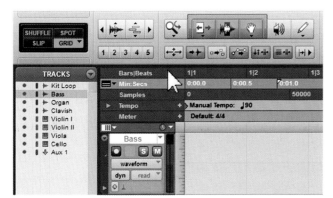

Figure 2.35
Switching the Main Time Scale using Rulers

Sub Time Scale

The Sub Time Scale in a Pro Tools session is set to Samples by default, meaning that Timeline locations are represented as sample-based values, relative to the start point of the session. The Sub Time Scale provides a convenient secondary timing reference.

Like the Main Time Scale, the Sub Time Scale can be set to Bars|Beats, Minutes:Seconds, Time Code, Feet+Frames, or Samples. To display the Sub Time Scale in the Edit menu, select **SHOW SUB COUNTER** from the Main Time Scale pop-up menu. To set the Sub Time Scale, select the desired timebase from the Sub Time Scale pop-up menu.

Figure 2.36
Sub Time Scale pop-up menu

Ruler Display Options

Pro Tools provides two types of Rulers that can be displayed in the Edit window: *Timebase Rulers* and *Conductor Rulers*.

The Pro Tools Timebase Rulers include the following:

- Bars|Beats
- Min:Sec
- Samples
- Time Code
- Time Code 2
- Feet+Frames

Tip: Timebase Rulers are commonly referred to as *Timelines* in the industry.

The Pro Tools Conductor Rulers include the following:

- Markers
- Tempo
- Meter
- Key
- Chords

You can customize your sessions to display only the Timebase and Conductor Rulers you want to work with. To display a Ruler, do one of the following:

- Choose VIEW > RULERS and select the desired Ruler from the submenu.
- Click the RULER VIEW SELECTOR and select the desired Ruler from the pop-up menu.

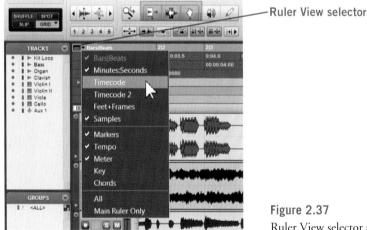

Ruler View selector

Figure 2.37
Ruler View selector and pop-up menu

To remove a Ruler from the display, do one of the following:

■ Choose VIEW > RULERS and click on a checked Ruler to deselect it.

■ From the Ruler View selector pop-up menu, click on a checked item to deselect it.

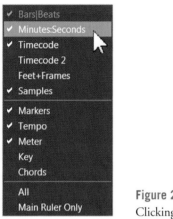

Figure 2.38
Clicking on a Ruler to deselect it

■ ALT-CLICK (Windows) or OPTION-CLICK (Mac) directly over the Ruler's nameplate in the Timeline display area.

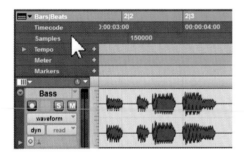

Figure 2.39
Alt-clicking/Option-clicking on the Samples Ruler nameplate to hide the Ruler

Hide Views with the Alt/Option Key

A handy feature of the Alt/Option key (Windows/Mac, respectively) is the Hide Views function. By holding the Alt/Option key while clicking on the nameplate of a Ruler or Edit window column view, you can cause Pro Tools to instantly hide that Ruler or column view.

Tip: The Ruler that corresponds to the session's Main Time Scale cannot be deselected/hidden. (The Main Time Scale Ruler is indicated by a highlight across the Ruler.)

You also have the option to change the display order of the Rulers, arranging them as needed to best fit your work style. To change the display order for the Rulers, do the following:

- Click directly on the Ruler's nameplate and drag up or down to the desired location.

In the following example, the Min:Secs Ruler is moved below the Timecode Ruler:

Figure 2.40
Rulers before and after moving the Min:Secs display

MIDI Control Features

The Edit and Transport windows provide access to various MIDI controls with options for playing back your session and recording MIDI data. The available MIDI controls include Wait for Note, Metronome, MIDI Merge, Tempo Ruler Enable, Countoff, Meter, and Tempo.

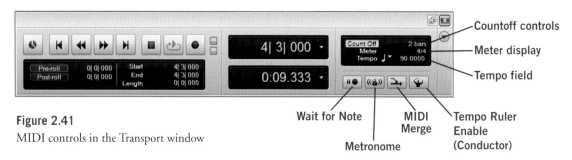

Figure 2.41
MIDI controls in the Transport window

Wait for Note

When Wait for Note is selected, recording does not begin until a MIDI event is received. This ensures that you begin recording when you're ready to play and that the first MIDI event is recorded precisely at the beginning of the record range.

Tip: You can set a preference in the MIDI Preferences page (SETUP > PREFERENCES > MIDI) to use the F11 key for Wait for Note.

Metronome

When the Metronome button is selected, a metronome will sound during playback and recording, as specified by the settings in the Click/Countoff Options dialog box (SETUP > CLICK/COUNTOFF). The simplest way to enable metronome playback is to set up a click track for your session, as described in Lesson 4.

To modify the click settings, choose SETUP > CLICK/COUNTOFF or double-click the METRONOME button in the Edit or Transport window. Enter the desired settings in the Click area of the Click/Countoff Options dialog box.

Figure 2.42
Click/Countoff Options dialog box

Tip: With the Numeric Keypad mode set to Transport (default), you can press [7] to enable the click.

Tip: To set the mode for the numeric keypad, choose SETUP > PREFERENCES > OPERATION. Select the desired mode under Numeric Keypad in the Transport section.

Countoff Controls

When Count Off is selected (highlighted) in the MIDI controls section, Pro Tools counts off a specified number of bars (measures) before playback or recording begins. The number of bars used for Count Off is indicated in the Count Off field.

To change the Count Off settings, choose SETUP > CLICK/COUNTOFF or double-click the Count Off field in the Edit or Transport window. Enter the desired settings in the Countoff area of the Click/Countoff Options dialog box.

Tip: With the Numeric Keypad mode set to Transport, you can press [8] to enable the countoff.

MIDI Merge Mode

When MIDI Merge is selected (MIDI Merge mode), recorded MIDI data will be merged with existing track material, overdubbing the track. When deselected (Replace mode), recorded MIDI data will replace existing track material.

To engage MIDI Merge mode, click on the MIDI Merge button in the Edit or Transport window. Click a second time to return to Replace mode.

Tip: With the Numeric Keypad mode set to Transport, you can press [9] to enable MIDI Merge.

Tempo Ruler Enable

When selected, Pro Tools uses the tempo map defined in the Tempo Ruler to control the tempo during playback and recording. When deselected, Pro Tools switches to Manual Tempo mode and ignores the tempo map.

In Manual Tempo mode, the tempo can also be adjusted by typing a value directly into the Tempo field or by tapping in a tempo (see "Tempo Field," below).

Meter Display

The Meter display indicates the session's current meter based on the play location. Double-click the Meter display to open the Meter Change dialog box.

Tempo Field

The Tempo field displays the session's current tempo based on the play location. In Manual Tempo mode, you can enter a BPM value directly into this field. In addition, when the Tempo field is selected, you can tap in a tempo from a MIDI controller or from the computer keyboard using the **T** key.

Review/Discussion Questions

1. Name some of the folders and files that Pro Tools creates as part of the session hierarchy. Where is the session file (.ptx) stored? (See pages 37 through 39.)

2. What is the WaveCache.wfm file used for? What happens if the WaveCache file gets deleted or goes missing? (See pages 37 and 38.)

3. Where are audio files stored in the session hierarchy? (See page 38.)

4. Where are Pro Tools' MIDI files normally stored? (See page 38.)

5. Which component should you turn on first when powering up a Pro Tools system? Which component should you turn on last? (See page 40.)

6. What type of processing does the Hardware Buffer Size affect? What type of processing does it *not* affect? (See page 42.)

7. What kinds of commands can be found under the Pro Tools View menu? How does the View menu differ from the Window menu? (See page 44.)

8. What kinds of commands can be found under the Pro Tools Options menu? How does the Options menu differ from the Setup menu? (See page 45.)

9. Which main Pro Tools window displays audio waveforms and can be used to work directly with audio, MIDI, and video files on tracks? (See page 46.)

10. Which Pro Tools window provides access to Pan controls and Volume Faders for each track? (See page 53.)

11. What icon/button is used for the Zoomer tool in the Edit window? How can you use this tool to quickly zoom out to fill the Edit window with the longest track in the session? (See pages 59 and 60.)

12. Which Edit tool is represented by a hand icon? What is this tool used for? (See page 62.)

13. Which tool is active when the Trim, Selector, and Grabber icons are all selected (highlighted in blue) in the Edit window toolbar? (See page 63.)

14. Which Pro Tools windows provide access to MIDI controls, such as Wait for Note, Metronome, and MIDI Merge? (See page 70.)

The Software Interface

In this exercise worksheet, you will identify various Pro Tools windows as well as various controls and components within those windows. This exercise reviews the material covered in Lesson 2.

Duration: 10 to 15 Minutes   **Media: None Required**

Pro Tools Windows

Refer to Figures EX2.1 through EX2.3 when answering the questions below. Refer to the section on "The Pro Tools Software Interface" in Lesson 2 for assistance.

Questions 1 through 5 refer to Figure EX2.1.

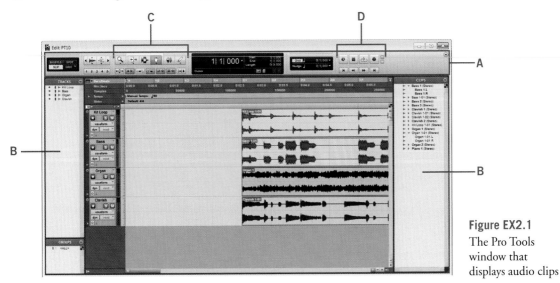

Figure EX2.1
The Pro Tools window that displays audio clips

1. The window shown in Figure EX2.1 is called the

   _____ window.

2. The area labeled **A** across the top of the window is called the

   _____.

3. The areas labeled **B** on the sides of the window are called

   _____.

4. The buttons labeled **C** at the top of the window are called

   _____.

5. The controls labeled **D** on the top-right side of the window are called

   _____ controls.

Questions 6 through 11 refer to Figure EX2.2.

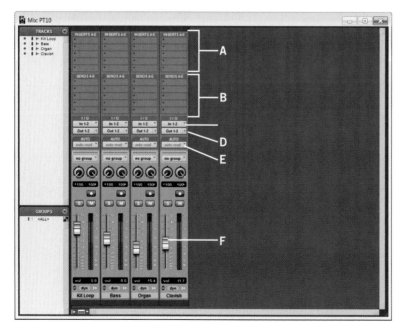

Figure EX2.2

The Pro Tools window that displays channel strips

6. The window shown in Figure EX2.2 is called the

   _____ window.

7. The signal routing controls labeled A at the top of the window are called

   _____.

8. The signal routing controls labeled B at the top of the window are called

   _____.

9. The signal routing controls labeled C and D in the I/O section are called

   the _____ selector and the

   _____ selector, respectively.

10. The control labeled E in the middle of the window is called the

    _____ selector.

11. The slider labeled F toward the bottom of the window is called the

    _____.

Questions 12 through 15 refer to Figure EX2.3.

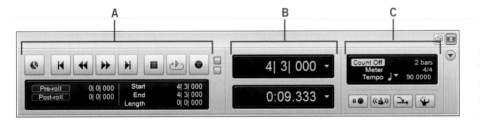

Figure EX2.3
The Pro Tools window that displays playback controls

12. The window shown in Figure EX2.3 is called the

    _____ window.

13. The controls labeled **A** on the left side of the window are called

    _____.

14. The controls labeled **B** in the middle of the window are called

_____.

15. The controls labeled **C** on the right side of the window are called

_____.

Tools and Controls

Refer to Figures EX2.4 through EX2.6 when answering the questions below. Refer to the sections on "Edit Tool Functions" and "MIDI Control Features" in Lesson 2 for assistance.

Questions 16 through 18 refer to Figure EX2.4.

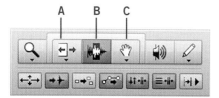

Figure EX2.4
Tool cluster in the Pro Tools Edit window

16. The button labeled **A** in Figure EX2.4 is called the

_____ tool.

17. The button labeled **B** in Figure EX2.4 is called the

_____ tool.

18. The button labeled **C** in Figure EX2.4 is called the

_____ tool.

Question 19 refers to Figure EX2.5.

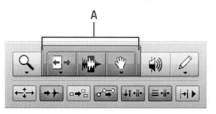

Figure EX2.5
Specialized tools in the Pro Tools Edit window

19. The combo button labeled **A** in Figure EX2.5 is called the

_____ tool.

Questions 20 through 23 refer to Figure EX2.6.

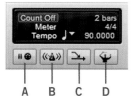

Figure EX2.6
MIDI Controls in Pro Tools

20. The button labeled **A** in Figure EX2.6 enables the

_____ function.

21. The button labeled **B** in Figure EX2.6 enables the

_____ function.

22. The button labeled **C** in Figure EX2.6 enables the

_____ function.

23. The button labeled **D** in Figure EX2.6 is the

_____ button.

Working with Sessions

OVERVIEW

Part II provides information and instructions for working with Pro Tools sessions to accomplish common audio production tasks. In the early lessons, you will learn processes for creating and configuring sessions, creating audio and MIDI recordings, and keeping session files organized. As you progress through the lessons, you will learn how to import audio and movie files, how to set up virtual instrument plug-ins, how to use selection and navigation techniques to work with audio and MIDI recordings, and how to edit your work using Edit modes, edit commands, and moving and trimming operations. In the final lessons, you will learn about Pro Tools' mixing and automation functions, plug-in operations, and mixdown and bouncing operations, as well as suggestions for sharing a completed mix on SoundCloud or burning it to a CD.

COMPONENTS

Creating Your First Session

This lesson covers the basics of working with Pro Tools sessions. It introduces session configuration options, playback and navigation options, and session saving and opening operations.

Duration: 90 Minutes

GOALS

- Choose appropriate session parameters for a project

- Create and name tracks

- Recognize the difference between the playback cursor and the edit cursor

- Navigate your session for playback and editing

- Save, locate, and open sessions on available hard drives

Before you can begin working with audio or MIDI in Pro Tools, you need to have a Pro Tools session open. This lesson covers the basics of creating a session, adding tracks to your session, navigating your session, and saving and reopening sessions.

Quick Start

When you first launch Pro Tools, the Quick Start dialog box is displayed, giving you quick access to options for creating or opening a session. The Quick Start dialog box lets you choose any of the following four actions:

- Create a new session from a template.
- Create a new blank session.
- Open any of the 10 most recent sessions.
- Open any other session on your system.

Shortcut: Press CTRL+UP ARROW or DOWN ARROW (Windows) or COMMAND+UP ARROW or DOWN ARROW (Mac) to select different session Quick Start options.

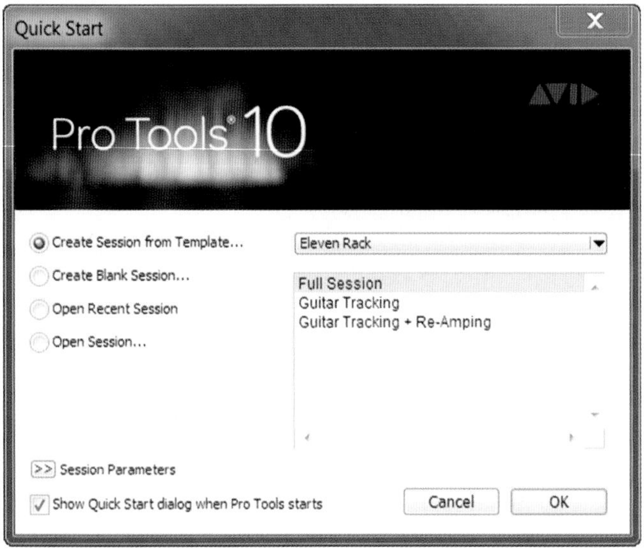

Figure 3.1
Quick Start dialog box

Creating and Configuring a Pro Tools Session

From the Quick Start dialog box, you can begin a new recording project either by selecting CREATE SESSION FROM TEMPLATE and choosing a session template from the list or by selecting CREATE BLANK SESSION. As discussed in Lesson 2, creating a session sets up a standard hierarchy of folders for the session and its associated files. The characteristics of your recording will be determined by the session parameter settings. To specify these settings, click the Session Parameters reveal button in the Quick Start dialog box. The dialog box will expand to display configurable audio and I/O parameters.

Pro Tools Session Templates

The Pro Tools installer disc includes factory session templates that are preconfigured with common track and mixer setups. You can use these templates and/or create your own to avoid having to configure your studio setup from scratch every time you start a new session.

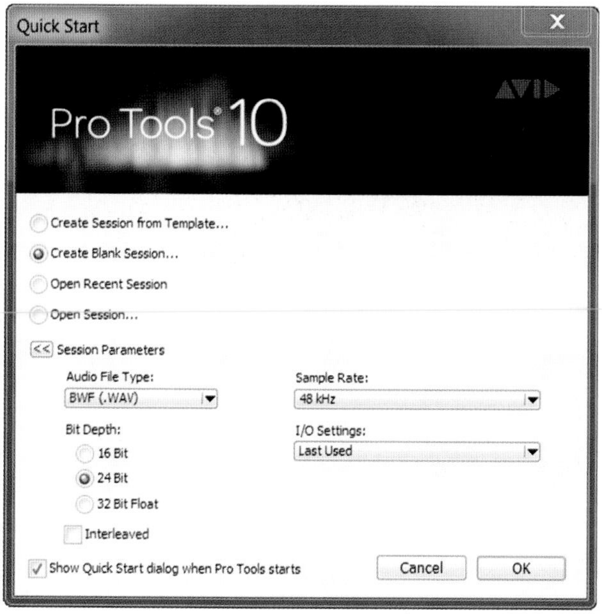

Figure 3.2

Session parameters in the Quick Start dialog box

Tip: To create a new session when the Quick Start dialog box is not being displayed, choose FILE > NEW SESSION. The New Session dialog box will appear, allowing you to specify the session parameters.

Choosing Session Parameter Settings

The session parameter settings include selections for audio file type, sample rate, I/O settings, and session bit depth.

Audio File Type

Pro Tools stores audio as WAV or AIFF files. WAV is the default file type on all platforms. Use the default (WAV) format unless you intend to work primarily with imported files in another format.

Sample Rate

Pro Tools supports sample rates up to 192 kHz with a compatible audio interface. To optimize the file sizes in your session, choose the lowest sample rate that meets the needs of the project.

A sample rate of 44.1 kHz, the industry standard for audio CDs, is often adequate for home- and project-studio recordings. Higher sample rates can be chosen for demanding projects, to capture a greater frequency response from the source audio and to minimize sound degradation throughout the project lifecycle. However, with higher sample rates come greater disk space requirements for your session. (See Table 3.1 in the "Bit Depth" section of this lesson.)

For more details on sample rates, see the "How Sample Rate Affects Frequency Resolution" section in Lesson 1.

I/O Settings

Pro Tools provides preset input and output configurations for Stereo Mix or various surround sound options (Pro Tools HD), such as 5.1 Mix I/O. You can also choose Last Used to load the settings from your last session. Use the settings that match the intended output of your final mix. For the Pro Tools 101 course, we will use the Stereo Mix setting only.

> **Tip:** Use the Stereo Mix setting whenever you are recording music or other audio intended for a general consumer market, such as music to be burned to audio CDs or to be posted as MP3 files.

Bit Depth

Pro Tools 10 works with files in 16-bit, 24-bit, or 32-bit floating-point audio resolution. The 16-bit option generates smaller files and is typically adequate for basic recordings destined for audio CDs. The 24-bit and 32-bit float options provide greater dynamic range in your recorded audio (see the "How Bit Depth Affects Amplitude Resolution" section in Lesson 1) and lower the noise floor.

These options should be used for high-end recordings that include very quiet passages (such as a classical orchestra piece), recordings that require intensive processing, and recordings intended for media that support higher resolution audio, such as DVD.

Tip: For the highest quality audio, record at 24-bit or 32-bit float and properly dither down, if needed, during the final mix. Dithering is covered in the Pro Tools 110 course.

Warning: The option for 32-bit floating-point files is new to Pro Tools 10. To provide maximum compatibility and interchange with earlier versions of Pro Tools, use 16- or 24-bit resolution.

Table 3.1 shows the relationship between sample rate, bit depth, and hard disk space consumption for the standard configurations supported in Pro Tools 10.

Table 3.1　Audio Recording Storage Requirements (Approximate)

Session Sample Rate	Session Bit Depth	Megabytes/Track Minute (Mono)	Megabytes/Track Minute (Stereo)
44.1 kHz	16-bit	5 MB	10 MB
44.1 kHz	24-bit	7.5 MB	15 MB
44.1 kHz	32-bit float	10 MB	20 MB
48 kHz	16-bit	5.5 MB	11 MB
48 kHz	24-bit	8.2 MB	16.4 MB
48 kHz	32-bit float	11 MB	22 MB
88.2 kHz	16-bit	10 MB	20 MB
88.2 kHz	24-bit	15 MB	30 MB
88.2 kHz	32-bit float	20 MB	40 MB
96 kHz	16-bit	11 MB	22 MB
96 kHz	24-bit	16.5 MB	33 MB
96 kHz	32-bit float	22 MB	44 MB
176.4 kHz	16-bit	20 MB	40 MB
176.4 kHz	24-bit	30 MB	60 MB
176.4 kHz	32-bit float	40 MB	80 MB
192 kHz	16-bit	22 MB	44 MB
192 kHz	24-bit	33 MB	66 MB
192 kHz	32-bit float	44 MB	88 MB

Creating the Session

After choosing your session parameters and clicking **OK** in the Quick Start dialog box (or the New Session dialog box), you will be prompted to choose a save location and a name for the new session.

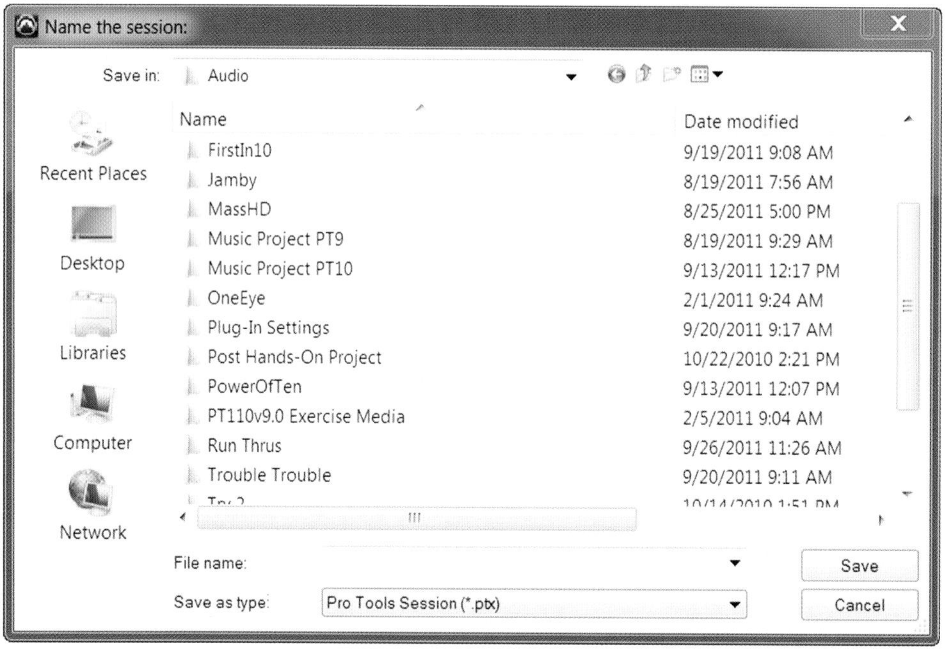

Figure 3.3
Dialog box for naming and saving a session

Using the dialog box, navigate to a valid audio drive, enter a name, and click **SAVE** to save your session-related files to the selected location. The new Pro Tools session will open, with no tracks in the Edit and Mix windows.

Tip: You can configure Pro Tools to automatically add a click track to new sessions. Choose SETUP > PREFERENCES and select the MIDI tab. Enable the option for AUTOMATICALLY CREATE CLICK TRACK IN NEW SESSIONS.

Adding Tracks

Once you've created a new session, you will need to create and name new tracks. In Pro Tools, tracks are where audio, MIDI, and automation data are recorded and edited. Audio and MIDI data can be edited into clips that are copied or repeated in different locations to create loops, to rearrange sections or entire songs, or to assemble material from multiple takes. You add tracks to a Pro Tools session using the New Tracks dialog box.

Figure 3.4
The New Tracks
dialog box

To add tracks to your session, choose **TRACK > NEW** to open the New Tracks dialog box and then choose the number of tracks and the track format, type, and timebase using the dialog box controls.

Shortcuts for Creating Tracks

Numerous shortcuts are available to speed up the process of creating new tracks. All share the Ctrl/Command modifier (Windows/Mac, respectively).

Use **CTRL/COMMAND+SHIFT+N** to open the New Tracks dialog box. Once it is displayed, use the following shortcuts to modify the settings within the New Tracks dialog box:

Change track format	Ctrl/Command+Left/Right arrow
Change track type	Ctrl/Command+Up/Down arrow
Change track timebase	Ctrl/Command+Alt/Option+Up/Down arrow
Add/remove rows	Ctrl/Command+Shift+Up/Down arrow

Track Number

The New Tracks dialog box allows you to add multiple tracks to your session simultaneously. To add multiple tracks with the same format, type, and timebase, enter the number of tracks to add in the Track Total field. To add multiple tracks using different configurations, click on the **ADD ROW** button (plus sign).

You can simultaneously add as many tracks with as many different configurations as your session will allow.

Tip: Tracks will be added to your session in the order shown in the New Tracks dialog box. To rearrange the track order, click on the Move Row control and drag the row to a new position.

Figure 3.5

Arranging tracks using the Move Row control

Track Format

Within the New Tracks dialog box, you can choose a format for the track or tracks you are adding to your session. Available options include mono, stereo, or multi-channel formats, depending on the type of track you are adding and the type of system you are using. Stereo tracks provide the added benefit of automatically linking both channels for editing, mixing, and clip renaming, although separate control over each individual channel of the stereo pair is not possible.

Track Type

Track types supported in Pro Tools include the following:

- Audio tracks
- MIDI tracks
- Instrument tracks
- Video tracks (Pro Tools HD required for multiple tracks)
- Auxiliary inputs
- VCA Masters (Pro Tools HD only)
- Master faders

Any combination of the supported track types can be added using the New Tracks dialog box.

Tip: Standard Pro Tools software does not include Video tracks in the New Tracks dialog box, since only a single Video track is supported. A Video track will be created only if you import video into your session.

Audio Tracks

Audio tracks allow you to import/record and edit an audio signal as a waveform. Audio tracks can be mono, stereo, or any supported multi-channel format.

Standard Pro Tools software can create up to 128 audio tracks in a session (up to 96 voiced tracks), while Pro Tools HD software can create up to 768 audio tracks, with voice count dependent on hardware. However, the session sample rate, the number of voices your hardware supports, and the continuity of your audio will determine how many tracks you can actually play back and record simultaneously.

Tip: **Pro Tools software uses the host computer's CPU to mix and process Audio tracks. Computers with faster clock speeds support higher track counts and more plug-in processing.**

MIDI Tracks

MIDI tracks store MIDI note and controller data. Pro Tools includes an integrated MIDI sequencer that lets you import/record and edit MIDI data in much the same way that you perform these operations when working with audio files. MIDI data appears in tracks in the Pro Tools Edit window, referencing the same Timeline as Audio tracks.

Note that you do not specify a track format (mono or stereo) for MIDI tracks, since no audio passes through the track; MIDI tracks are data-only.

Instrument Tracks

Instrument tracks combine the functions of MIDI tracks and auxiliary inputs (see the upcoming "Auxiliary Inputs" section) into a single track type, making them ideal for composing with virtual instrument plug-ins, sound modules, and all your other MIDI devices.

Video Tracks

Video tracks let you add or import video to the Timeline. Standard Pro Tools software lets you add or import one Video track per session and use a single video clip on the track. Pro Tools HD software lets you add multiple Video tracks to the Timeline and use multiple video files and video clips on each Video track. Only one Video track can be active, or *online*, at any time.

Auxiliary Inputs

An Aux Input track can be used as an effects return, a destination for a submix, an input to monitor or process live audio (such as the output of a synthesizer triggered from a MIDI source), or a control point for any other audio routing task. Auxiliary inputs can be mono, stereo, or any supported multi-channel format.

VCA Master Tracks

VCA Master tracks are available in Pro Tools HD software or Pro Tools with Complete Production Toolkit only. These tracks emulate the operation of voltage-controlled amplifier channels on analog consoles. Traditional VCA channel faders are used to control, group, or offset the signal levels of other channels on the console. In similar fashion, a Pro Tools VCA Master track is associated with a Mix group, and the controls of the tracks in the Mix group can then be modified by the controls on the VCA Master.

▲▼▍▶
*In the Avid
Learning Series*   VCA Masters are covered in the Pro Tools 201 course.

Master Faders

A master fader is a single fader used to control hardware output levels and bus paths. Master Fader tracks control the overall level of the Audio tracks that are routed to the session's main output paths or busses. In Pro Tools, you can create a Master Fader track for mono, stereo, or any supported multi-channel format.

Example: Suppose you have 24 tracks in a session with Tracks 1 through 8 routed to Analog Output 1–2, Tracks 9 through 16 routed to Analog Output 3–4, and Tracks 17 through 24 routed to Analog Output 5–6. You might want to create three master faders, one to control each of the output pairs.

Timebase

The track *timebase* refers to the type of Time Scale that material on the track is associated with. All track types can be set to either sample-based (for the Samples Time Scale) or tick-based (for the Bars|Beats Time Scale), with different tracks set to different timebases, as needed.

Audio tracks are sample-based by default, meaning that audio clips and events have absolute locations on the Timeline, correlated to specific sample locations. Material on sample-based tracks maintains a constant absolute position on the track, regardless of tempo or meter changes specified in the session.

By contrast, MIDI and Instrument tracks are tick-based by default, meaning that MIDI clips and events are fixed to bar and beat positions and move relative to the sample Timeline as meter and tempo changes occur.

Although Audio tracks are sample-based by default, Elastic Audio–enabled tracks can be switched to tick-based in order to automatically follow tempo changes in your session and conform to the session's tempo map.

You select whether a track is sample-based or tick-based when you create it; however, you can change timebases later as needed.

In the Avid Learning Series   Sample-based editing and tick-based editing are covered in more detail in the Pro Tools 110 and 210M courses.

Naming Tracks

When you create tracks in Pro Tools, they are added to the session using generic names, such as Audio 1, Audio 2, MIDI 1, and so on. To change a track name to something more meaningful, double-click the track name within the Edit window or the Mix window. A dialog box will appear, allowing you to rename the track.

Aux 1   X

Name the track:
Aux 1
Comments:

Previous   Next   Cancel   OK

Figure 3.6
The Track Name dialog box

Tip: You can also name a track by right-clicking on the track name and choosing RENAME from the pop-up menu.

Using the Track Name dialog box, you can also add comments to a track and cycle through the tracks in your session, renaming and adding comments to each, using the NEXT and PREVIOUS buttons. Comments you add will be visible in the Comments area, if displayed, at the bottom of the channel strip (Mix window) or at the head of a track (Edit window).

Shortcut: Press CTRL+LEFT/RIGHT ARROW (Windows) or COMMAND+LEFT/ RIGHT ARROW (Mac) in the Track Name dialog box to cycle through your tracks and rename each without leaving the keyboard.

Deleting Tracks

When you delete tracks, your audio or MIDI clip data will remain in the Clip List, but your arrangement of the clips on the deleted track (the track's playlist) will be lost. This is also true of video clips in Pro Tools HD.

Note: The Track Delete command cannot be undone.

To delete a track, follow these steps:

1. Click the track nameplate to select the track; SHIFT-CLICK or CTRL-CLICK (Windows)/COMMAND-CLICK (Mac) to select multiple tracks.

2. Choose TRACK > DELETE.

3. If all selected tracks are empty, they will be deleted immediately; if any tracks contain data, you will be prompted with a verification dialog box. Click DELETE to permanently remove the selected tracks from the session.

Tip: You can also right-click on a track name and choose DELETE from the pop-up menu to remove all selected tracks.

Adding Audio to Your Session

Once you have created one or more Audio tracks in your session, you can begin adding audio, either by recording to your track(s) or by importing existing audio files. When you record audio or import audio from a hard drive (or other volume) into tracks in your session, Pro Tools also places the audio files in the Clip List.

Audio recording is covered in Lesson 4, and audio importing is covered in Lesson 5.

The Playback Cursor and the Edit Cursor

The Edit window displays two different cursors: a *playback* cursor and an *edit* cursor. The two cursors are linked by default; however, you can unlink them to meet the needs of a particular situation. When unlinked, the different cursors allow you to play one area of your session while simultaneously editing an entirely different area. This can be useful when you are working with a film or video scene or when you are trying out edits within an area that you need to audition repeatedly.

Throughout this book, we will assume that the playback and edit cursors remain linked, unless otherwise noted.

In the Avid
Learning Series
Workflows that involve unlinking the edit and playback cursors are included in the Pro Tools 210M and 310M courses.

To link or unlink the playback and edit cursors, choose OPTIONS > LINK TIMELINE AND EDIT SELECTION. The option should be checked (linked) for this course.

Playback Cursor

The playback cursor is a solid, non-blinking line that moves across the screen during playback and indicates where the current playback point is. The playback cursor's exact time location is displayed in the Main and Sub Counters in the Transport window (mirrored in Counters in the Edit window when LINK TIMELINE AND EDIT SELECTION is active).

Edit Cursor

The edit cursor is a flashing line that appears when you click the Selector tool in a track. The blinking edit cursor indicates the starting point for any editing tasks that you perform. By making a selection with the edit cursor, you define an area for Pro Tools to perform a desired editing task. With the Timeline and Edit Selections linked and the Pro Tools Transport stopped, the playback cursor's location will always match the edit cursor's location.

Setting the Playback Point

With the Timeline and Edit Selections linked, you can set the playback point using the Selector tool by clicking directly on a track. To set the playback point on a track using the Selector tool, follow these steps:

1. In the Edit window, click the SELECTOR tool. The cursor will turn into an I-beam.

2. Click and release the mouse button at any point in an existing track.

3. Press the SPACE BAR to begin playback from this point.

4. To stop playback, press the SPACE BAR again.

5. To move to a different playback point in the track, click the SELECTOR at the new position and press the SPACE BAR again.

You can also set the playback point with any tool selected by clicking on any Ruler in the Timeline display area of the Edit window. This allows you to set the playback point without changing tools. Clicking on a Timebase Ruler provides a common way to set the playback point regardless of whether the Timeline and Edit Selections are linked.

Locating the Playback Cursor

At times, the playback cursor might be difficult to find in a session. For example, if the No Scrolling option is selected (see "Scrolling Options," below), the playback cursor will move off screen after it has played past the location currently visible in the Edit window.

To make navigation easier, Pro Tools provides a Playback Cursor Locator, which you can use to jump to the playback cursor when it is off screen.

If the playback cursor is not visible in the Edit window, the Playback Cursor Locator will appear in the Main Timebase Ruler, as follows:

- On the left if the playback cursor is located before the visible area
- On the right if the playback cursor is located after the visible area

Playback Cursor Locator

Figure 3.7
Playback Cursor Locator

The Playback Cursor Locator is red when any track is record-enabled and blue when no tracks are record-enabled.

To locate the playback cursor when it is off screen, click the **PLAYBACK CURSOR LOCATOR** in the Main Timebase Ruler. The Edit window's waveform display will jump to the playback cursor's current onscreen location.

Scrolling Options

Pro Tools offers several different display options that affect how the contents of the Edit window are displayed during playback and recording. Three options available on all Pro Tools systems are discussed in the following sections. Additional options are discussed in advanced courses.

No Scrolling

Scrolling can be turned off by choosing **OPTIONS > SCROLLING > NO SCROLLING**. This option prevents Pro Tools from scrolling the Edit window during playback and recording as the playback cursor moves off screen and does not reposition the window when playback or recording is stopped.

After Playback

To prevent scrolling during playback but have the Edit window reposition to the stop point during playback and recording, use the After Playback scrolling option. To select this option, choose **OPTIONS > SCROLLING > AFTER PLAYBACK**.

Page

To scroll the Edit window one screen (or "page") at a time as the playback cursor moves across the Timeline, enable the Page Scrolling option. To select this option, choose OPTIONS > SCROLLING > PAGE.

When Page Scrolling is enabled, the playback cursor moves across the Edit window until it reaches the right edge of the window. Each time the playback cursor reaches the right edge, the entire contents of the window are scrolled, one screen at a time, and the playback cursor continues from the left edge of the Edit window.

Note: When the zoom magnification of the Edit window is too high, Page Scrolling may not function properly. If you experience problems, decrease the zoom magnification to enable Page Scrolling.

Saving, Locating, and Opening Existing Sessions

As with most software applications, Pro Tools provides commands for saving and opening your files under the File menu. The following sections describe the options for saving, locating, and opening your session files and other files related to your Pro Tools projects.

Saving a Session

While working in Pro Tools, it is important to save your work often. When you save a session using the two commands explained in the following sections, you are saving only the Pro Tools session file, not its associated files. (A session's audio files are written directly to disk, so you don't have to save them independently.) Consequently, even very large sessions can be saved quickly.

Save Command

Saving can be done manually by choosing the Save command from the File menu. This saves the changes you have made since the last time you saved and writes the session in its current form over the old version. You cannot undo the Save command.

Save As Command

The Save As command is useful for saving a copy of the current session under a different name or in a different hard drive location. Because the Save As command closes the current session and lets you keep working on the renamed copy, it is particularly useful if you are experimenting and want to save successive stages of a session. This way, you can save each major step under a different name, such as Student Session-2, Student Session-3, and so on. By working this way, you can always retrace your steps if you should want to go back to an earlier version.

To use the Save As feature, follow these steps:

1. Choose FILE > SAVE AS.

2. Type a new name for the session.

3. Click SAVE.

The renamed, newly saved session will then remain open for you to continue your work.

> Tip: A third Save command, Save Copy In, allows you to create a copy from your current session with different session parameters and place it, along with copies of all associated audio files, in a new location. The Save Copy In command is discussed in Lesson 10.

Locating and Opening a Session

Pro Tools provides specialized windows, called *DigiBase browsers*, that you can use to quickly locate, manage, and open Pro Tools sessions and related media files. DigiBase browsers provide more meaningful search, navigation, file information, and audition capabilities than standard operating system–level functions.

If you know the location of the session you want to open, you can open it directly from the File menu (choose FILE > OPEN SESSION). For recently used sessions, choose FILE > OPEN RECENT and select the session that you wish to open from the submenu. In other cases, you can use the DigiBase *Workspace* browser to help locate a session on your system.

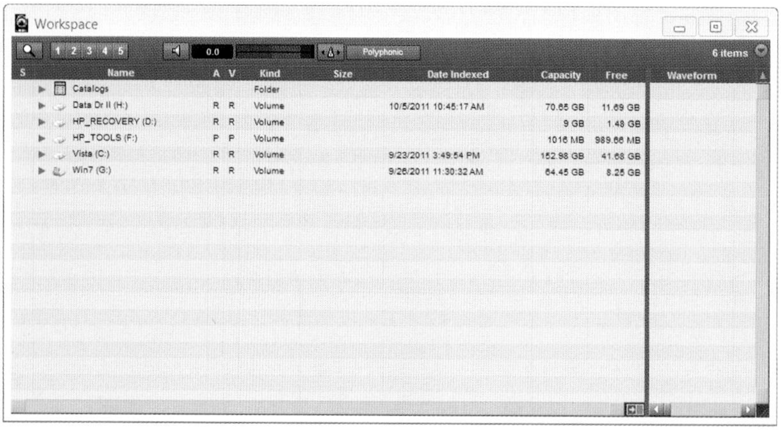

Figure 3.8
The DigiBase Workspace browser window

Locating a Session

The DigiBase Workspace browser has a powerful search tool that lets you search for Pro Tools file types, such as session files, audio files, and video files.

To search for Pro Tools sessions in the DigiBase Workspace browser, follow these steps:

1. Choose **WINDOW > WORKSPACE**. The Workspace browser will open as the active window.

2. In the Workspace window, click the **FIND** button (magnifying glass) to show the search tools.

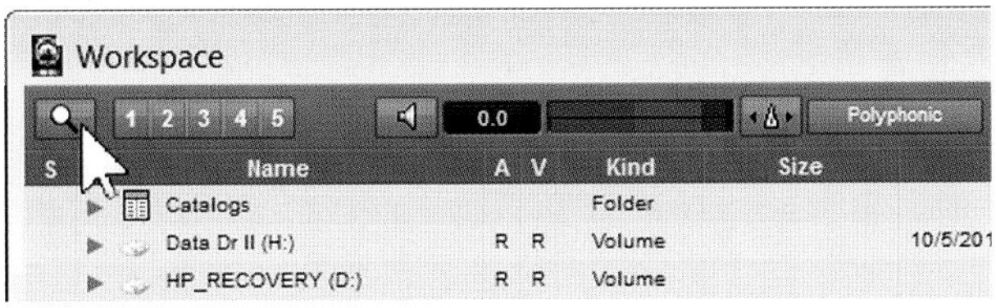

Figure 3.9
Clicking the Find button in the Workspace browser

3. Choose the volumes or folders you want to search by selecting the appropriate check boxes in the Workspace browser window. Note that you can navigate through the file system by clicking the triangle icons to expand or collapse volumes and folders.

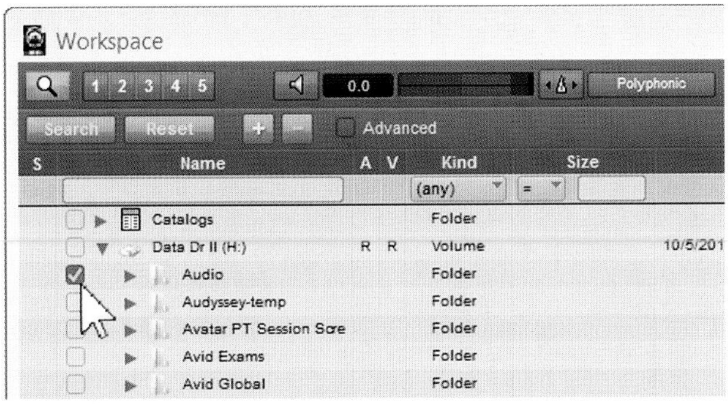

Figure 3.10
Selecting a folder to search

4. Click the drop-down button in the Kind column and select **SESSION FILE**.

5. Click the **SEARCH** button. The search results will be shown in the bottom half of the Workspace browser.

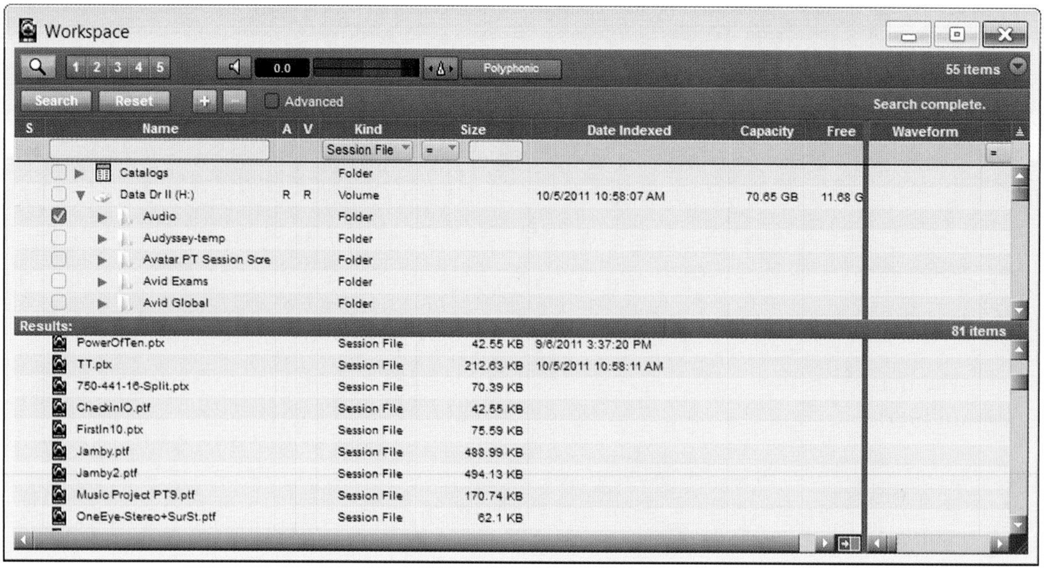

Figure 3.11
Search results shown in the Workspace browser

Opening a Session

Once you have located the session you are interested in, you can open the session directly from the DigiBase Workspace browser window. (You can also open Pro Tools sessions from the computer's hard drive by double-clicking on the session file in an Explorer or Finder window.)

Note: Pro Tools can have only one session open at a time. If you attempt to open a session while another session is open, Pro Tools will prompt you to save the current session and close it before opening the selected session.

To open a Pro Tools session using a DigiBase browser, follow these steps:

1. Locate the session file you want to open in the Workspace browser.

2. Double-click the session file.

The Pro Tools session will open with all windows and display options appearing exactly as saved. Any previously created tracks will appear in the Edit and Mix windows, and all audio and MIDI clips associated with the session will appear in the Clip List at the right of the Edit window.

Tip: If the Edit or Mix window is not displayed in a session you have opened, you can display it by choosing the corresponding command in the Window menu.

Review/Discussion Questions

1. What four actions can be initiated from the Quick Start dialog box? How can you display and specify the Session Parameter settings in this dialog box? (See pages 84 and 85.)

2. What audio file types are supported in Pro Tools? What is the default file type? (See page 86.)

3. What is the maximum sample rate supported in Pro Tools? What is the maximum bit depth? (See page 86.)

4. What command lets you add tracks to your session? How many tracks can you add at one time? (See page 89.)

5. Describe some track types supported in Pro Tools. (See page 90.)

6. Which timebase do Audio tracks use by default? Which timebase do MIDI and Instrument tracks use by default? (See page 92.)

7. What happens to the audio and MIDI data on a track when the track gets deleted from your session? Can the Track > Delete command be undone? (See page 93.)

8. Name the two types of cursors available in the Edit window. How can the two types of cursors be linked or unlinked? (See page 94.)

9. Which tool can be used to set the playback point by clicking directly on a track? (See page 95.)

10. What is the Playback Cursor Locator used for? Where will the Playback Cursor Locator appear (in what Ruler)? (See page 96.)

11. What is the purpose of the Save As command? Which session will be open after completing the Save As command, the original or the renamed copy? (See pages 97 and 98.)

12. How can you open a session after locating it in the Workspace browser? (See page 100.)

Creating a Session

In this exercise tutorial, you will create a Pro Tools session, add three tracks to the session, name each of the tracks, and set the Main Time Scale for the session. You will then save the session for use in subsequent exercises.

Duration: 10 to 15 Minutes   **Media: None Required**

Getting Started

To get started, you will need to open Pro Tools and create a new 44.1 kHz, 24-bit session.

To create the session:

1. Power up your computer and any connected hardware, as described in Lesson 2.

2. Do one of the following to launch Pro Tools:

   - Double-click on the **PRO TOOLS** shortcut icon on the desktop.

   - Click **START > PRO TOOLS 10** (Windows).

   - Click the **PRO TOOLS** icon in the Dock (Mac).

3. In the Quick Start dialog box, select **CREATE BLANK SESSION**.

4. At the bottom of the Quick Start dialog box, set the session parameters as follows and then click **OK**:

   - Audio File Type: BWF (.WAV)

   - Bit Depth: 24 Bit

   - Sample Rate: 44.1 kHz

   - I/O Settings: Stereo Mix

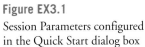

Figure EX3.1

Session Parameters configured in the Quick Start dialog box

Tip: You may need to expand the Session Parameters section to access the Sample Rate and Bit Depth settings in the Quick Start dialog box. Click on the arrow or triangle icon next to Session Parameters to expand the dialog box.

5. In the resulting dialog box, name your session *Exercise3-YourName* and navigate to an appropriate location to save your session.

6. Click **SAVE** to save the session in the selected location.

Creating Tracks and Setting the Main Time Scale

In the next series of steps, you will create three new tracks and rename them with descriptive names for this session. You will also set the Main Time Scale and other display options for the session.

To create the tracks:

1. Choose **TRACK > NEW** to open the New Tracks dialog box.

Shortcut: Try using the keyboard shortcut for the TRACK > NEW command: CTRL+SHIFT+N **(Windows) or** COMMAND+SHIFT+N **(Mac).**

2. Configure the first row in the New Tracks dialog box for two stereo Audio tracks.

Figure EX3.2
New Tracks dialog box configured for two Audio tracks and one Master Fader

3. Click the Plus sign on the right side to add a second row; configure this row as a Stereo Master Fader.

4. Click **CREATE** to create the tracks.

To name the tracks:

1. Double-click on the track nameplate of the first track (Audio 1). A dialog box will open prompting you to name the track.

2. Rename the track to Guitar without closing the dialog box.

3. Click the **NEXT** button at the bottom of the dialog box. The dialog box will update to show the Audio 2 track.

4. Rename the Audio 2 track to Drums and then click **OK** to close the dialog box.

To set the Main Time Scale and other display options:

1. If needed, choose **WINDOW > EDIT** or press **CTRL+=** or **COMMAND+=** to display the Edit window.

2. Choose **VIEW > MAIN COUNTER > BARS|BEATS** to set the Main Time Scale to Bars|Beats. The Bars|Beats ruler will display above the tracks in the Edit window, and the Main Counter will display its location information in Bars|Beats.

3. If needed, click the arrow icons in the bottom corners of the Edit window to display the Edit window side columns. The Track List will display in the left side column, and the Clip List will display in the right side column.

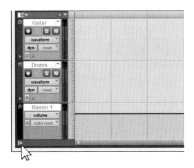

Figure EX3.3
Clicking the arrow icon to display the left side column

Finishing Up

To complete this exercise tutorial, you will need to save your work and close the session. Note that you will be reusing this session in Exercise 4, so it is important to save the work you've done.

To finish your work:

1. Choose FILE > SAVE to save the session.

2. Choose FILE > CLOSE SESSION to close the session.

Tip: You cannot close a Pro Tools session by closing the Mix and Edit windows. This common mistake leaves the session open with no active windows.

Making Your First Audio Recording

This lesson covers the steps required to begin recording audio in your Pro Tools sessions. It also describes the types of audio clips your session will include and covers processes for keeping your clips and audio files organized.

Duration: 90 Minutes

GOALS

- Set up Pro Tools hardware and software for recording audio
- Create and configure a click track
- Record audio onto tracks in your session
- Recognize clips and whole-file clips
- Organize your clips and audio files after recording to minimize clutter and optimize your session

Many Pro Tools projects require extensive audio recording. After all, multi-track recording is a cornerstone of what Pro Tools is all about. Whether your projects involve a simple setup in a home studio or an elaborate system in a professional environment, knowing how to get your audio onto tracks in Pro Tools is the first step to creating a successful recording.

Before Recording

Before you begin recording in a session, you should ensure that your system has enough storage space for the project. The amount of storage space consumed by audio clips in a project will vary, depending on the bit depth and sample rate of the session. (See the "Analog-to-Digital Conversion" section in Lesson 1 for a detailed discussion of bit depth and sample rate.)

Audio Storage Requirements

Pro Tools records all audio using sample rates ranging from 44.1 kHz to 192 kHz, with bit depths of 16-bit, 24-bit, or 32-bit floating point. At a sample rate of 44.1 kHz, each track consumes approximately 5 megabytes (MB) of disk space per minute for 16-bit audio (mono), 7.5 MB per minute for 24-bit audio (mono), and 10 MB per minute for 32-bit floating-point audio. With increasing bit depth and sample rates, hard disk space consumption increases correspondingly; recording at a sample rate of 88.2 kHz, therefore, consumes twice as much space as recording at 44.1 kHz. Similarly, recording in stereo consumes twice the space of recording in mono.

Table 3.1 in Lesson 3 shows approximate storage consumption at the different data rates supported by Pro Tools.

Tip: Pro Tools audio files require a small amount of additional disk space to store associated clip metadata; this can add up to 0.3 MB per minute to the total file size.

Disk Space Window

With a session running, you can monitor storage space and estimate the amount of available record time remaining for your project using the Disk Space window.

To access the disk space window, choose WINDOW > DISK SPACE.

The Disk Space window shows the number of continuous track minutes available on each mounted hard drive, using the current session's sample rate and bit depth.

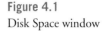

Disk Name	Size	Avail	%	48 kHz 24 Bit Track Min.	Meter
Vista (C:)	153.0G	49.6G	32.4%	6162.7 Min	
HP_RECOVERY (D:	9.0G	1.5G	16.5%	184.5 Min	
HP_TOOLS (F:)	1016.0M	989.7M	97.4%	120.1 Min	
Win7 (G:)	64.5G	2.2G	3.4%	271.6 Min	
Data Dr II (H:)	70.7G	12.7G	17.9%	1575.0 Min	
Win7Beta (I:)	153.0G	117.4G	76.8%	14592.9 Min	
Data Dr XP (J:)	488.3G	421.8G	86.4%	52424.0 Min	
Betalll (K:)	43.3G	6.5G	15.0%	806.6 Min	
Win7Clean (L:)	70.6G	41.0G	58.0%	5090.9 Min	

Figure 4.1
Disk Space window

Calculating File Sizes

The sample rate and bit depth of the audio you record are directly related to the size of the resulting files. In fact, you can calculate file sizes in mathematical terms using these two parameters:

Sample Rate × Bit Depth = Bits per Second

Or, stated another way:

Sample Rate × Bit Depth × 60 = Bits per Minute

In the binary world of computers, 8 bits make a byte, 1,024 bytes make a kilobyte (KB), and 1,024 KB make a megabyte (MB). Therefore, this equation can be restated as follows:

(Sample Rate × Bit Depth × 60) / (8 bits per byte × 1,024 bytes per kilobyte × 1,024 kilobytes per megabyte) = Megabytes (MB) per Minute

Reducing terms gives us the following:

Sample Rate × Bit Depth / 139,810 = MB per Minute

So by way of example, recording audio at a sample rate of 44,100 samples per second with a bit depth of 24 bits per sample would generate files that consume space at the following rate:

44,100 × 24 / 139,810 = 7.57 MB per Minute

Preparing to Record

Once you have created a session, added an Audio track (or tracks) to record onto, and verified that you have adequate disk space available for your project, you will need to prepare your hardware and software for recording. If your session does not already include a click track, you might want to add one to use as a tempo reference while recording.

Whether or not you use a click track, the general processes you will use to prepare for recording audio are as follows:

1. Check the hardware connections.

2. Record-enable the Audio track(s).

3. Set the track input path, level, and pan.

Creating a Click Track (Optional)

When you're working with a song or other composition that is bar- and beat-based, you might want to record tracks while listening to a MIDI-generated metronome click in Pro Tools. This ensures that recorded material, both MIDI and audio, will align with your session's bar and beat boundaries.

Aligning track material with beats allows you to take advantage of many useful MIDI editing functions in Pro Tools. It also enables you to arrange your song in sections by copying and pasting measures in Grid mode.

To set up a click track, use the **TRACK > CREATE CLICK TRACK** command. This command inserts the Click plug-in on a new Auxiliary Input track. The Click plug-in is a mono plug-in that creates an audio metronome click during session playback. You can use this audio click as a tempo reference when performing and recording. The Click plug-in receives its tempo and meter data from the Pro Tools application, enabling it to follow any changes in tempo and meter that have been set in a session. Several click sound presets are included for you to choose from.

To create a click track, do the following:

■ Choose **TRACK > CREATE CLICK TRACK**. A new click track will be created in your session.

To configure the Click plug-in, do the following:

1. Choose **OPTIONS > CLICK** to enable the Click option, if not already active (or enable the Metronome button in the Transport window).

2. From the Insert panel for the click track (Mix or Edit window), click on the **CLICK** insert nameplate. The Click plug-in window will open.

Figure 4.2
The Click plug-in window

Tip: Details on inserts and plug-ins are presented in Lesson 5 and Lesson 9.

3. Click on the drop-down labeled <FACTORY DEFAULT> to select a click sound preset, and set other options as desired.

- **Accented.** Control the output level for the accented beat (Beat 1 of each bar) of the audio click.

- **Unaccented Beats.** Control the output level for the unaccented beats of the audio click.

4. Click the **CLOSE** icon in the upper-right corner (Windows) or upper-left corner (Mac) to exit the Click plug-in window.

5. Choose **SETUP** > **CLICK/COUNTOFF** to open the Click/Countoff Options dialog box; set the Click and Countoff options as desired.

Figure 4.3
Click/Countoff Options dialog box

Note: The Note, Velocity, Duration, and Output options in this dialog box are used with MIDI instrument–based clicks and do not affect the Click plug-in.

When you begin playback, a click is generated according to the tempo and meter of the current session and the settings in the Click/Countoff Options dialog box.

Checking Hardware Connections

Recording audio involves connecting an instrument, microphone, or other sound source to your Pro Tools system. Most audio interfaces have inputs designated for different sound sources and input types. Before starting to record, you should verify that your sound source is connected to the appropriate inputs of the audio interface and that the signal is being passed through correctly. For basic recording, it is simplest to use the lowest available inputs on your audio interface that match your needs (for example, Input 1 for a mono source or Inputs 1 and 2 for a stereo pair).

If necessary, check the configuration of your audio interface and/or the Hardware Setup of your system to ensure correct routing of inputs or to change existing settings. Depending on your audio interface, you can use physical controls or switches, the controls in the Hardware Setup dialog box, or a separate control panel to define which physical inputs and outputs on your audio interface are routed to available inputs and outputs in Pro Tools.

Example: Suppose you are using an Mbox with a guitar and bass connected to the front-panel instrument inputs and microphones connected to the rear-panel XLR/TRS inputs. Using the source selector switches on the front panel, you can choose which source (front or rear) is routed to each Pro Tools input.

Record-Enabling Tracks

To set up a Pro Tools Audio track for recording, click the track's RECORD ENABLE button in either the Edit window or the Mix window. The button will flash red when the track is record-enabled.

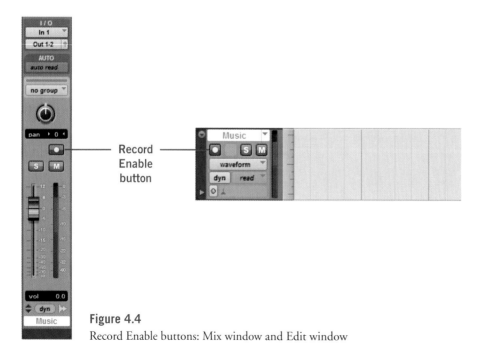

Record
Enable
button

Figure 4.4
Record Enable buttons: Mix window and Edit window

When a track has been record-enabled, the Track Fader turns red, indicating that it is now functioning as a record monitor level control.

Tip: To record-enable multiple Audio tracks, click the RECORD ENABLE buttons on additional tracks. To record-enable all tracks of a particular type in the session, ALT-CLICK (Windows) or OPTION-CLICK (Mac) on any track's RECORD ENABLE button.

Setting Input Path, Level, and Pan

With your sound source connected to the inputs of your Pro Tools interface, you are now ready to set Pro Tools to receive a signal from your source and to pass the signal through the system for recording and monitoring purposes.

Input Path

Each Audio track has an *Audio Input Path selector*, which allows you to route a signal from an input on your interface to the track for recording. To set the incoming signal, do the following:

1. Locate the channel strip for the track you will record to in the Mix window.

2. Verify that the input displayed on the Input Path selector matches the input that your sound source is plugged into on your audio interface.

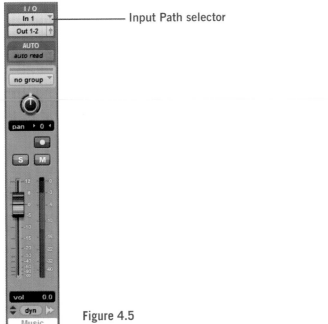

Input Path selector

Figure 4.5
The Input Path selector in the Mix window

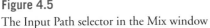

3. If necessary, click the INPUT PATH SELECTOR to make changes, selecting the correct input path from the pop-up menu. (Note: Stereo tracks will have a pair of inputs routed to the track.)

✔	no input	
	interface ▶	In 1 (Mono)
	bus ▶	In 2 (Mono)
	plug-in ▶	S/PDIF Left-Right.L (Mono)
		S/PDIF Left-Right.R (Mono)

Figure 4.6
Input Path selector pop-up menu

Example: Suppose you are recording a vocalist and acoustic guitar accompaniment onto Tracks 1 and 2 of your session, with the vocalist's mic plugged into Input 1 of your Mbox and the guitar mic plugged into Input 2. In the Pro Tools Mix window, you should have the Input Path selector for your first track set to IN 1 (MONO) (to receive signal from Input 1) and the Input Path selector for your second track set to IN 2 (MONO) (to receive signal from Input 2).

Input Level

As a general rule, input levels should be adjusted to obtain a strong, clean signal without clipping. Unlike when recording to tape, however, you do not need to record at the highest possible level in Pro Tools. Recording too hot can leave little room for subsequent gain-based processing (such as EQ) and can lead to digital clipping, which is always detrimental to audio quality. For best results, aim for an average peak input level around –6 dB, keeping the track meter in the yellow range. To do this, adjust the level of your analog source while monitoring the indicator lights on your onscreen track meter.

Adjusting the input level will typically require you to change the source volume, adjust the microphone placement, or modify the incoming signal strength using a mixer or pre-amplifier, because record levels cannot be adjusted within Pro Tools. Note that although a track's Volume Fader can be used to increase or decrease playback levels, the Volume Fader *does not* affect record levels.

Many Pro Tools, M-Audio, and third-party I/O devices provide pre-amplifier gains for their inputs. For all other I/O devices, record levels are set entirely from the source or pre-I/O signal processing.

In the case of direct digital recording, which involves a one-to-one transfer, the source levels are copied directly to Pro Tools, typically with no level adjustment possible. (Some digital playback devices support digital output gain adjustment, allowing levels to be modified at the source.)

Pan Position

To set the pan position of the incoming signal (the placement of the signal in the stereo field), change the position of the Pan knob(s) for the track in the Mix window. The pan is initially set to >0<, signifying the center of the stereo field. Pan settings range from <100 (hard left) to 100> (hard right). Setting the pan affects the stereo placement of a signal for monitoring and playback purposes only; it has no effect on how the audio files are actually recorded.

Recording and Managing Audio

With your sound source routed to one or more tracks and the desired tracks record-enabled, you are ready to begin recording audio. Pro Tools offers a variety of recording modes that can be used in different audio recording situations. We will use the default mode (Nondestructive Record) for all work done in this course.

In the Avid Learning Series Other record modes are covered in the Pro Tools 110, 201, and 210M/210P courses.

To begin recording audio, do the following:

1. Display the Transport window, if it is not already showing (**WINDOW > TRANSPORT**).

2. To display or hide the expanded view, click the **EXPANDED VIEW** toggle button in the upper-right corner (Windows) or upper-left corner (Mac) of the Transport window, or click the Transport window menu icon and select **EXPANDED TRANSPORT**.

3. Verify that one or more tracks have been record-enabled. (See the "Record-Enabling Tracks" section earlier in this lesson.)

4. Click the **RECORD** button in the Transport window to enter Record Ready mode. The button will turn red and begin to flash.

Figure 4.7
The Transport window in Record Ready mode

5. When you're ready, click **PLAY** in the Transport window to begin recording (or press the **SPACE BAR**).

Tip: You can also press CTRL+SPACE BAR (Windows), COMMAND+SPACE BAR
       (Mac), or F12 to start recording immediately without first entering Record
       Ready mode.

6. When you have finished your record take, click the STOP button in the
    Transport window (or press the SPACE BAR).

Organizing after Recording

You should complete several housekeeping steps immediately after making a successful audio recording to stay organized and to prevent accidents while editing.

Return to Playback Mode

Returning record-enabled tracks to Playback mode will prevent unintended
recording onto those tracks during subsequent operations in your session. To return
a track to Playback mode and adjust the playback settings, do the following:

1. Click the RECORD ENABLE button on the Audio track to take it out of
    Record Ready mode. The track's Volume Fader will now function as a
    playback level control rather than as an input-monitoring level control.

2. Click PLAY in the Transport window.

3. Adjust the playback level and panning as necessary.

Note: If you have overloaded your audio inputs during recording and caused
        clipping, the topmost indicator on the level meter will stay lit. Click the
        indicator light to clear it.

Organize Audio Files and Clips

Each time you record audio into Pro Tools, you create a single audio file that
appears in both the Clip List and the Track Playlist. An *audio file* is an entire
unedited, continuous audio recording. Audio files—or *whole-file clips*, as they are
known in Pro Tools—are written and stored externally from your session file.
Organizing audio files involves maintaining information both within the Pro Tools
session and within the external files.

Tip: When you record audio into Pro Tools, the audio files are stored in your
       session's Audio Files folder by default.

As you begin to edit, you also create smaller, more manageable pieces of the original sound file, called *subset clips*, or simply *clips*. An audio clip is an electronic pointer, normally stored within the session document, that references some portion of an audio file. Clips can range in length from one sample to several hours. Clips do not store audio information directly, but instead store information used to display, edit, and play back audio information contained in the whole-file clip or audio file. Organizing audio clips is generally internal to Pro Tools only.

Recognizing Audio Files and Clips

The Clip List in the Edit window shows all clips and whole-file clips that have been used in your session.

Pro Tools lists all whole-file clips in boldface type and all other clips in normal type. When sound files are recorded onto stereo Audio tracks, in addition to appearing in boldface type, the word *stereo* is shown in parentheses at the end of the file name. Examples of these file and clip types are shown in the following figure.

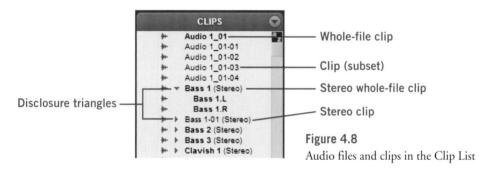

Figure 4.8
Audio files and clips in the Clip List

Note that clips on stereo Audio tracks also allow you to view both left and right channels of the clip separately by clicking the disclosure triangle.

Audio clips represent pieces of audio data that can be moved or edited within Pro Tools. They are created during normal editing, either by the user or automatically by Pro Tools, and can refer to any type of audio, such as music, dialogue, sound effects, Foley, or automated dialogue replacement (ADR).

Clips and whole-file clips can also appear in the Track Playlist. As shown in the following figure, each audio clip on a track is displayed using a solid rectangle to clearly delineate the clip boundaries.

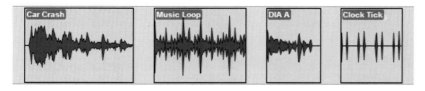

Figure 4.9
Audio clips as displayed in a Track Playlist

Naming Audio Files and Clips

During recording and editing, Pro Tools gives your audio files and clips default file names. At times, you might want to change the names of the files and/or clips in your session to make them easier to recognize and more meaningful for your purposes.

Default Naming Conventions

When you record audio on a track, Pro Tools names the resulting file (a whole-file clip) using the name of the Audio track followed by an underscore and the take number for that track (a sequential number based on the number of times you've recorded on that track). Following are examples of the file names Pro Tools automatically creates after recording for the first time on a mono track and on a stereo track:

Audio 1_01	Where *Audio 1* is the mono track name and *01* is the take number
Music 1_01 (Stereo)	Where *Music 1* is the stereo track name and *01* is the take number

When you edit a whole-file clip on a track, Pro Tools retains the original file and creates a new, edited clip, appending a hyphen followed by the edit number (a sequential number based on the number of edits you have created from that whole-file clip) onto the end of the clip name. Following are examples of the clip names Pro Tools automatically creates for the first edit to whole-file clips on a mono track and on a stereo track:

Audio 1_02-01	Where *Audio 1_02* is a whole-file clip on a mono track and *01* is the edit number for that clip
Music 1_02-01 (Stereo)	Where *Music 1_02* is a whole-file clip on a stereo track and *01* is the edit number for that clip

Changing File and Clip Names

You can change the default name that Pro Tools assigns to a clip or whole-file clip at any time. To rename a clip, do one of the following:

■ Double-click the file or clip in the Edit window (with the **Grabber** tool) or in the Clip List.

Tip: **Double-clicking on a MIDI clip opens the MIDI Editor window by default. This behavior can be changed using the associated Preferences setting (Setup > Preferences > MIDI tab).**

- Right-click on the file or clip in the Edit window or Clip List and select RENAME from the pop-up menu.

The Name dialog box will open.

Figure 4.10
The Name dialog box

When renaming a whole-file clip, you can select from the following options in the Name dialog box:

- **Name Clip Only.** Renames the file clip in Pro Tools but leaves the original file name on the hard drive unchanged.

- **Name Clip and Disk File.** Renames the clip in Pro Tools and renames the file on the hard drive as well.

Note that when you rename a stereo file or clip, both corresponding left and right channels are renamed accordingly.

Removing Audio Clips and Deleting Audio Files

Pro Tools makes an important distinction between removing clips from a session and deleting files from a hard drive:

- When you remove a clip from a session, the parent audio file remains on the hard drive and can be used in other clips elsewhere in the session or in other sessions.

- When you delete an audio file from the hard drive, all clips referring to that file are removed from the session, and the file is permanently deleted.

Removing Audio Clips

As your Clip List grows in your session, you might want to periodically remove the audio clips you no longer need, in order to reduce clutter. However, because removing audio clips does not delete the audio files, it will have no effect on hard drive usage of the session.

To remove unwanted audio clips from the Clip List, do the following:

1. Select the clips in the Clip List that you want to clear. To select multiple clips, **CTRL-CLICK** (Windows) or **COMMAND-CLICK** (Mac) on clips individually; to select a continuous range, **SHIFT-CLICK** on the top and bottom of the range.

2. Choose **CLEAR** from the Clips pop-up menu.

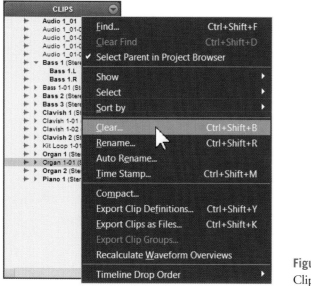

Figure 4.11
Clips pop-up menu

3. In the resulting Clear Clips dialog box, click **REMOVE** to remove the clips from the session, while leaving the audio files of any whole-file clips that are cleared on the hard drive.

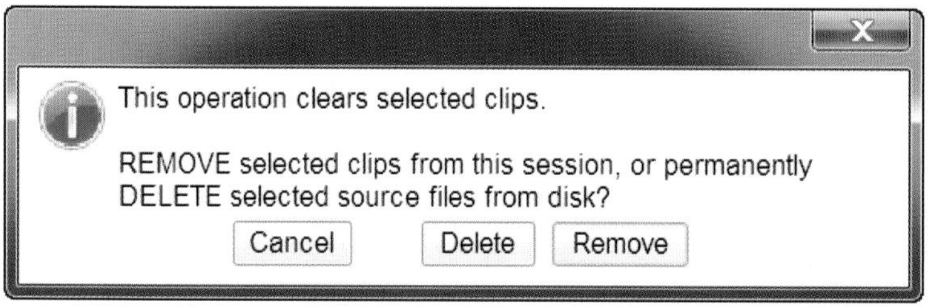

Figure 4.12
The Clear Clips dialog box

Pro Tools requires that all clips used on any Track Playlist, in the Undo queue, or on the Clipboard remain in the Clip List. If you attempt to remove a clip that has been placed on a track, on the Clipboard, or in the Undo queue, the following warning appears:

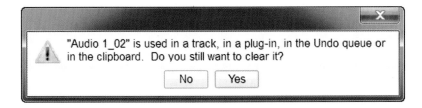

Figure 4.13
Clear warning dialog box

Choose one of the following:

■ **Yes.** This option clears the clip from the Clip List and the corresponding track, Undo queue, or Clipboard.

■ **No.** This option cancels the Clear command.

Deleting Audio Files

As you work on your session, you will probably accumulate unwanted whole-file clips from test recordings or unusable takes. As you reduce clutter in your Clip List, you might want to delete these unneeded audio files from your hard drive.

By removing audio files from the hard drive, you can free up additional drive space and reduce the overall storage requirements of your session. In addition to utilizing hard drive space more effectively, this will also help reduce the file backup time of your sessions.

To remove clips from the Clip List and delete any associated audio files from the hard drive permanently, do the following:

1. Complete Steps 1 and 2 in the "Removing Audio Clips" section earlier in this lesson.

2. In the Clear Clips dialog box, click **DELETE** to remove the selected clips from the Clip List *and* permanently delete the files for any selected whole-file clips from your hard drive.

Note: The Delete option permanently and irreversibly deletes audio files from your hard drive for the current session and all other sessions that reference the audio file. It cannot be undone. Use this command with caution.

Just like when you are removing audio clips, if you attempt to delete a file that has been placed on a track, on the Clipboard, or in the Undo queue, you will receive a warning message.

■ Click **YES** to permanently remove the file from the session and from the hard drive.

■ Click **NO** to leave the file untouched in the session and on the hard drive.

Pro Tools will prevent you from permanently deleting an audio file that is referenced by clips within the same session. If you attempt to delete an audio file that is referenced by other clips in the session, the following dialog box will appear:

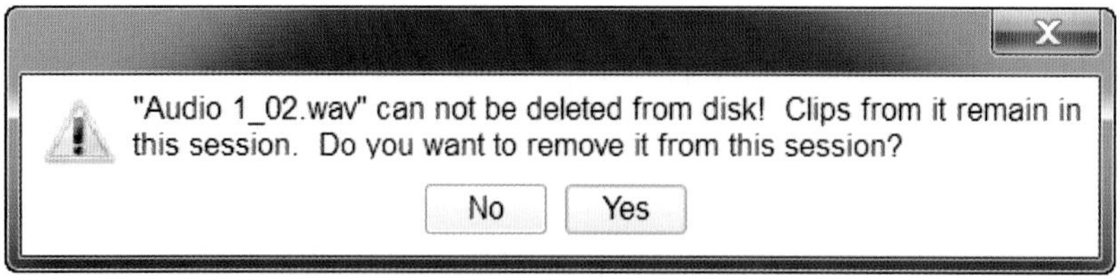

Figure 4.14
Dialog box displayed when unable to delete

- Click **YES** to remove the whole-file clip from the Clip List, while leaving the audio file on the hard drive.

- Click **No** to leave the whole-file clip untouched in the Clip List and on the hard drive.

If no other confirmation dialog box appears first, Pro Tools will prompt you with the following warning before completing the Delete command:

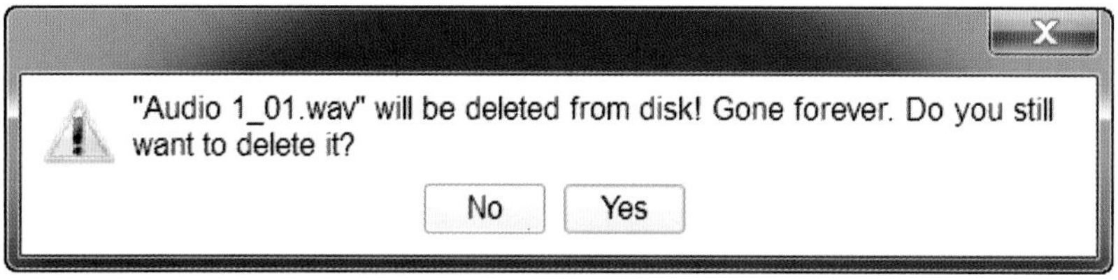

Figure 4.15
Delete warning dialog box

- Click **YES** to permanently remove the file from the session and from the hard drive.

- Click **No** to leave the file untouched in the session and on the hard drive.

Tip: To bypass repeated warnings when you are clearing or deleting multiple files or clips, ALT-CLICK (Windows) or OPTION-CLICK (Mac) on the YES or No button. This will prevent multiple warnings from appearing.

Review/Discussion Questions

1. How much disk space is consumed per minute by a mono track at a sample rate of 44.1 kHz and bit depth of 16-bit? What happens to disk space consumption if the sample rate is doubled to 88.2 kHz with the same bit depth? (See page 108.)

2. How can you monitor the storage space available on your system to determine the amount of record time remaining for each mounted hard drive? (See page 108.)

3. How can you create a click track for a session? What kind of track is used for a click track? (See page 110.)

4. What window(s) can you use to record-enable an Audio track? (See page 112.)

5. What selector can you use to route a signal from an input on your interface to a track for recording? (See page 113.)

6. How can you adjust the input level going to a record-enabled track? Can you use the Volume Fader to achieve a strong signal going to disk? (See page 114.)

7. How can you place a session in Record Ready mode after record-enabling a track? What modifiers/ shortcuts are available to initiate recording without first entering Record Ready mode? (See pages 115 and 116.)

8. Where are recorded audio files stored for Pro Tools sessions? (See page 116.)

9. What term is used to describe an unedited audio file in Pro Tools? What term is used to describe the smaller, edited pieces of the original sound file? (See page 116 and 117.)

10. What types of clips are represented by boldface type in the Clip List? What type is represented by normal type? (See page 117.)

11. How do track names affect the default names of the audio files you record in Pro Tools? (See page 118.)

12. Describe two ways to rename an audio file after recording into Pro Tools. (See pages 118 and 119.)

13. How would you go about removing unwanted audio from the Clip List without deleting the files from disk? (See page 120.)

14. How would you go about deleting unused whole-file clips to erase them from your hard drive? Can this action be undone? (See page 121.)

Importing and Working with Media in a Session

This lesson introduces various processes for importing audio and video files into a Pro Tools session. It describes file formats and types that can be imported, explains the functions of the Import Audio dialog box and other methods of importing audio, and discusses importing video files.

Duration: 90 Minutes

GOALS

- Determine whether an audio file's parameters are compatible with your session
- Understand how Pro Tools treats stereo files
- Understand the functions of each part of the Import Audio dialog box
- Import audio files to the Clip List or to Audio tracks in the Edit window
- Import video files to a Video track in the Edit window

Many music and post-production projects require you to work with media files that have been created outside of your current session. Whether you need to import music loops, add tracks recorded by others, copy audio sound effects files from a CD, or place a video clip in your session, you will need to know how to use the import options provided in Pro Tools.

Considerations Prior to Import

Pro Tools allows you to import audio and video files that already reside on a hard drive (or other volume) into your session. You can import media using one of several techniques, depending upon the type of media you are importing. Pro Tools can read some file formats directly and can convert many other audio formats on import. Prior to importing a file, you should understand whether the file can be read by your session and how the file will change if it needs to be converted.

Bit Depth, Sample Rate, and File Format

The types of media files that you can successfully import into a Pro Tools session will depend in part on how your session was originally configured. Some important considerations for audio files can include the bit depth, sample rate, and native file format of your session and of the files you plan to import. Important considerations for video files include the frame rate, sample rate, and file format.

Audio Bit Depth and Sample Rate

The bit depth (or bit resolution) of a Pro Tools session will be 16-bit, 24-bit, or 32-bit floating point, and the sample rate may be any of the following: 44.1 kHz, 48 kHz, 88.2 kHz, 96 kHz, 176.4 kHz, or 192 kHz. These settings are specified when a session is created. (See the "Choosing Session Parameter Settings" section in Lesson 3.) The sample rate of an imported file must match those of the current session in order to play back correctly.

In Pro Tools 10, an imported file can be any supported bit depth (16-, 24-, or 32-bit float) without requiring conversion. In earlier versions, the file bit depth was required to match the session bit depth.

Audio File Formats

The native audio file formats used in a Pro Tools session include Audio Interchange File Format (AIFF) and Waveform Audio File Format (WAV). You specify the session format when the session is created. (See the "Choosing Session Parameter Settings" section in Lesson 3.)

Tip: To determine the bit depth, sample rate, and file format of an open session, choose SETUP > SESSION.

Pro Tools recognizes compatible file formats that match the sample rate of your session, allowing you to add them to the Clip List without requiring any file translation. All WAV and AIFF files can coexist in a session without requiring conversion. However, any files in another format as well as any files that have a different sample rate from the session, regardless of format, must be converted.

Pro Tools will convert files on import, if necessary. Pro Tools can import many common audio file formats, including the following:

■ **Sound Designer II (SD II).** SD II is a monophonic or stereo interleaved file format supported on Macintosh systems only. This format supports only 44.1- and 48-kHz sample rates and can be imported into sessions on either platform with conversion.

■ **Audio Interchange File Format (AIFF).** This file format is used primarily on Macintosh systems, although the Windows versions of Pro Tools also support this file format. AIFF files can be recorded directly or imported without requiring conversion. The AIFF file format is commonly used with multimedia software programs for Macintosh, such as Final Cut, and is the standard audio file format used by Apple's QuickTime software.

■ **Audio Interchange File Compressed (AIFC).** A variant of the original AIFF audio file standard for the Macintosh, AIFC allows users to apply audio compression standards to AIFF files. In Avid systems, AIFC file compression is usually turned off; as such, there is essentially no difference between the Avid AIFC format and the standard AIFF file format.

■ **Waveform Audio File Format (WAV/WAVE).** Pro Tools reads and plays back any standard WAV (WAVE) format files. However, it records and exports WAV files exclusively in the Broadcast WAV or BWF format. (Like other WAV files, BWF files are denoted by the *.wav* extension.) BWF files store timestamps in a way that makes them ideal for file interchange operations. BWF is the default file format for both Mac- and Windows-based Pro Tools systems. BWF/WAV files can be recorded directly and imported (without conversion) on either platform, allowing seamless audio file exchange between Mac and Windows.

■ **MP3 (MPEG-1 Layer-3).** MP3 files are supported on all common computer platforms and employ file compression of 10:1, while still maintaining reasonable audio quality. Because of their small size and cross-platform support, they are well suited for use in email messages, web publishing, bulk file transfer, and storage. MP3 files must be converted for import to a Pro Tools session.

- **Windows Media Audio (WMA).** Like MP3, the WMA Standard format is a popular compressed audio format. The WMA Professional format offers higher quality and scales well at smaller file sizes; this format also supports multi-channel surround-sound files, sample rates up to 96 kHz, and 24-bit resolution. Pro Tools converts WMA files on import.

Tip: Pro Tools 10 supports the RF64 audio file format and the WAVE Extensible file format. The RF64 file format addresses the 4 GB size limitation of other WAV audio file formats. The WAVE Extensible file format specifies multiple audio channel data (surround sound) along with speaker positions within the audio file header.

Video File Formats

Pro Tools can import video files in the QuickTime format. Pro Tools HD can also import Avid video files. Windows systems also have the ability to import Windows Media (VC-1 AP) files.

Before you import a video file, you should verify the correct frame rate and sample rate, when applicable.

Note: QuickTime software is required for working with QuickTime files in Pro Tools. If you do not have the software installed on your system, you can obtain a free download from the Apple website (www.apple.com).

Configuration of Stereo Files

No universal stereo file configuration standard exists for software programs on Macintosh and Windows systems. However, two main stereo file configuration formats are common on both platforms: split stereo and interleaved stereo.

These two stereo file formats have no audible difference between them. The difference is primarily in how the audio is stored in the files. Either format can be imported into Pro Tools 10 without requiring conversion, although the format that Pro Tools uses for recording depends on the current session parameter configuration.

- **Split stereo.** In split stereo files, the stereo information is split between two separate mono files for the left and right channels. The split stereo file format is supported on all Pro Tools systems (and Avid picture-editing systems).

- **Interleaved stereo.** In an interleaved stereo file, the stereo information is combined (interleaved) into one single file that contains both left and right channel information. The stereo interleaved file format is not directly compatible with Pro Tools 9.x and earlier.

Pro Tools 10 supports interleaved audio files for stereo and greater multichannel files. Earlier versions require that interleaved files be converted to split stereo (or multiple mono files) on import. For Pro Tools 10 sessions with the INTERLEAVED option enabled, all stereo or greater multichannel audio will be recorded as interleaved audio files.

Importing Audio

When you import audio from a hard drive (or other volume) into your session, Pro Tools places the audio files in the Clip List. Pro Tools provides several options for importing audio into a session.

Import Audio Dialog Box

Audio files and clips can be imported directly to the Clip List or imported to new tracks using the Import Audio dialog box. This dialog box can be used to add, copy, and/or convert audio files for use in your session.

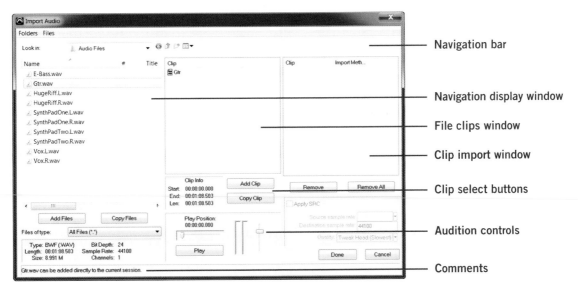

Figure 5.1
Import Audio dialog box (Windows)

The Import Audio dialog box includes seven main areas.

■ **File navigation.** A standard navigation bar at the top of the dialog box combined with the navigation display window on the left side allows you to locate and select audio files within an available hard drive or other volume.

■ **File properties.** The area below the navigation window lists the file type, length, size, bit depth, sample rate, and number of channels (1=mono, 2=stereo interleaved) for the file selected in the navigation window.

■ **Comments.** The area along the bottom of the dialog box describes how the selected file can be imported into the session and provides other information about the file's use in the session.

■ **File clips.** The file clips window in the middle of the dialog box shows the currently selected file and lists the whole-file clip (parent soundfile) and any internal clips (pointers to portions of the parent soundfile) that have been created from the original source file. Two types of icons can appear in the window, indicating whether the item is an audio file or an audio clip.

 Audio file. An icon that looks like a document with the upper-left corner turned down and dual audio waveforms is used to identify an audio file.

 Audio clip. An icon that looks like reverse highlighted dual-audio waveforms is used to identify an audio clip.

■ **Clip select buttons.** The Add Clip and Convert Clip/Copy Clip buttons below the file clips window are used to select audio to add, copy, or convert for use in your session. Clicking one of these buttons adds the selected audio file or clip to the clip import window on the right side of the dialog box.

■ **Audition controls.** The controls beneath the clip select buttons allow you to start, stop, rewind, and fast-forward playback of the currently selected file or clip.

■ **Clip import.** The area on the right side of the dialog box displays the audio files and clips that you have selected to import to the Clip List of your current session and the import method that will be used. You can remove clips from this list using the buttons beneath the display window.

Importing Audio with the Import Command

Audio files can be imported to tracks or directly to the Clip List, making the files available to be placed into tracks later. Compatible files or clips can be imported directly without adding them to the Audio Files folder, by referencing the existing files in their current location. Files that are not directly compatible must be converted to match; the converted files are placed in the session's Audio Files folder by default.

Tip: In Pro Tools 10, files in a supported format (WAV or AIFF) that match the
      session sample rate are directly compatible with the session. Earlier versions
      of Pro Tools require supported files to also match the session bit depth to be
      compatible. Files that are not directly compatible must be converted to match
      the session parameters during import.

To import audio, follow these steps:

1. Choose FILE > IMPORT > AUDIO. The Import Audio dialog box will appear.

2. Select an audio file in the navigation window to display its properties and
   any clips it contains.

3. Place a file or clip in the clip import window by clicking any of the following buttons:

   ● **Add/Add All.** Use these buttons to add compatible files or clips to the
     Clip List without copying them to the Audio Files folder. Clips that do
     not match the sample rate of the current session can also be added using
     these buttons, but they will not play back at the correct speed and pitch.

Note: The Add and Add All buttons reference the original audio file(s) and do not
       copy them into your session's Audio Files folder. If the original files are
       moved or become unavailable, or if the session is transferred to a different
       system, the session may no longer be able to play the referenced files.

   ● **Copy/Copy All.** Use these buttons to add compatible files or clips to the
     Clip List and force-copy them to the session's Audio Files folder. The Copy/
     Copy All buttons change to Convert/Convert All buttons when the selected
     audio file or clip is not directly compatible with the current session.

   ● **Convert/Convert All.** Use these buttons to convert files or clips that are
     not directly compatible with your session and add them to the session's
     Audio Files folder. All converted files will automatically be copied into
     new files that match the session parameters, with the correct speed, length,
     and pitch.

4. Click DONE to begin importing the audio to your session.

5. If any audio files or clips are being copied or converted, a dialog box will
   appear, prompting you to select a target destination for the newly created
   files. In the CHOOSE A DESTINATION FOLDER dialog box, the Audio Files
   folder for the current session will be selected by default; you can choose
   an alternate folder or directory location, if desired. Navigate to the desired
   folder location and choose USE CURRENT FOLDER.

6. When the AUDIO IMPORT OPTIONS dialog box appears, do one of the following:

- Select NEW TRACK and choose a start location from the drop-down list. New Audio tracks will be created for each separate clip you import, and each clip will be placed at the specified location on its track. The imported audio will also appear in the Clip List.

- Select CLIP LIST to import the audio to the Clip List for later use. The imported audio will appear in the Clip List in the session but will not be added to any tracks during import.

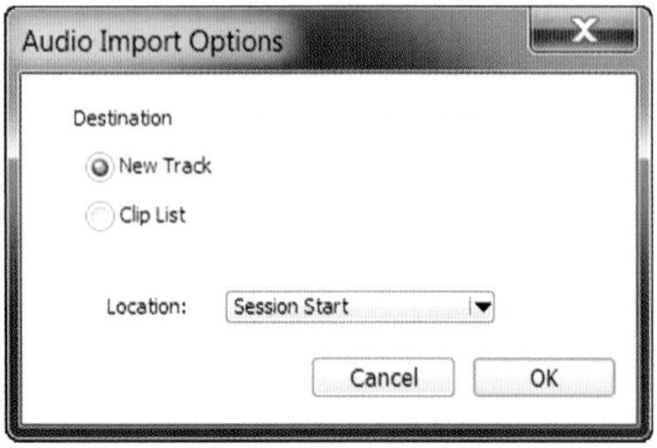

Figure 5.2
The Audio Import Options dialog box

Importing Audio with DigiBase Browsers

As discussed in Lesson 3, Pro Tools provides specialized DigiBase browsers that you can use to quickly locate, manage, and open Pro Tools sessions and compatible files. DigiBase browsers provide powerful search, navigation, file information, and audition capabilities for Pro Tools.

You can import audio into Pro Tools by dragging files into a session from a DigiBase browser window. All files imported in this manner are automatically converted to be compatible with the session parameters, if needed. If no conversion is necessary, the original files will be referenced and not copied.

Like the Import Audio dialog box, the DigiBase Workspace browser can be used to import audio directly into the Clip List or to import audio into new tracks in a session.

Importing to the Clip List

To import audio directly into the Clip List using the DigiBase Workspace browser, follow these steps:

1. Choose **WINDOW** > **WORKSPACE**.

2. To refine file choices so you can pick from only audio files in specific locations, follow these steps:

   a. In the Workspace window, click the **FIND** button (magnifying glass) on the left side of the toolbar. When the button is activated, the toolbar will expand to display the Search tools, and the browser window will divide into two panes.

   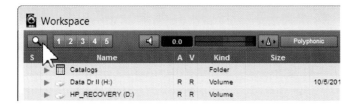

   Figure 5.3
   Clicking the Find button in the Workspace browser

   b. Select the volumes and/or folders you want to search by selecting/ deselecting the check boxes in the top pane. Note that you can drill down through the file system by clicking the arrow icons to expand volumes and folders.

   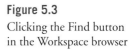

   Figure 5.4
   Selecting a search location

   c. Click the drop-down button in the **KIND** column and select **AUDIO FILE**.

   d. Click the **SEARCH** button. The search results will be shown in the bottom half of the Workspace browser.

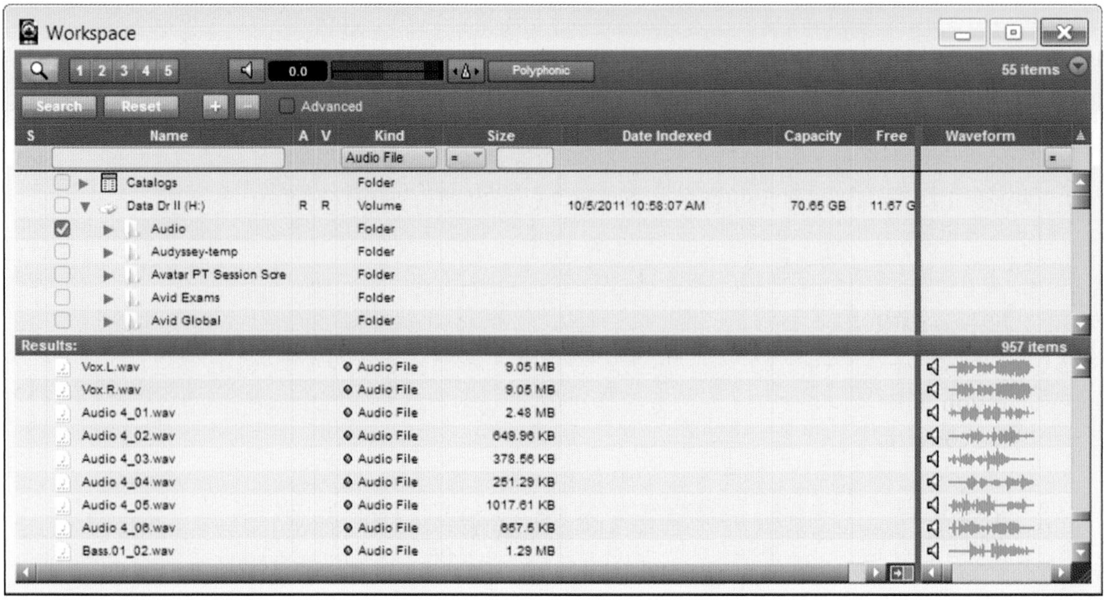

Figure 5.5
Search results displayed in the Workspace browser

3. Drag the audio files you want to import from the Workspace browser onto the Clip List.

The files are automatically converted to the file format, bit depth, and sample rate of the session, if necessary, and will appear in the Clip List.

Tip: Imported audio that is directly compatible with the session parameters will be referenced in its original location and not copied into the session's Audio Files folder. To force-copy a file, hold ALT (Windows) or OPTION (Mac) while dragging the file to the Clip List.

Importing to Tracks

To import audio to tracks using the DigiBase Workspace browser, follow these steps:

1. Choose WINDOW > WORKSPACE and use the Workspace browser to locate the audio files you want to import. (See Step 2 in the preceding "Importing to the Clip List" section.)

2. Drag the audio files from the browser onto an existing track or tracks in the Pro Tools Edit window.

The files will be automatically converted to match the session parameters, as needed, and will appear on the selected track or tracks.

Tip: To create new tracks for audio when importing from the Workspace browser, Shift-drag the audio files from the Workspace browser to the Edit window or drag the files to the Track List. Each of the imported audio files will appear on a new track.

Batch Importing Audio

With a Pro Tools session open, you can quickly import multiple audio files directly into the session. Files that have a different sample rate from the session will automatically be converted on import, as will any files with a non-native file format.

Tip: In Pro Tools 9.x and earlier, files with a different bit depth from the session will also convert on import.

To batch import files, follow these steps:

1. With a Pro Tools session open, browse the files on available volumes using your operating system's Explorer or Finder window.

2. Locate the audio files you want to import and drag them onto the Pro Tools application icon or its alias/shortcut.

Each of the files will appear in the Clip List in the session.

Importing Audio from an Audio CD

Pro Tools lets you import tracks from an audio CD using the DigiBase drag-and-drop feature. Since the transfer is made in the digital domain, there is no signal loss. The sample rate for audio CDs is 44.1 kHz. Therefore, if your session's sample rate is set to 48 kHz or higher, Pro Tools will convert the sample rate for the imported audio. Before importing CD audio, set the Sample Rate Conversion Quality Preference accordingly. (Choose **SETUP > PREFERENCES** and select the **PROCESSING** tab.)

To transfer audio from an audio CD using a DigiBase browser, follow these steps:

1. Insert the audio CD into your CD-ROM drive.

2. From within your Pro Tools session, choose **WINDOW > WORKSPACE**.

3. Browse to the CD and select the audio track(s) you want to import.

4. Drag the file(s) onto the Clip List, Track List, or Tracks Display area in the Edit window of the current session.

Importing Video

To import a video file into Pro Tools, follow these steps:

1. Check the time code settings of the session to make sure they match those of the movie you want to import and then save the session.

2. Choose FILE > IMPORT > VIDEO. A dialog box will open, allowing you to select the video file to import.

3. Navigate to and select the desired QuickTime movie or other video file that is compatible with your system.

4. Click OPEN. The Video Import Options dialog box will appear.

Figure 5.6
The Video Import Options dialog box

5. Select the desired import options as follows:

   - Select a start location from the LOCATION drop-down list.

   - If you wish to import audio embedded in a QuickTime movie, select IMPORT AUDIO FROM FILE.

6. Click OK.

Pro Tools will import the movie and display it in its own Video track in the Edit window as well as in a floating Video window. The first frame of the movie will be automatically placed at the selected start time in your session, unless otherwise specified during import. If you chose to import audio, you will be prompted to choose a destination folder for the audio file. After you've selected the desired folder, the audio will appear in a new Audio track in the session.

Depending on the setting of your Video track view, the movie will display in the Edit window as blocks or as a picture-icon (picon) "thumbnail" overview of the frames of the movie it represents. The Video track will show greater or lesser detail depending on your current zoom level in the Edit window—the closer in you zoom, the greater the number of individual frames that are displayed in the Video track; the farther out you zoom, the fewer the number of individual frames that are visible.

The Video track behaves much like a Pro Tools audio or MIDI track in that you can move the Video clip with the Grabber or other editing tools. This allows you to offset the movie to any start point.

Only one video file can be associated with a standard Pro Tools session at a time. If you want to import a different movie into a session, repeat the preceding steps. The new movie will replace the original in the session.

Pro Tools HD software lets you use multiple Video tracks in your session and add multiple video files and video clips to each Video track. However, only one Video track can be *active* at any time.

The Video track will take its name from the imported video file. Video tracks can subsequently be renamed, in the same manner as other tracks in your session. (See the "Naming Tracks" section in Lesson 3 for details.) However, if you later import a new video file, the track will be renamed to match the imported file.

Tip: Using Frames view to view movie content in the Video track may cause your computer to exhibit reduced or sluggish performance. If this happens, switch the Video track to Blocks view. You can also hide the Video track to further optimize performance, if necessary.

Adding Insert Processors

The Pro Tools Mix window provides channel inserts for Audio tracks, Instrument tracks, Auxiliary Input tracks, and Master Faders. Each channel insert position can be used to add a plug-in insert or external hardware signal processor directly into the signal path of the track.

To display track insert positions, follow these steps:

1. Choose **WINDOW > MIX** to display the Mix window.

2. If needed, choose **VIEW > MIX WINDOW VIEWS > INSERTS A-E** to display the first five insert positions (or choose **INSERTS F-J** to display the next five insert positions).

As discussed in Lesson 1, Pro Tools includes software plug-ins from the DigiRack collection and Pro Tools Creative Collection. (See Appendices A and B for complete lists of the included plug-ins in each collection.) These and other plug-ins can be used to add dynamics, EQ, and effects processing to individual tracks in your session.

To add a plug-in insert to an Audio track, follow these steps:

1. Display the track insert positions, as described above.

2. Click on an insert position on the Audio track and choose **PLUG-IN** from the pop-up menu.

Figure 5.7
Clicking on an insert position

3. Choose a plug-in category from the submenu, such as **REVERB**, and select the desired plug-in for your track. The plug-in window will open onscreen.

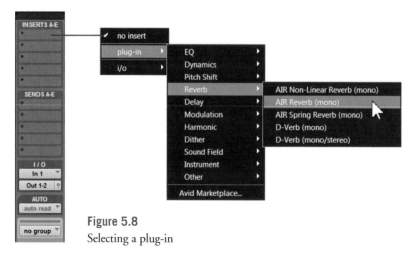

Figure 5.8
Selecting a plug-in

4. Adjust the plug-in parameters as needed.

Review/Discussion Questions

1. What audio file formats can be imported to Pro Tools without requiring conversion? What condition would cause a file in one of these formats to require conversion on import? (See pages 126 and 127.)

2. Name some common audio file formats that Pro Tools can convert on import. (See pages 127 and 128.)

3. What video file format can be imported by all Pro Tools systems? What additional format can be imported by systems running Pro Tools HD? (See page 128.)

4. What two stereo file configuration formats are common on Mac and Windows systems? Which format does Pro Tools 10 support directly? (See page 128.)

5. What is the difference between the Add/Add All buttons in the Import Audio dialog box and the Copy/Copy All buttons? Which buttons can you use to force-copy the files to your session's Audio Files folder? (See page 131.)

6. What happens when you use the Workspace browser to import audio that is not compatible with your session's parameters (in other words, audio that requires conversion)? What happens when you import audio that does not require conversion? (See page 132.)

7. How can you conduct a search for an audio file using the Workspace browser? Where are the search results displayed? (See page 133.)

8. What parameter will Pro Tools convert when importing audio from a CD into a 48-kHz Pro Tools session? Why? (See page 135.)

9. How would you go about importing a QuickTime movie file to Pro Tools while simultaneously importing the audio embedded in the file? (See page 136.)

10. How many video files can be associated with a standard Pro Tools session at once? (See page 137.)

Importing Audio

In this exercise tutorial, you will import several audio files into the session you started in Exercise 3. First, you will import audio files to existing tracks in the session; next, you will import additional audio files to new tracks.

Duration: 10 to 15 Minutes   **Media: DrumLoop.wav, Guitar.wav, 10_01.wav, 10_03.wav**

Getting Started

You will start by opening the Pro Tools session you created in Exercise 3. If that session is not available, use the Ex03.ptxt session template in the Completed Exercises folder on the DVD.

To create the session:

1. Launch Pro Tools and open the session you created in Exercise 3.

2. Choose FILE > SAVE AS and name your session Exercise4-YourName.

3. If needed, toggle the display to show the Edit window by choosing WINDOW > EDIT or pressing CTRL+= (Windows) or COMMAND+= (Mac).

Importing Audio for Existing Tracks

In this part of the exercise, you will import audio files to the Clip List for use on existing tracks. You will then drag the audio onto the appropriate tracks in your session.

To import audio files to the Clip List:

1. Choose FILE > IMPORT AUDIO and navigate to the Exercise Media folder on the DVD.

2. Copy the following audio files into your session by selecting them and clicking the **COPY** or **COPY FILES** button:

- DrumLoop.wav
- Guitar.wav

Note: Be sure you choose the button to *copy* files, not the button to *add* files.

3. Click **DONE** to import the audio. A dialog box will open, prompting you to select a save location.

4. Save the files in the Audio Files folder for your session (the default) by clicking **USE CURRENT FOLDER** (Windows) or **OPEN** (Mac). Next, the Audio Import Options dialog box will appear.

5. In the dialog box, choose the option to import to the Clip List and click **OK**. The files will appear selected in the Clip List on the right side of the Edit window.

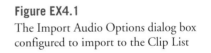

Figure EX4.1
The Import Audio Options dialog box configured to import to the Clip List

To place the imported audio files on existing tracks:

1. Select the **GRABBER** tool (hand icon) in the Edit window toolbar.

2. **CTRL+SHIFT-CLICK** (Windows) or **COMMAND+SHIFT-CLICK** (Mac) on the Guitar clip in the Clip List to select just this one clip and drag it onto the Guitar track.

3. Next, click on the DrumLoop clip in the Clip List and drag it onto the Drums track.

4. If needed, reposition the Guitar and DrumLoop clips with the Grabber tool to position them at the very start of their respective tracks.

5. Choose **FILE > SAVE** to save your work in progress.

Importing Audio to Tracks

In this part of the exercise, you will import additional audio files, placing them directly onto new Audio tracks. You will then rename the Audio tracks with descriptive names for the session.

1. Choose FILE > IMPORT > AUDIO and again navigate to the Exercise Media folder on the DVD.

2. Copy the following audio files into your session (select the files and click the COPY or COPY FILES button):

   - 10_01.wav

   - 10_03.wav

3. Click DONE to import the audio. As before, the Audio Import Options dialog box will appear.

4. Save the files in the Audio Files folder for your session (the default) by clicking USE CURRENT FOLDER (Windows) or OPEN (Mac).

5. When prompted, choose the option to import to a new track, with the Location set to Session Start.

6. Click OK. Two new tracks will appear in your session, with one audio file placed on each track.

7. Double-click on the track nameplate of the 10_01 track and rename it to Vox1; click the NEXT button and rename the 10_03 track to Vox2.

Finishing Up

To complete this exercise tutorial, you will need to save your work and close the session. You will be reusing this session in Exercise 5, so it is important to save the work you've done.

1. Choose FILE > SAVE to save the session.

2. Choose FILE > CLOSE SESSION to close the session.

Making Your First MIDI Recording

This lesson covers the basics of recording and working with MIDI data in Pro Tools. It describes how to set up and record onto MIDI-compatible tracks, how to use virtual instrument plug-ins, and how to select different views for the MIDI data on your tracks.

Duration: 120 Minutes

GOALS

- Understand the basics of the MIDI protocol
- Identify the two types of MIDI-compatible tracks that Pro Tools provides
- Recognize the difference between sample-based operation and tick-based operation
- Set the Main Time Scale to Bars|Beats
- Prepare a system to record MIDI data
- Set up a virtual instrument to play MIDI data recorded on an Instrument track

Recording and editing MIDI data is similar to working with audio; many of the tools, modes, and menu functions work in a similar fashion. However, MIDI data is fundamentally different from audio; therefore, some of the processes and operations you use to work with this data will be different. This chapter introduces Pro Tools features that will allow you to record and edit MIDI data in ways that are specific to this protocol.

MIDI Basics

MIDI, or *Musical Instrument Digital Interface*, is a protocol for connecting electronic instruments, performance controllers, and computers so they can communicate with one another. MIDI data is different from data stored in an audio file in that MIDI data does not represent sound waves; instead, it represents information about a performance, such as the pitch, duration, volume, and order of notes to be played.

MIDI devices transmit performance data via MIDI messages, which are composed of 8-bit numbers (or *bytes*) and include information such as *note* or *pitch number* (indicating an individual note in a scale) and *velocity* (typically affecting an individual note's volume). Up to 16 separate channels of MIDI information can be sent over a single MIDI cable, allowing a single cable path to control multiple MIDI devices or to control a single device that is capable of multi-channel (also known as *multi-timbral*) operation.

The Format of a MIDI Message

The most significant bit of a MIDI message byte is reserved to distinguish between status bytes and data bytes. The remaining seven bits represent the unique data of the message byte, encompassing a range of values from 0 to 127. The maximum length for a standard MIDI message is three bytes, consisting of one status byte and one or more data bytes.

Status Byte	Data Byte 1	Data Byte 2
1tttnnnn	0xxxxxxx	0xxxxxxx

Where:

t is used to specify the type of status message being sent

n is used to specify the associated MIDI Channel Number

x is used to specify the associated data value, such as a note number (pitch) or velocity value

Many other kinds of information can be conveyed via MIDI messages, such as pan and general MIDI volume information for instruments that support these, as well as program change events, or commands that tell MIDI instruments which of their available sounds, or *patches*, to use.

A *MIDI sequencer* allows you to store, edit, and play back MIDI information that can be used to control MIDI-compatible devices, such as synthesizers, sound modules, and drum machines. These devices don't have to be external hardware devices—today many software synthesis and sampling packages are available, enabling you to add internal devices to your host computer.

MIDI in Pro Tools

Pro Tools includes an integrated MIDI sequencer that lets you import, record, and edit MIDI in much the same way that you work with audio. MIDI data appears in tracks in the Pro Tools Edit window, referencing the same Timeline as your Audio tracks. Corresponding channel strips appear in the Pro Tools Mix window and include familiar mixer-style controls that affect MIDI data in the track. MIDI Editor windows are also available in Pro Tools for detailed MIDI composition and editing tasks.

As you learned in Chapter 3, Pro Tools provides two types of tracks for working with MIDI data: MIDI tracks and Instrument tracks.

■ A *MIDI track* stores MIDI note, instrument, and controller data only; no audio can pass through a MIDI track. MIDI tracks are often used in conjunction with Auxiliary Input tracks for monitoring and playback of a synthesizer or virtual instrument associated with MIDI data.

■ An *Instrument track* provides MIDI and audio capability in a single channel strip. Like MIDI tracks, Instrument tracks store note, instrument, and controller data. Instrument tracks can also route audio signals for monitoring and playback of an instrument associated with the MIDI data on the track. This capability simplifies the process of recording, editing, and monitoring MIDI data.

Creating MIDI-Compatible Tracks

If your session does not already contain them, you will have to create one or more MIDI-compatible tracks for your MIDI recording. The type of track you use (MIDI track or Instrument track) will depend on how you prefer to work with your MIDI devices. Some considerations include whether you will be using a virtual instrument with the track (see the "Using Virtual Instruments" section later in this chapter) and the complexity of your setup. For basic MIDI recording or working with virtual instruments, you will probably find Instrument tracks to be easier to use, due to the simplified manner in which they allow you to route audio from your MIDI devices through your session.

To add MIDI-compatible tracks, do the following:

1. Chose **TRACK** > **NEW** to open the New Tracks dialog box.

2. Input the number of desired tracks in the **TRACK TOTAL** field.

3. Select either **MIDI TRACK** or **INSTRUMENT TRACK** in the Track Type drop-down list. The Track Time Base drop-down will default to Ticks.

4. For Instrument tracks, choose between **MONO** and **STEREO** in the Track Format drop-down list. (Additional multi-channel formats are available with Pro Tools HD software.)

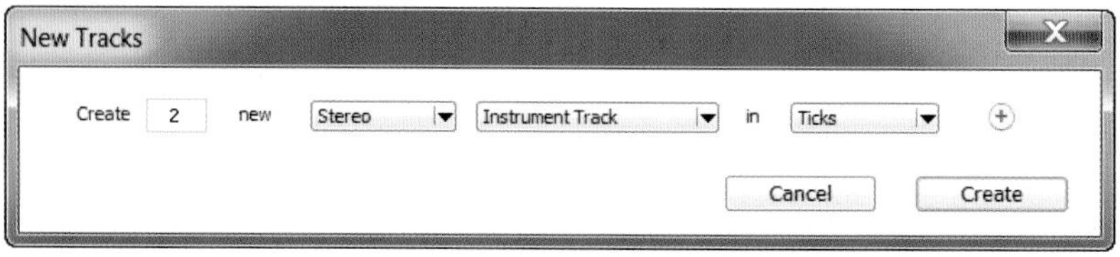

Figure 6.1
Creating stereo Instrument tracks in the New Tracks dialog box

5. Click **CREATE**.

When you create a track for working with MIDI data, the track timebase defaults to Ticks, indicating that the track uses tick-based timing (also known as *bar-and-beat-based timing*). MIDI operations are typically bar-and-beat-based, whereas audio operations are typically sample-based.

Sample-Based Operation versus Tick-Based Operation

The differences between sample-based operation and tick-based operation are essentially the differences between how audio data is stored and how MIDI data is stored.

Sample-Based Operation

In sample-based operation, recorded information is tied to fixed points in time relative to the beginning of the session. In Chapter 4, you learned how to record audio in Pro Tools. Recorded audio data is stored in audio files as individual audio samples. In Pro Tools, the corresponding audio clips are represented on sample-based tracks by default. Audio material that resides on sample-based tracks is located at particular sample locations on the Timeline. You can think of these sample-based locations as *absolute locations* in time, measured by the number of samples that have elapsed since the beginning of the session. The audio material will not move from its absolute locations in time if the session tempo is later modified—though the audio clips' *relative* bar and beat locations in the session will change.

Audio tracks can also be set to tick-based operation to perform specialized functions, such as tempo matching for REX-like clip groups or Elastic Audio. For the purposes of this course, whenever we discuss recording and editing audio, we will assume sample-based operation unless otherwise stated.

Tick-Based Operation

In tick-based operation, recorded information is tied to specific Bar|Beat locations in an arrangement. When you record MIDI data, Pro Tools uses tick-based timing to determine the locations of your MIDI events. MIDI events are recorded relative to particular bar and beat locations within the composition (such as Bar 16, Beat 1), and their absolute locations adjust based on the session tempo—if the tempo increases, the MIDI data will play back faster, and individual events will occur earlier in time; if the tempo decreases, the MIDI data will play back slower, and the same events will occur later in time. The Elastic Audio capabilities in Pro Tools provide the same functionality for audio on tick-based tracks, enabling audio clips to automatically compress or expand to conform to the session tempo.

Pro Tools subdivides the bars and beats in your session into ticks, with 960 ticks comprising a quarter note. Timing can thus be specified with a precision (or resolution) of up to 1/960th of a quarter note when using tick-based operation. You can think of the tick-based locations as *relative locations* in time, measured by the number of bars, beats, and ticks that have elapsed since the beginning of the session. A tick-based event maintains its rhythmic location relative to other tick-based events in the song if the session tempo is later modified—but a tempo change will cause the event to occur earlier or later in *absolute* time, thereby changing its location relative to any sample-based audio in the session.

Tick-based tracks and data coexist with sample-based tracks and data within the same Pro Tools session.

Tip: Pro Tools displays relationships between audio and MIDI accurately in the Edit window at all zoom levels, with MIDI event durations drawn proportionally to the Timeline, according to tempo.

Though MIDI tracks are typically tick-based, they can also be set to sample-based to perform specialized functions. For the purposes of this course, whenever we discuss MIDI recording and editing, we will assume tick-based operation unless otherwise stated.

In the Avid Learning Series   Sample-based MIDI operations are discussed in the Pro Tools 110 and 310M courses.

Time Scale and Rulers for Working with MIDI

When you are working with MIDI data in a session, you will frequently reference the Bars|Beats Time Scale. This Time Scale can be displayed in the Location Indicators at the top of the Edit window and is represented on the Bars|Beats Ruler. You will also commonly work with tempo, meter, and key signature settings, which are displayed in the Tempo, Meter, and Key Signature Rulers, respectively.

Setting the Timebase Ruler and Main Time Scale

For MIDI recording and editing, you will find it helpful to display the Bars|Beats Timebase Ruler and to set the Main Time Scale to Bars|Beats. This will let you reference any recorded material, track selections, and edits to the bar numbers and beats of the project.

To set the Timebase Ruler and Main Time Scale, do the following:

1. Display the Bars|Beats Ruler by choosing VIEW > RULERS > BARS:BEATS.

2. Set the Main Time Scale to Bars|Beats by doing one of the following:

   - Click on BARS|BEATS in the Ruler View area of the Edit window.

   - Select VIEW > MAIN COUNTER > BARS:BEATS.

   - Click on the MAIN COUNTER SELECTOR in either the Edit window or the Transport window and select BARS|BEATS from the pop-up menu.

Figure 6.2
Main Counter selector in the Edit window

Figure 6.3
Selecting Bars|Beats from the Main Counter pop-up menu

Tip: Refer to Chapter 2 for more information on the Main Time Scale.

The Bars|Beats Time Scale displays information in the following format:

1|1|000 (Bar Number|Beat Number|Tick Number)

The first number in this format represents the bar number with respect to the zero point on the session Timeline. The second number represents the beat number within the current bar. The final number represents the tick number within the current beat, based on the division of 960 ticks per quarter note.

Tempo, Meter, and Key Signature Rulers

The Tempo, Meter, and Key Signature Rulers allow you to specify the default tempo, meter, and key signature for your session and to set tempo, meter, and key changes at any point along the session Timeline. To display the Tempo, Meter, and Key Signature Rulers, choose VIEW > RULERS > TEMPO, VIEW > RULERS > METER, and VIEW > RULERS > KEY SIGNATURE, respectively.

Preparing to Record MIDI

Once you have added MIDI-compatible tracks to your session, you will need to prepare your MIDI device and software for recording. The general processes you will use to prepare for recording MIDI are as follows:

1. Connect a MIDI device.
2. Check the track inputs/outputs.
3. Record-enable the track(s).
4. Set record options.

Connecting a MIDI Device

Recording MIDI data typically involves connecting a keyboard, a drum machine, or another MIDI device as an input to your Pro Tools system. Before starting to record, you should verify that the MIDI device you will use for input (also called a *MIDI controller*) is connected to your system through an input on your MIDI interface or a USB port on your computer, if applicable. You might also need to connect a MIDI output from your interface as a return to this device or as an input to a separate MIDI device, such as a synthesizer, for monitoring and playback purposes.

Example: For basic recording in a home or project studio, you can connect a MIDI cable from the MIDI Out port on the back of a keyboard to the MIDI In port on an Mbox or similar interface. For monitoring and playback purposes, you can also connect the MIDI Out port of the Mbox to the MIDI In port on the keyboard (assuming onboard sound capabilities) or to a separate synthesizer unit.

Tip: Connecting a MIDI device to Pro Tools with a USB cable provides both MIDI input and MIDI output for the device.

Checking MIDI Inputs/Outputs

Once your MIDI device is connected, you will need to configure the inputs and outputs of your MIDI-compatible track(s) with the appropriate settings to route the MIDI signals into and out of the tracks.

MIDI Input

The MIDI Input selector in the Edit or Mix window for a MIDI-compatible track is the functional equivalent to the Audio Input Path selector for an Audio track. This selector determines which incoming MIDI data gets recorded onto the track in Pro Tools.

On MIDI tracks, the MIDI Input selector is located in the track display (Edit window) or channel strip (Mix window), where the Audio Input Path selector would be on an Audio track. On Instrument tracks, however, the MIDI Input selector appears in the Instrument MIDI controls section. This section of the track display or channel strip is used only for Instrument tracks and needs to be displayed separately.

To display the Instrument MIDI controls, do one of the following:

- Choose **VIEW > MIX WINDOW > INSTRUMENTS**. The Instrument MIDI controls will appear at the top of the channel strip.

- Choose **VIEW > EDIT WINDOW > INSTRUMENTS**. The Instrument MIDI controls will appear at the head of the track display.

The MIDI Input selectors for MIDI-compatible tracks are set to All by default, such that the MIDI signals from all connected and enabled input devices are received in the track. If you prefer, you can set the MIDI Input to a specific device (port) and channel to more tightly control the routing of MIDI data.

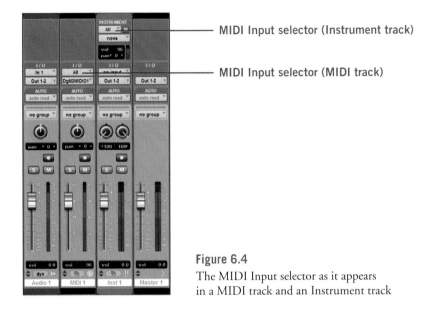

MIDI Input selector (Instrument track)

MIDI Input selector (MIDI track)

Figure 6.4
The MIDI Input selector as it appears
in a MIDI track and an Instrument track

To limit the MIDI input on a track to a specific device, do the following:

1. Click on the **MIDI INPUT SELECTOR** in the Edit or Mix window.

2. Select the MIDI device or interface and port that you want to route to the track.

3. Do one of the following:

   ● Select **ALL CHANNELS** to route all channels from the selected device to the track.

   ● Select a specific channel to route only the data being transmitted on that channel to the track.

MIDI Output

The MIDI Output selector for a MIDI-compatible track determines which device or port is used for monitoring and playing back MIDI data. Live MIDI signals can be routed to an audio sound source for monitoring purposes when MIDI Thru is enabled. (See the "MIDI Thru" section later in this chapter.) Similarly, recorded MIDI signals can be routed to an audio sound source for playback purposes. You use the MIDI Output selector to configure the device or port and the MIDI channel that the signal is routed to for both of these purposes. On MIDI tracks, the MIDI Output selector is located where the Audio Output Path selector would be on an Audio track; on Instrument tracks, it is located in the Instrument MIDI controls section of the channel strip (Mix window) or track display (Edit window).

To set the MIDI Output, do the following:

1. Click on the **MIDI OUTPUT SELECTOR** in the Edit or Mix window.

2. Select the instrument or port and channel you wish to route the output to for MIDI playback.

Record-Enabling MIDI-Compatible Tracks

The process you use to enable recording on a Pro Tools MIDI track or Instrument track is the same as you use for an Audio track: Simply click the track's **RECORD ENABLE** button in either the Edit window or the Mix window. As with an Audio track, the Record Enable button flashes red when a MIDI-compatible track is record-ready.

Setting Record Options

Pro Tools provides various record options that are specific to working with MIDI data. You will need to set the MIDI Controls, quantizing, and MIDI Thru options as desired prior to beginning to record onto your MIDI tracks.

MIDI Controls

As discussed in Chapter 2, the Pro Tools Transport window or Edit window can be set to show MIDI Controls that you can use when recording MIDI data.

To display MIDI Controls in the Pro Tools Transport window, do the following:

1. Select **WINDOW** > **TRANSPORT** to display the Transport window, if it is not currently showing.

2. Select **VIEW** > **TRANSPORT** > **MIDI CONTROLS** to display the MIDI Controls, if they are not currently showing.

Tip: The MIDI Controls can also be displayed in the Edit window. Choose MIDI CONTROLS from the Edit Window Toolbar menu in the upper-right corner of the window.

Before you begin recording MIDI data, you can take any of the following optional steps to set the MIDI Controls:

1. Enable **WAIT FOR NOTE** and/or **COUNT OFF** in the Transport window or Edit window, if desired. Use Wait for Note to begin recording automatically when you begin playing; use Count Off to count off a specified number of measures before recording begins.

2. Enable the **METRONOME**, if desired, and specify the settings in the Click/Countoff Options dialog box (**SETUP** > **CLICK/COUNTOFF**).

Tip: The simplest way to enable playback of the metronome click is to set up a
      click track. See the "Creating a Click Track" section in Chapter 4 for details.

3. Disable **MIDI MERGE** for initial recording. Once you have recorded a
   MIDI pass that you want to keep, you can enable this control to layer
   additional MIDI data on top of the existing recording.

4. Set the tempo for recording by doing one of the following:

   ● Engage the **TEMPO RULER ENABLE** button (Conductor Track) to follow
     the tempo map defined in the Tempo Ruler. See the "Setting the Session
     Tempo" section later in this chapter for more information.

   ● Disengage the **TEMPO RULER ENABLE** button (Conductor Track) to set the
     tempo using the Tempo field in the Transport window or Edit window.

5. Set the meter as needed by double-clicking the **CURRENT METER** display.
   See the "Setting the Session Meter" section later in this chapter for more
   information.

The functions of each of the MIDI Controls are described in detail in the "MIDI
Controls" section in Chapter 2.

Input Quantize

The Input Quantize feature enables you to automatically align, or *quantize*, all
recorded MIDI notes to a specified timing grid. This creates a style of recording
similar to working with a hardware sequencer or drum machine. Do not use this
feature if you want to preserve the original "feel" of the performance.

To enable Input Quantize, do the following:

1. Choose **EVENT** > **EVENT OPERATIONS** > **INPUT QUANTIZE.** The Event
   Operations window will open with Input Quantize selected in the Operation
   drop-down list.

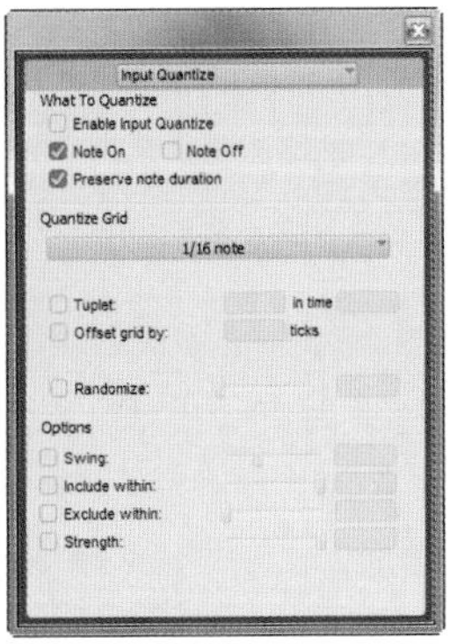

Figure 6.5
The Event Operations window

2. Select the **ENABLE INPUT QUANTIZE** option.

3. In the **WHAT TO QUANTIZE** section of the window, choose the MIDI note attributes to quantize:

   - **Attacks.** Aligns note start points to the nearest grid value (commonly used).

   - **Releases.** Aligns note end points to the nearest grid value (used only for specific situations).

   - **Preserve Note Duration.** Preserves the note durations of the performance by moving end points in concert with start points. If this option is not selected, note start and end points can be moved independently, changing the duration of the note.

4. Set the quantize grid to the smallest note value that will be played. All notes in the performance will be aligned to the nearest value on this grid.

5. In the **OPTIONS** section of the Input Quantize window, select any other desired options.

MIDI Thru

To monitor MIDI-compatible tracks while recording, you need to enable MIDI Thru. When it is enabled, Pro Tools routes the MIDI signals it receives from your controllers out to the devices and channels assigned by the MIDI Output selectors for your MIDI-compatible tracks.

To enable MIDI Thru, select **OPTIONS > MIDI THRU.**

Caution: When using MIDI Thru, you might need to disable Local Control on your MIDI keyboard controller. Otherwise, your keyboard could receive double MIDI notes, which can lead to stuck notes.

Tip: You must enable MIDI Thru when using an Instrument track to record MIDI data; if MIDI Thru is not enabled, the track will not receive a MIDI signal.

Using Virtual Instruments

Virtual instruments are the software equivalents of outboard synthesizers or sound modules. Many virtual instruments are available for Pro Tools in the form of real-time plug-ins. The Xpand![2], Boom, and Structure Free plug-ins are examples of virtual instruments installed as standard components of Pro Tools.

Virtual instrument plug-ins can be added to Auxiliary Input tracks or Instrument tracks and triggered by MIDI events routed through the respective tracks.

For basic recording with a virtual instrument, you will want to create an Instrument track and connect a MIDI controller as described earlier in this chapter.

Placing a Virtual Instrument on an Instrument Track

A virtual instrument plug-in can be placed directly on an Instrument track, allowing the instrument to be triggered by the MIDI data on the track during playback or by MIDI data passing through the track for live input monitoring.

To add a virtual instrument such as Xpand!^{2}, Boom, or Structure Free to an Instrument track in Pro Tools, do the following:

1. Display the track inserts, if not already displayed, by choosing **VIEW** > **MIX WINDOW** or **VIEW** > **EDIT WINDOW** and selecting **INSERTS**.

2. Click an insert on the Instrument track, choose **PLUG-IN** > **INSTRUMENT**, and select the virtual instrument to use on the track. The track's MIDI Output will automatically be assigned to the virtual instrument plug-in, and the instrument's user interface will open.

Figure 6.6
Selecting the Xpand!^{2}
virtual instrument plug-in

Tip: Stereo Instrument tracks provide two options for plug-ins: multi-channel plug-ins and multi-mono plug-ins. Choose multi-channel plug-ins for stereo virtual instruments; choose multi-mono plug-ins for mono virtual instruments.

3. Assign the appropriate hardware outputs, if not already selected, using the AUDIO OUTPUT PATH selector (for monitoring and playback purposes).

4. Set the track's VOLUME FADER to the desired output level.

5. Play notes on your MIDI controller. The meters on the Instrument track will register the instrument's audio output.

Tip: The MIDI signal received on an Instrument track is displayed by the MIDI meter in the Instrument MIDI Controls section of the channel strip or track display. If the MIDI meter on an Instrument track does not register a signal, verify that the MIDI output has been assigned with the MIDI Output selector.

Using Xpand!²

Xpand!² is an A.I.R. virtual instrument designed to provide fast access to high-quality sounds directly from within Pro Tools. Xpand!² comes equipped with more than 2,300 *Patches* (plug-in settings) and more than 1,200 combinable *Parts* (sound presets). The Xpand!² sound library includes synth pads, leads, acoustic and electric pianos, organs, strings, vocals, brass and woodwinds, mallet percussion, ethnic instruments, loops, and more.

Figure 6.7
The Xpand!² virtual instrument plug-in user interface

Xpand!² provides four synthesizer slots (A, B, C, and D), each with individual MIDI Channel, Mix, Arpeggiator, Modulation, and Effects settings. Each slot can hold one of the included preset Parts. Each Xpand!² Patch is composed of a blend of the individual Parts in slots A through D, which can be layered together to produce a rich, dynamic texture.

To use the Xpand!² plug-in, add the plug-in to an Instrument track as described in the "Placing a Virtual Instrument on an Instrument Track" section earlier in this chapter. The Xpand!² user interface will open, displaying selectors for each of the four parts.

The plug-in initially opens to the <factory default> setting with a Part assigned for Slot A only. Xpand!² includes numerous additional Patches to choose from, organized into folders by type.

To select a different Patch setting, click either the **LIBRARIAN MENU** or the **PLUG-IN SETTINGS SELECT** button in the plug-in window and navigate to the desired folder and Patch. Each Patch calls up a preset Xpand!² configuration.

Each of Xpand!²'s sound Parts can be turned on or off at any time by clicking on the On/Off power indicator above the Part letter. (When toggled off, the power indicator turns a dimmed gray color.) Slot assignments can also be changed individually by clicking on the sound selector in the Xpand!² user interface.

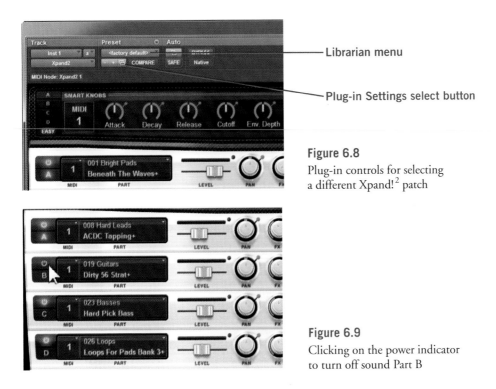

Librarian menu

Plug-in Settings select button

Figure 6.8
Plug-in controls for selecting a different Xpand!² patch

Figure 6.9
Clicking on the power indicator to turn off sound Part B

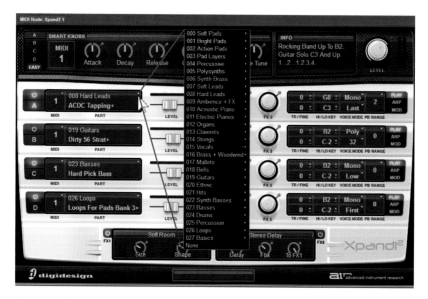

Figure 6.10
Clicking on the sound selector to change the Part assigned to Slot A

Smart Knobs

Xpand!^{2} includes a row of controls in the user interface called *Smart Knobs*. These six knobs are displayed across the top of Xpand!^{2}. Smart Knobs provide access to assignable or variable parameters. The Smart Knobs in Xpand!^{2} give you quick access to the most useful parameters for a given task. For example, in Part mode, the Smart Knobs display parameters for the selected Part in Slot A, B, C, or D. Selecting a different slot or changing a slot assignment changes the parameters that are displayed on the Smart Knobs.

You can modify the behavior of Smart Knobs in Xpand!^{2}. You can also use the MIDI Learn function to assign MIDI controllers to Smart Knob parameters for real-time control from a MIDI keyboard or control surface.

Using Boom

Boom is a virtual drum machine featuring a broad range of percussion sounds. The Boom user interface provides a simple, drum-machine-style pattern sequencer. Boom comes with 10 drum kits inspired by classic electronic drum machines.

To use the Boom plug-in, add the plug-in to an Instrument track as described in the "Placing a Virtual Instrument on an Instrument Track" section earlier in this chapter. The Boom user interface will open, displaying the pattern for the <factory default> preset.

Figure 6.11
The Boom virtual instrument plug-in user interface

The Matrix Display on the left side of the plug-in window presents a visual overview of the current pattern in Boom's sequencer. The Matrix provides a way to work with patterns and to keep track of the step that Boom is playing at any given time. Each lit LED in the sequencer corresponds to an instrument that is sequenced to play at that step. The brighter the LED, the higher the velocity of the instrument trigger. You can click each LED directly to add a note on that step. Successive clicks toggle through velocity levels or toggle the note on/off.

Figure 6.12
The Boom Matrix Display

The Kit Selector menu at the bottom of the plug-in window provides access to the 10 preset drum kits in Boom: Urban 1, Urban 2, Dance 1, Dance 2, Electro, Eight-O, Nine-O, Fat 8, Fat 9, and Retro.

Figure 6.13
The Boom Kit Selector menu

You can use MIDI data on your Instrument track to control Boom playback. Boom responds to two main ranges of MIDI notes:

■ From C1–D#2, Boom plays each of the instruments in the current drum kit. This allows you to use Pro Tools' MIDI sequencer to create drum tracks, rather than using Boom's built-in pattern sequencer.

■ From C3–D#4, each note triggers one of the 16 patterns in the current preset, switching between them on the fly.

Using Structure Free

Structure Free is a sample playback plug-in that brings various sample libraries to Pro Tools. Structure Free comes with 60 preset patches and a 64-voice multi-timbral sound engine. The Structure Free sample library includes drum kits, drum loops, bass and guitar patches, leads, electric pianos, organs, pads, and more.

Structure Free loads a variety of sample libraries, including native Structure, SampleCell, SampleCell II, Kontakt, Kontakt 2, and EXS 24. The plug-in supports all common bit depths, sample rates, and surround formats.

To use Structure Free, add the plug-in to a stereo Instrument track as described in the "Placing a Virtual Instrument on an Instrument Track" section earlier in this chapter. The Structure Free user interface will open with the Sine Wave Patch loaded.

To select a different Patch preset, click the QUICK BROWSE menu and navigate to the desired folder and Patch. Each Patch calls up a preset Structure Free configuration.

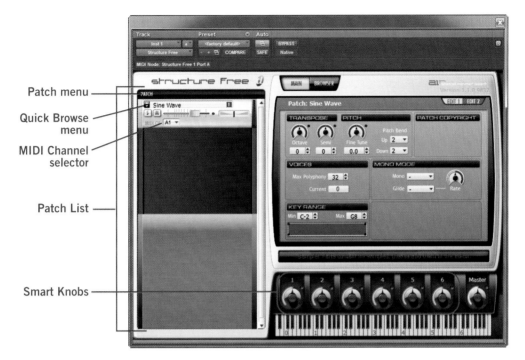

Patch menu —

Quick Browse menu —

MIDI Channel selector —

Patch List —

Smart Knobs —

Figure 6.14
The Structure Free sample player user interface

Figure 6.15
Selecting a Patch from the Quick Browse menu

Additional Patches can be added to the preset using the Patch menu at the top of the Patch List. To add a Patch, select **PATCH > ADD PATCH** and navigate to the desired folder and Patch. To configure a new Patch to play back concurrently with existing patches, set its MIDI channel correspondingly (to MIDI Channel A1, for example).

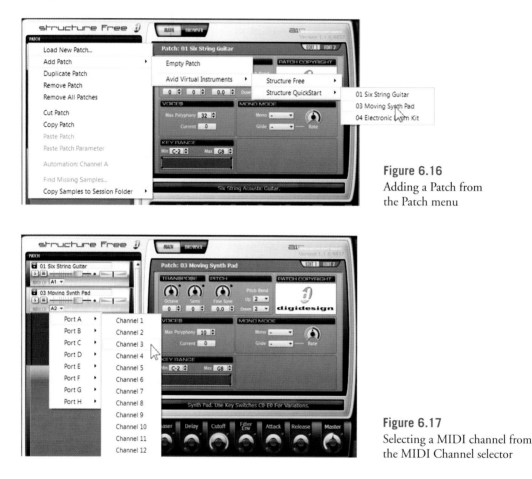

Figure 6.16
Adding a Patch from the Patch menu

Figure 6.17
Selecting a MIDI channel from the MIDI Channel selector

Many of the Structure Free patches include *Key Switches*, special MIDI notes or keys that are assigned to change control values rather than trigger notes. Key Switches can toggle between different settings or mute parts within a Patch. For example, a Key Switch can be assigned to Smart Knobs that control effect settings, allowing you to mix in effects by pressing the corresponding key on your MIDI controller.

All available Key Switches appear blue on the screen keyboard. The currently activated Key Switch appears green.

Setting the Session Meter, Tempo, and Key Signature

Before you begin recording MIDI data, you will need to verify the meter and tempo settings for your session and make any necessary changes. You may also want to set the key signature for your session. The following sections describe how to set the meter, tempo, and key signature for your composition.

Setting the Session Meter

When you open a new session in Pro Tools, the meter defaults to 4/4. If you intend to record with the click and you are working with a different meter, make sure to set the session meter accordingly. Meter events, which can occur anywhere within a Pro Tools session, are registered and displayed using the Meter Ruler.

To set the meter for a session, do the following:

1. With the Meter Ruler displayed in the Edit window, click on the **ADD METER CHANGE** button (or double-click on the **CURRENT METER** display in the Transport window). The Meter Change dialog box will open.

Figure 6.18
The Add Meter Change button on the Meter Ruler

Figure 6.19
The Meter Change dialog box

2. Enter the meter you will use for the session and enter 1|1|000 in the **LOCATION** field.

3. Choose a note value that corresponds to the desired click timing.

4. Click **OK** to insert the new meter event at the beginning of the session, replacing the default meter.

Setting the Session Tempo

When you open a new session in Pro Tools, the tempo defaults to 120 beats per minute (BPM). If you intend to record with the click, and you are working with a different tempo, make sure to set the session tempo accordingly. If you know the tempo you will use for the session, you can insert a tempo event at the beginning of the session.

Tempo events, which can occur anywhere within a Pro Tools session, are registered and displayed using the Tempo Ruler.

To set the session tempo, do the following:

1. With the Tempo Ruler displayed and the Tempo Ruler Enable option selected (see the "Tempo Map Mode" section later in this chapter), click on the **ADD TEMPO CHANGE** button.

Figure 6.20
The Add Tempo Change button on the Tempo Ruler

2. Enter the BPM value you will use for the session and enter 1|1|000 in the **LOCATION** field.

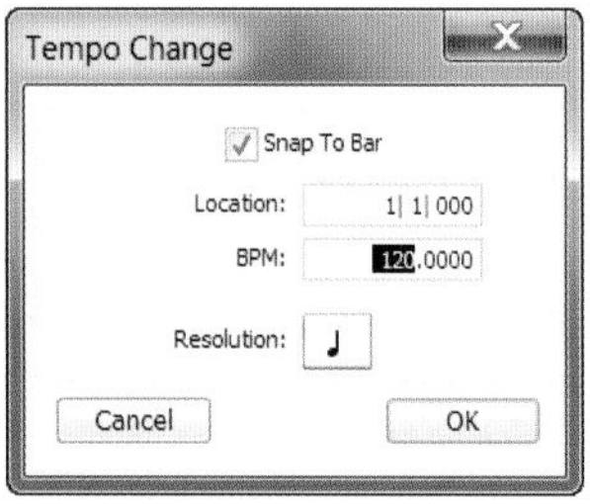

Figure 6.21
The Tempo Change dialog box

3. To base the beat on something other than the default quarter note, select the desired note value.

4. Click **OK** to insert the new tempo event at the beginning of the session, replacing the default tempo.

Tempo Map Mode

When you create a new Pro Tools session, the session is configured by default to follow the tempo events in the Tempo Ruler (also known as the session tempo map). The tempo map can be toggled on and off as needed. To use the tempo map, ensure that the **TEMPO RULER ENABLE** (Conductor Track) button is activated in the Transport or Edit window.

Figure 6.22
Enabling the Tempo Ruler in the Transport window

Manual Tempo Mode and Tap Tempo

In Manual Tempo mode, Pro Tools will ignore the tempo events in the Tempo Ruler. In this mode, the tempo can be adjusted by typing a value directly into the **CURRENT TEMPO** field in the Transport window. The tempo can also be tapped in using a MIDI controller or the **T** key on your computer. Manually adjusting the tempo during playback will momentarily interrupt playback.

To put Pro Tools into Manual Tempo mode, click to deselect the **TEMPO RULER ENABLE** button in the Transport window.

Setting the Session Key Signature

When you open a new session in Pro Tools, the key signature defaults to C major. If you intend to use the key signature functionality in Pro Tools, make sure to set the key signature for your session correctly. If you know the key you will use for the session, you can insert a Key Change event at the beginning of the session to change the key of the session.

Key Change events, which can occur anywhere within a Pro Tools session, are registered and displayed using the Key Signature Ruler.

To set the session key signature, do the following:

1. With the Key Signature Ruler displayed, click on the **ADD KEY SIGNATURE** button.

Figure 6.23
The Add Key Signature button on the Key Signature Ruler

2. Select the mode (major or minor) and key signature you will use for the session and enter 1|1|000 in the **FROM** field.

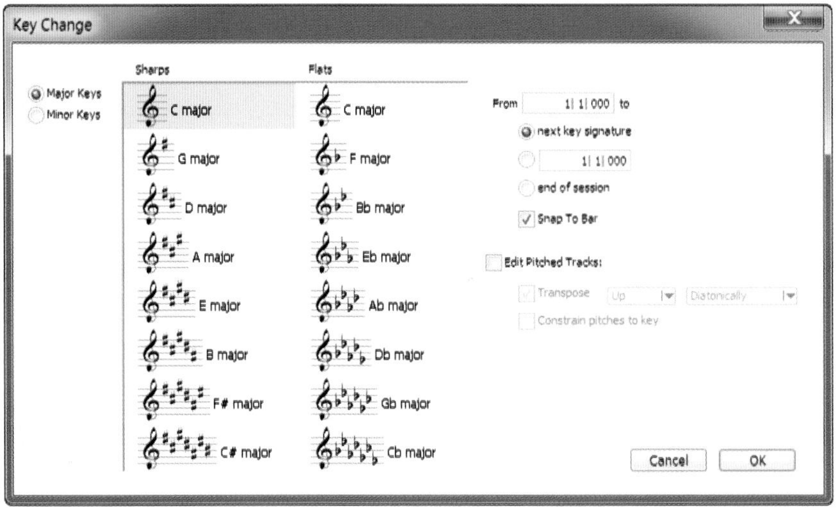

Figure 6.24
The Key Change dialog box

3. Click **OK** to insert the Key Change event at the beginning of the session.

Recording MIDI

With a MIDI controller connected to your Pro Tools system, the MIDI signal routed to a MIDI-compatible track, and the track record-enabled, you are ready to begin recording.

To record to a MIDI-compatible track, do the following:

1. Display the Transport window, if it is not already showing (**WINDOW > TRANSPORT**).

2. In the Transport window, click the **RETURN TO ZERO** button so the start and end times are cleared. This ensures that you'll start recording from the beginning of the track.

3. Verify that one or more tracks have been record-enabled. (See the "Record-Enabling MIDI-Compatible Tracks" section earlier in this chapter.)

4. Click the **RECORD** button in the Transport window to enter Record Ready mode. The button will turn red and begin to flash. If you are using Wait for Note, the Play button will also flash green.

Figure 6.25
The Transport window in Record Ready mode

5. When you're ready, click **PLAY** in the Transport window, or if you're using Wait for Note, simply begin playing. Recording will begin.

Tip: If you are using countoff, the Record and Play buttons will flash during the countoff, after which recording will begin.

6. When you have finished recording, click **STOP**.

To play back the track through a connected virtual instrument or outboard device, do the following:

1. Click the **RECORD ENABLE** button on the Instrument track to disable recording.

2. In the Transport window, click the **RETURN TO ZERO** button.

3. Click **PLAY** in the Transport window to begin playback.

Viewing MIDI Data on MIDI-Compatible Tracks

After you've completed a recording, your MIDI data will appear in the Edit window, arranged in a Track Playlist, against the same Timeline as audio. Your MIDI information can be viewed in a variety of ways in Pro Tools, allowing you to perform editing tasks that affect different attributes of the data. The Edit window allows you to select from several view formats, including *Notes* view, *Clips* view, and *Velocity* view. Alternatively, you can view and work with your MIDI data in a MIDI Editor window, giving you access to multiple types of data at once.

Tip: You can quickly toggle between Notes and Clips views in the Edit window by pressing START + – (Windows) or CONTROL + – (Mac) whenever your insertion point is located in a MIDI-compatible track.

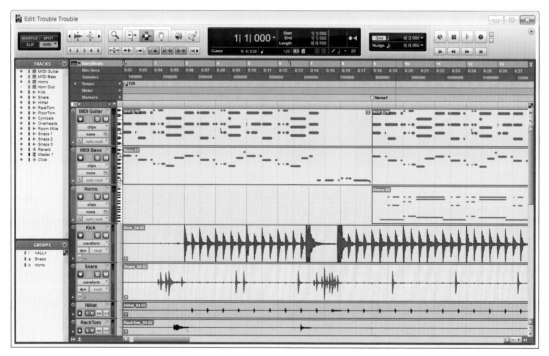

Figure 6.26
MIDI-compatible tracks and Audio tracks in the Edit window

MIDI Clips View

MIDI data is initially displayed in Clips view by default. MIDI Clips view shows MIDI notes grouped together into clips, similar to clips on Audio tracks. MIDI clips act as containers for the MIDI data that falls within the clip boundaries.

While notes are visible in Clips view, they cannot be individually edited in this view.

Figure 6.27
An Instrument track in Clips view

MIDI clips can be selected, copied, cut, and trimmed in the same way as audio clips, allowing you to quickly arrange song phrases or sections.

To switch to Clips view, do one of the following:

■ Click anywhere in the track with the **Selector** tool and press **Start+minus (-)** (Windows) or **Control+minus (-)** (Mac) to toggle to Clips view. Depending on the currently selected view, you might have to toggle twice.

■ Click on the **Track View selector** for the track and choose **Clips** from the pop-up list.

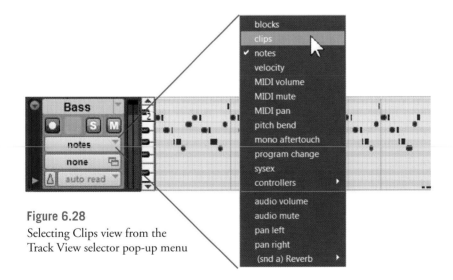

Figure 6.28
Selecting Clips view from the
Track View selector pop-up menu

Tip: When Zoom Toggle is active, pressing Start + – (Windows) or Control + –
      (Mac) will toggle between Notes view and Velocity view.

MIDI Notes View

MIDI Notes view shows individual MIDI notes in a piano-roll format, with pitch shown on the vertical axis and durations shown on the horizontal axis. The pitch range displayed in a track depends on the track height and the current zoom value. A mini-keyboard on the left side of the track allows you to scroll up or down to see all pitches in the track.

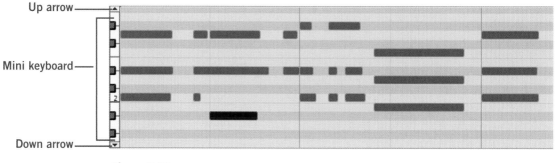

Figure 6.29
Mini keyboard with scroll arrows

When a track's notes do not fit within the track's current height, notes above or below the viewed area are shown as single-pixel lines at the very top and bottom of the track display.

Tip: You can audition pitches on the mini-keyboard by clicking on any key in Notes view. The selected note is played through your connected virtual instrument or outboard device.

If a MIDI-compatible track has been set to a different view, you can easily change back to Notes view using the key command or the Track View selector.

To switch to Notes view, do one of the following:

■ Click anywhere in the track with the **SELECTOR** tool and press **START+MINUS (-)** (Windows) or **CONTROL+MINUS (-)** (Mac) to toggle to Notes view.

■ Click on the **TRACK VIEW SELECTOR** for the track and choose **NOTES** from the pop-up list.

Velocity View

The MIDI Velocity view shows the attack velocity of each note in the MIDI track with a vertical indicator called a *velocity stalk*. Velocity stalks can be dragged up or down, individually or in groups, to change the velocities of their associated notes.

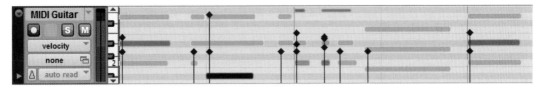

Figure 6.30
MIDI track in Velocity view

MIDI Editor Window Views

MIDI data on your tracks can also be viewed using a MIDI Editor window. MIDI Editor windows can show MIDI data and automation data simultaneously for all of your Auxiliary Input, Instrument, and MIDI tracks. When displaying multiple tracks, the MIDI Editor window superimposes the MIDI notes from each of the tracks in the MIDI Notes pane. The MIDI Editor window can also display automation and controller lanes at the bottom of the window for velocity stalks, volume automation playlists, and other continuous controller and automation data.

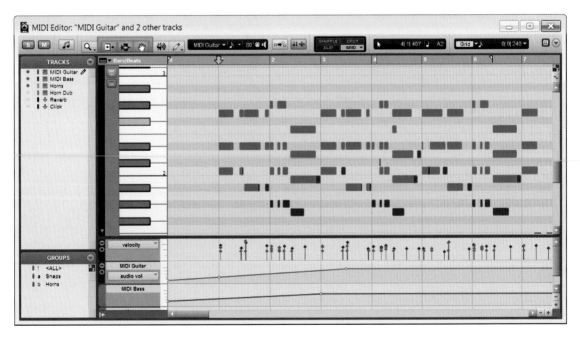

Figure 6.31
MIDI notes, velocity stalks, and volume automation displayed in a MIDI Editor window

To display MIDI data in a MIDI Editor window, do one of the following:

- Double-click on a MIDI clip in the Edit window (Clips view) with the Grabber tool.

- Select **WINDOW > MIDI EDITOR** or press **START+=** (Windows) or **CONTROL+=** (Mac).

MIDI Editor windows allow you to toggle between Notes view and Notation view for the displayed MIDI and Instrument tracks. To toggle the view, click on the **NOTATION DISPLAY ENABLE** button on the left side of the MIDI Editor window toolbar.

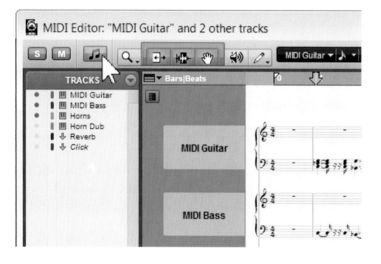

Figure 6.32

Toggling to Notation view in the MIDI Editor window

Review/Discussion Questions

1. What does the term MIDI stand for? How is MIDI data different from the data stored in an audio file? (See page 144.)

2. How many channels of MIDI information can be sent over a single MIDI cable? (See page 144.)

3. What two types of tracks does Pro Tools provide for working with MIDI data? What is the difference between the two track types? (See page 145.)

4. How many ticks are in a quarter note in Pro Tools? (See page 147.)

5. Describe three ways to set the Main Time Scale to Bars|Beats. (See page 148.)

6. What physical connections can you use to connect a MIDI controller to your system for recording on a MIDI or Instrument track? (See page 149.)

7. Give some examples of virtual instrument plug-ins that are installed as standard components of Pro Tools. On which track types are virtual instrument plug-ins placed? (See pages 154 and 155.)

8. How many synthesizer slots are included in Xpand!²? How can each part be turned on/off? (See page 157.)

9. What kind of virtual instrument is Boom? What does the Boom Matrix Display show? (See pages 158 and 159.)

10. What is the Structure Free virtual instrument used for? What are some of the sample library formats that Structure Free can load and play back? (See page 160.)

11. What is the default meter in Pro Tools? How would you go about changing the meter? (See page 163.)

12. What is the default tempo in Pro Tools? What is the default key signature? (See pages 164 and 165.)

13. What track views are available for MIDI data in the Edit window? Which view allows you to scroll up or down to see notes at different pitches? (See pages 168 and 170.)

14. What track types can display data in MIDI Editor windows? What is the Notation Display Enable button used for in the MIDI Editor window? (See pages 171 and 172.)

Selecting and Navigating

This lesson covers various selection and navigation techniques that are available in Pro Tools. It includes descriptions of how to use Timeline and Edit selections, how to modify your session view (including setting track sizes and zoom displays), and how to use memory markers for quickly navigating to preset locations and views in your session.

Duration: 120 Minutes

GOALS

- Navigate a session with the Universe view
- Recognize the difference between a Timeline selection and an Edit selection
- Mark and adjust selection in and out points
- Use the Tab key to navigate a Track Playlist
- Adjust the session view for different needs
- Add, delete, and work with location markers

Understanding selection and navigation techniques can dramatically improve your efficiency in working with Pro Tools. Whether you need to audition material you have just added to your session or you need to edit a transition between clips, being able to quickly find and select the right material is of key importance. The sections in this lesson introduce you to various processes that you can use to streamline your work in all phases of your project.

Using the Universe View

Pro Tools provides a Universe view that can be displayed at the top of the Edit window. The Universe view displays an overview of your entire session, providing a miniature representation of all video, audio, and MIDI material on your displayed tracks.

Material residing on each track is represented by a single horizontal line in the Universe view that is the same color as the clips on the track. Since Aux Inputs, VCA tracks (Pro Tools HD only), and Master Faders do not contain any audio, they are represented as blank areas in the Universe view.

To toggle the display of the Universe view, do the following:

■   Choose VIEW > OTHER DISPLAYS > UNIVERSE.

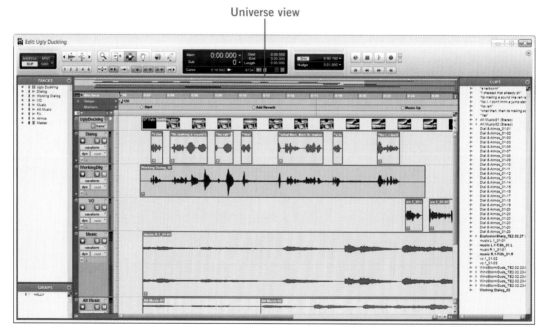

Figure 7.1
Universe view in the Edit window

Resizing the Universe

You can resize the height of the Universe view to fit the total number of tracks in the session or to show more of the Edit window.

To resize the height of the Universe view, do the following:

1. Click the area between the bottom of the Universe view and the top of the Timebase Rulers. The cursor will change to a double-headed arrow, indicating that you can resize the Universe view area.

2. Drag up or down to change the height of the Universe view.

If you resize the Universe view to less than its minimum size, the view will toggle off. This provides another method of hiding the view. When you toggle the view on again, it will restore to its previous height.

The Current View Indicator

The area of the session that is currently displayed in the Edit window is represented by a white rectangular frame in the Universe view.

If you change the display in the Edit window—by zooming, scrolling, hiding or showing tracks, or changing track heights—the framed area in the Universe view will relocate and resize accordingly. During playback, if the Edit window is set to scroll, the framed area in the Universe view will also scroll.

Current view
indicator frame

Figure 7.2

Framed area in the Universe view

Moving and Scrolling from the Universe View

By clicking in the Universe view, you can scroll the material displayed in the Edit window horizontally, vertically, or both. This provides a simple method of navigating within your session and controlling which sections of your tracks are visible in the Edit window.

To navigate the session using the Universe view, do the following:

1. If the Universe view is not currently displayed, choose VIEW > OTHER DISPLAYS > UNIVERSE.

2. Do one of the following:

   ● Click anywhere in the Universe view to move the framed area. The Edit window will update accordingly, jumping to the framed location.

   ● Click and drag on the framed area. The Edit window will scroll in real time to match your movements in the Universe view.

Types of Selection

Once you've navigated to the area where you would like to work, you will often need to make a specific selection. Pro Tools provides two types of selections: *Timeline selections* and *Edit selections*. Timeline selections can be made from any Timebase Ruler and are used to set a playback or record range. Edit selections can be made in any track or in multiple tracks and are used to set an edit range.

Timeline Selections

At any time while working in your Pro Tools session, you can create a Timeline selection. Timeline selections are frequently made by dragging with the SELECTOR tool and can also be created or adjusted using the TIMELINE SELECTION fields in the Transport window or the TIMELINE SELECTION IN/OUT POINTS in the Main Timebase Ruler.

> Tip: With LINK TIMELINE AND EDIT SELECTION enabled, a Timeline selection is also made whenever you select audio or MIDI data on a track. See the "Edit Selections" section later in this lesson.

Selecting with the Timebase Rulers

To make a Timeline selection with the Rulers, do the following:

1. With any tool selected, move your pointer over a TIMEBASE RULER in the Edit window. The Selector tool will become active.

2. Click and drag with the SELECTOR tool in any Timebase Ruler to select the desired area of the Timeline.

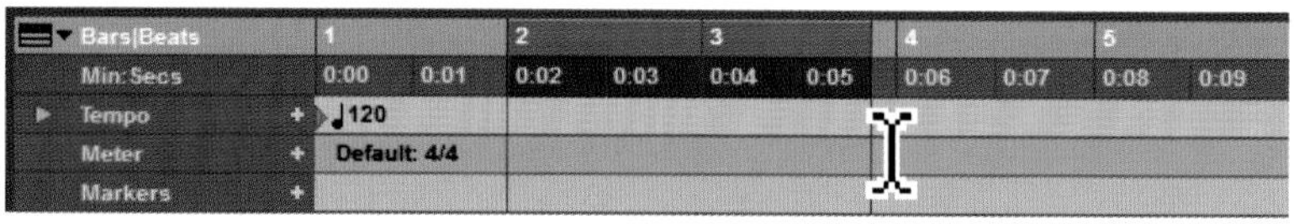

Figure 7.3
Making a Timeline selection with the Selector tool

The Timeline selection is indicated in the Main Timebase Ruler by blue Timeline Selection In/Out Points (red if a track is record-enabled). The start, end, and length values for the Timeline selection are also displayed in the Timeline Selection fields in the Transport window.

Timeline Selection In/Out Points

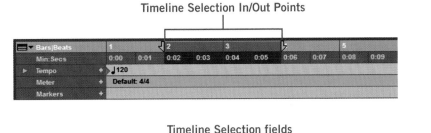

Timeline Selection fields

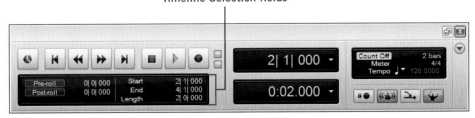

Figure 7.4
Timeline selection as indicated in the Timebase Rulers and the Transport window

Selecting with the Timeline Selection Fields (Transport Window)

You can use the Timeline Selection fields in the Transport window to create a new selection or to adjust a selection numerically from the keyboard.

To create a new selection using the Timeline Selection fields:

1. Click on the first field in the **START** Location Indicator to activate it. The selected field will become highlighted.

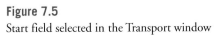

Figure 7.5
Start field selected in the Transport window

2. Enter the desired value or use the **UP** or **DOWN** arrow keys on the keyboard to increment or decrement the value one unit at a time.

3. Click on each successive field to select it (or use the **LEFT** and **RIGHT** arrow keys on the keyboard to cycle through the fields).

4. Enter the desired value in each field or select a value using the **UP** or **DOWN** arrow keys.

5. Press **RETURN** or **ENTER** to confirm your entry and move the insertion point to the specified location.

6. Do one of the following to complete the selection:

- Repeat this process, using the **END** fields to specify the end point for the Timeline selection. The Length indicator fields will update accordingly.

- Repeat this process, using the **LENGTH** fields to specify the duration of the Timeline selection. The End indicator fields will update accordingly.

Tip: When you type a value in a Timeline Selection field or an Edit Selection field, Pro Tools will zero out all fields to the right of the changed field. To change a value without affecting the other fields (to move to a different bar but retain the beat and tick number, for example), select the value and press the Up or Down arrow key as needed.

Tip: The plus (+) and minus (–) keys provide a calculator-like function, allowing you to add or subtract a number to offset the current field. To add to or subtract from a field, press PLUS or MINUS in any field, followed by the desired offset. Press RETURN or ENTER to calculate the new value or press ESCAPE to cancel.

Selecting with the Timeline Selection In/Out Points

You can also use the Timeline Selection In Point and Out Point on the Main Timebase Ruler to create a new selection or to adjust an existing selection. To set the Timeline selection by dragging the Timeline Selection In/Out Points, do the following:

1. With any tool selected, move your pointer over a **TIMELINE SELECTION IN POINT** or **OUT POINT** in the Main Timebase Ruler. The Time Grabber tool will become active.

2. Drag the **TIMELINE SELECTION OUT POINT** to set the selection end.

3. Drag the **TIMELINE SELECTION IN POINT** to set the selection start.

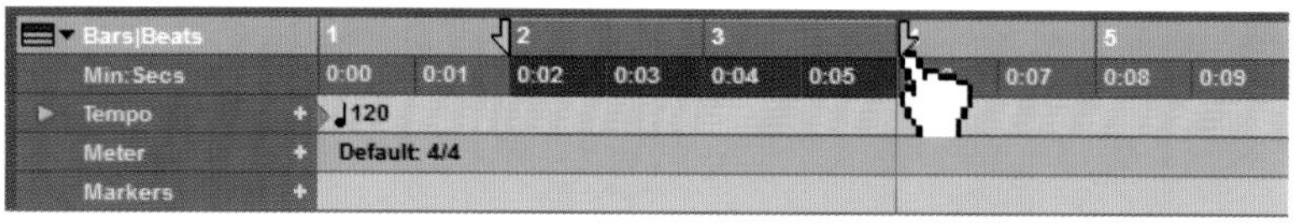

Figure 7.6
Dragging the Timeline Selection Out Point

Edit Selections

When you are working with audio or MIDI data in your Pro Tools session, you can create an Edit selection to work with a portion of the material on a track. Edit selections are frequently made using the Grabber tool or the Selector tool. Edit selections can also be created or adjusted using the Edit Selection fields in the Edit window.

Tip: With LINK TIMELINE AND EDIT SELECTION enabled, an Edit selection is also made whenever you select an area on a Timebase Ruler. See the "Timeline Selections" section earlier in this lesson.

Selecting with the Grabber Tool

You can use the Grabber tool to make an Edit selection on any clip that exists on a Track Playlist. To select a clip with the Grabber tool, click once on the clip you want to select. The selected clip will be highlighted. To select multiple clips, click on the first of the clips you want to select and then Shift-click on the last clip. Both clips will be selected, along with all clips in between them.

Selected clips can be moved, copied, cut, or deleted (cleared) from the track.

Tip: When MIDI and Instrument tracks are set to Notes view, the Grabber tool selects individual MIDI notes or note ranges. To select MIDI clips, first set the track to Clips view (see the "MIDI Clips View" section in Lesson 6) and then click on a clip to select it.

Selecting with the Selector Tool

Using the Selector tool, you can select any portion of audio or MIDI data on your tracks for editing. To make an Edit selection with the Selector tool, do one of the following:

■ Click and drag across the area on the track that you want to select.

■ Click once to define a starting point for the selection and then Shift-click to define an ending point for the selection.

The selected area becomes highlighted, and the selection can be moved, copied, cut, or deleted (cleared) from the track.

Tip: Double-clicking with the Selector tool will select an entire clip; triple-clicking will select the entire Track Playlist.

Selecting with the Edit Selection Fields (Edit Window)

You can use the Edit Selection fields in the Edit window to create a new selection or to adjust a selection numerically from the keyboard.

—— Timebase Rulers

Figure 7.7
The Edit Selection fields in the Edit window

To create a new selection using the Edit Selection fields:

1. Click on the first field in the **START** Location Indicator to activate it. The selected field will be highlighted.

2. Enter the desired value or use the **UP** or **DOWN** arrow keys on the keyboard to increment or decrement the value one unit at a time.

3. Click on each successive field to select it (or use the **LEFT** and **RIGHT** arrow keys on the keyboard to cycle through the fields).

4. Enter the desired value in each field or select a value using the **UP** or **DOWN** arrow keys.

5. Press **RETURN** or **ENTER** to confirm your entry and move the insertion point to the location you have specified.

Shortcut: Use the slash key (/) to rotate between the Start, End, and Length boxes in the Edit Selection fields. This shortcut also works for the Timeline Selection fields (Transport window).

6. Do one of the following:

   • Repeat this process, using the **END** fields to specify the end point for the Edit selection. The Length indicator fields will update accordingly.

   • Repeat this process, using the **LENGTH** fields to specify the duration of the Edit selection. The End indicator fields will update accordingly.

Working with Selections

Pro Tools provides various ways of making selections and adjusting the selection boundaries. The following sections describe some common selection techniques.

Creating Separate Timeline Selections and Edit Selections

The default setting in Pro Tools links Timeline selections and Edit selections together. This means that whenever you select an area on the Timeline, you simultaneously select the same area in each of your Track Playlists. Conversely, whenever you select a clip or area in any Track Playlist, you simultaneously select the same area in the Timeline. This is often the easiest way to work because it allows you to easily play back areas as you adjust your selection and to easily re-record selected areas on a track.

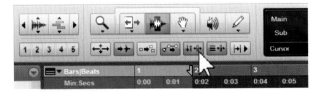

Figure 7.8
Using the toggle button to link the Timeline and Edit selections

However, in advanced workflows, you might encounter situations in which you want to unlink the Timeline selection from the Edit selection. You can link and unlink the Timeline selection and Edit selection using the LINK TIMELINE AND EDIT SELECTION toggle button in the Edit window. This button is blue when the Timeline and Edit selections are linked.

For the purposes of this book, we assume that selections are made with the Timeline and Edit selections linked. Workflows that require unlinking the Timeline and Edit selections are introduced in later courses.

Making Selections on Multiple Tracks

Edit selections can be extended across multiple tracks in several different ways. The method you use will depend on the needs of the situation.

Selecting Material on Adjacent Tracks

When you create a selection with the Selector tool, you can drag vertically to select the same area across several adjacent tracks.

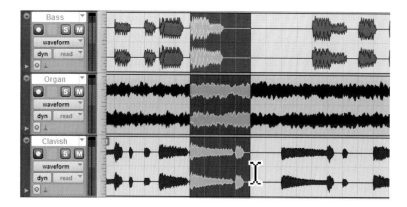

Figure 7.9

Making a selection across multiple tracks using the Selector tool

Selecting Material on Nonadjacent Tracks

After creating a selection on one or more tracks, you can add the selection to an additional track by Shift-clicking on the Track Playlist with the Selector tool. This technique allows you to make selections on *nonadjacent* tracks.

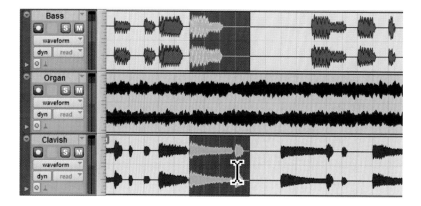

Figure 7.10

Making a selection across nonadjacent tracks using Shift-click on a Track Playlist

Selecting Material on Selected Tracks

The **LINK TRACK AND EDIT SELECTION** setting in Pro Tools provides an option for sharing Edit selections among tracks by selecting or deselecting the desired tracks. This option allows you to copy a selection to additional tracks, remove a selection from individual tracks, and move a selection among tracks by selecting or deselecting tracks as needed.

Enabling Link Track and Edit Selection

In normal operation, selecting a track in Pro Tools brings that track into focus for certain track-level operations, such as grouping, hiding, duplicating, making active/

inactive, deleting, and so forth. To select a track, you simply click on the track nameplate in the Edit or Mix window. The track nameplate becomes highlighted to indicate that the track is selected.

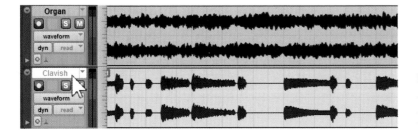

Figure 7.11
Selecting a track in the Edit window by clicking the nameplate

By enabling the Link Track and Edit Selection setting (**OPTIONS > LINK TRACK AND EDIT SELECTION**), tracks that receive an Edit selection become selected automatically. Conversely, tracks that are selected after an Edit selection is made inherit the Edit selection.

The Edit selection can also be linked or unlinked from selected tracks using the **LINK TRACK AND EDIT SELECTION** toggle button in the Edit window. This button turns blue when the track selection and Edit selection are linked.

Figure 7.12
Using the toggle button to link the Edit selection to selected tracks

Using Link Track and Edit Selection to Modify Playlist Selections

To copy an Edit selection (or playlist selection) to additional tracks with **LINK TRACK AND EDIT SELECTION** enabled, do one of the following:

■ To select a range of adjacent tracks, **SHIFT-CLICK** on the nameplate of the last track in the range. All tracks in the range will be selected and will inherit the Edit selection.

■ To select nonadjacent tracks, **CTRL-CLICK** (Windows) or **COMMAND-CLICK** (Mac) on the nameplates of the desired tracks. Each clicked track will be selected and will inherit the Edit selection.

To remove an Edit selection from a track while retaining it on others, **CTRL-CLICK** (Windows) or **COMMAND-CLICK** (Mac) on the nameplate of the unwanted track to deselect it. The Edit selection will be removed from that track.

To move a selection to a different track, click on the nameplate of the desired destination track to select it. The Edit selection will be removed from the previously selected track(s) and placed on the newly selected track.

Using the Tab Key

When working in a track, you can use the Tab key to move the cursor to clip boundaries on the Track Playlist. To advance the cursor to the next adjacent clip boundary to the right, press the **TAB** key. To withdraw the cursor to the previous clip boundary to the left, press **CTRL+TAB** (Windows) or **OPTION+TAB** (Mac). With each press of the Tab key, the cursor will move to the next successive clip boundary.

Using the Tab key to make selections can be quite useful when you want your selection to start or end exactly on a clip boundary, because it allows you to precisely locate the cursor to any clip start or end point.

■ To select from the current cursor position or extend a selection to the next clip boundary to the right, press **SHIFT+TAB**.

■ To select from the current cursor position or extend a selection to the previous clip boundary to the left, press **CTRL+SHIFT+TAB** (Windows) or **OPTION+SHIFT+TAB** (Mac).

Cursor position

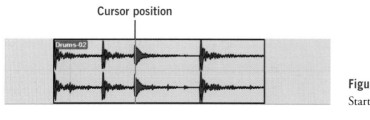

Figure 7.13
Starting cursor position

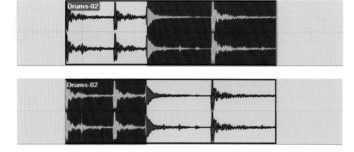

Figure 7.14
Result of pressing Shift+Tab (top)
or Ctrl/Option+Shift+Tab (bottom)

Note: The Tab key is a repeater key; do not hold it down. Doing so will cause your selection to tab rapidly to successive clip boundaries.

Tabbing to Transient Points

A variation on the standard Tab key behavior is provided by the Tab to Transients function. This function is extremely useful for finding the initial peak or modulation in an audio waveform, saving you time and trouble when locating the exact starting point of a sound or louder transition.

To use the Tab to Transients function, do the following:

1. Click on the **TAB TO TRANSIENTS** toggle button in the Edit window toolbar so that it becomes highlighted in blue.

Figure 7.15
Enabling the Tab to Transients function

2. Press the **TAB** key to move the cursor forward to the next transient to the right. Press **CTRL+TAB** (Windows) or **OPTION+TAB** (Mac) to move the cursor backward to the previous transient to the left.

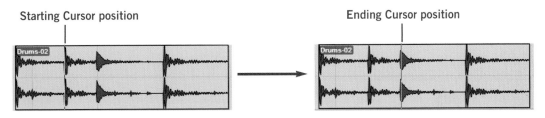

Figure 7.16
Cursor advanced to the next drum hit using Tab to Transients

Tip: The Tab to Transients threshold is set by Pro Tools and is not user-adjustable.

Using the Tab to Transients function is an easy way to make selections that start or end on a sound, because it allows you to locate the cursor immediately before an audio peak.

■ To select from the current cursor position or extend a selection to the next transient to the right, press **SHIFT+TAB**.

■ To select from the current cursor position or extend a selection to the previous transient to the left, press **CTRL+SHIFT+TAB** (Windows) or **OPTION+SHIFT+TAB** (Mac).

To disable the Tab to Transients function (so that the Tab key again moves to clip boundaries), click the **TAB TO TRANSIENTS** toggle button so that it is no longer lit blue.

Shortcut: Press CTRL+ALT+TAB (Windows) or COMMAND+OPTION+TAB (Mac) to toggle the Tab to Transients function on and off.

Adjusting the Session View

Pro Tools enables you to customize many aspects of your session display. You can change the display size of individual tracks, change the order in which tracks are displayed, change the Zoom settings for the current view, and create Zoom presets to store and recall commonly used magnification settings.

Adjusting Track Size

Pro Tools allows you to change the size of the track display in the Edit window by adjusting the track height. Track height can be adjusted on a track-by-track basis, allowing each track to be displayed at any of the following sizes:

- Micro
- Mini
- Small
- Medium
- Large
- Jumbo
- Extreme
- Fit to Window

Larger track heights are particularly useful for precision editing because they show more detail. Smaller track heights are useful for conserving screen space in large sessions.

Tip: Due to their small size, tracks using the micro or mini display options do not show Voice or Automation Mode selectors in the Edit window. These options remain available in the Mix window.

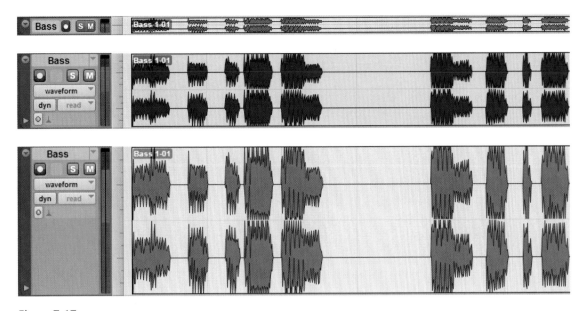

Figure 7.17
Bass track at different heights (mini, medium, and large track sizes shown)

You can select a track height at any time by clicking on the Track Height selector or the amplitude scale area of the track, or you can adjust the height incrementally by dragging the lower boundary of the track.

To select a track height from a pop-up menu:

1. Click anywhere within the amplitude scale area immediately to the right of the track meter or click directly on the **TRACK HEIGHT SELECTOR** button to the left of the track name.

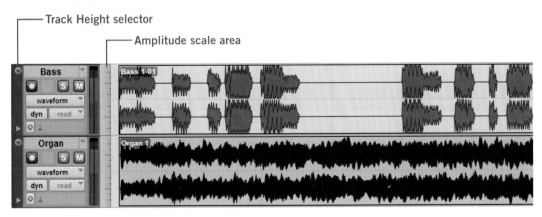

Figure 7.18
The Track Height selector button and amplitude scale area

2. Choose the desired height from the pop-up menu.

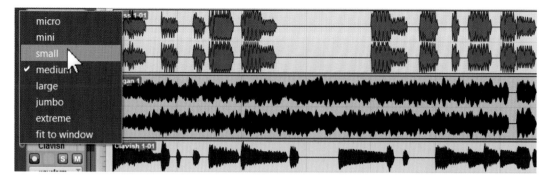

Figure 7.19
The Track Height pop-up menu

To incrementally resize the track height using the lower boundary of the track:

1. Position your pointer over the lower boundary at the head of any track; the cursor will change into a double-headed arrow.

2. Click on the track boundary and drag up or down. The track height will change in increments.

Shortcut: Press and hold CTRL (Windows) or COMMAND (Mac) while adjusting track height for continuous, non-incremental adjustment.

Shortcut: To set all tracks in the session to the same height, press the ALT key (Windows) or OPTION key (Mac) while selecting the desired height on any track.

Changing the Track Order

Pro Tools allows you to change the order of tracks in your session at any time to customize the onscreen layout. Changing the track order affects both the Mix and Edit windows, as well as the track layout on any connected control surface.

Arranging tracks in a logical order can simplify your navigation. This can be true even in relatively small sessions. Consider arranging the tracks in your session such that related tracks are displayed together, instruments are displayed in a logical order, or commonly used tracks are presented at the top. The order can be rearranged as needed as you work your way through the editing process.

To change the session's track order, do any of the following:

■ In the Edit window, click on the track nameplate and drag the track above or below other tracks in the session.

■ In the Mix window, click on the track nameplate and drag the track to the left or right of other tracks in the session.

■ In the Track List, click on the track name and drag it to a higher or lower position in the list.

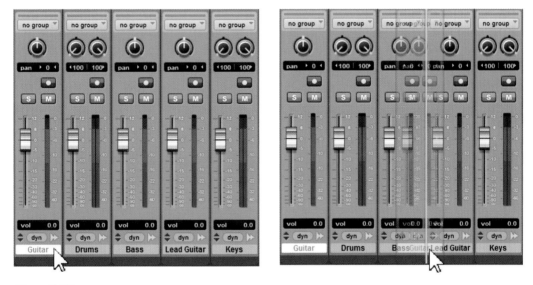

Figure 7.20
Clicking on a track nameplate and dragging the track to a new position (Mix window)

Figure 7.21
Track order after repositioning the track

Using the Zoomer Tool

The Zoomer tool can be used to examine a waveform up close for precision editing.

Figure 7.22
The Zoomer tool

Zooming In and Out

To zoom in, centering on a certain point in a track, do the following:

1. If it is not already selected, click the **ZOOMER** tool. The pointer will display a magnifying glass with a plus sign when positioned over a track.

2. Click once at the desired point within the track. The waveform will enlarge within the track display, with the zoom point centered horizontally in the Edit window.

3. To zoom in further, click multiple times. Each successive click zooms all tracks in by one additional level.

To zoom back out, **ALT-CLICK** (Windows) or **OPTION-CLICK** (Mac) with the **ZOOMER** tool. While you are pressing the **ALT** or **OPTION** key, the cursor will display a magnifying glass with a minus sign when positioned over a track. Each successive click zooms out by one additional level, with the zoom point centered horizontally in the Edit window.

Zooming In on a Range

The Zoomer tool can also be used to zoom in on a particular range, enlarging the range to fill the visible area of the track. To zoom into a range, do the following:

1. If it is not already selected, click the **ZOOMER** tool to select it.

2. Click and drag with the magnifying glass over the horizontal portion of a track that you want to view up close. (To zoom horizontally and vertically, **CTRL-DRAG** [Windows] or **COMMAND-DRAG** [Mac].) As you drag, a dashed box will appear, indicating the range that you will be zooming in on.

3. Release the mouse. The display will fill the screen with the portion of the waveform you selected, zooming in horizontally to the same level on all tracks simultaneously.

Tip: Double-click on the ZOOMER **tool to get a full track view that fills the screen with the longest displayed track in the session.**

Using Zoom Toggle

The Zoom Toggle button is located immediately beneath the Zoomer tool in the toolbar area. Use the **ZOOM TOGGLE** button to toggle the view between the current zoom state and a preset/defined zoom state.

Figure 7.23
Zoom Toggle button

When Zoom Toggle is enabled, the Edit window displays the stored zoom state, as specified in the Zoom Toggle preferences. When Zoom Toggle is disabled, the Edit window reverts to the pre–Zoom Toggle view.

Zoom Toggle behavior varies, based on the Zoom Toggle settings selected in the Editing Preferences page (**SETUP > PREFERENCES**).

Changing the Horizontal and Vertical Zoom

The Edit window includes Zoom buttons in the toolbar area that allow you to adjust the track waveform or MIDI view without using the Zoomer tool. These buttons adjust the display zoom levels, keeping the insertion cursor or selection start point centered as it changes. Like the Zoomer tool, the Zoom buttons change only the display of the data and do not affect playback.

Zoom buttons

Figure 7.24
The Zoom buttons in the Edit window toolbar

From left to right, the Zoom buttons are as follows:

■ **Horizontal Zoom Out button.** This button changes the time display of all tracks in the session by shrinking the track Timeline, audio waveform views, and MIDI displays to show more time on screen, with less detail. This adjustment is useful for obtaining a "big-picture" view of your Track Playlists.

■ **Audio Zoom In and Out button.** This button changes the waveform amplitude display of all Audio tracks in the session by enlarging or shrinking the track waveform views vertically, making the waveforms appear taller or shorter. Zooming in is useful to distinguish low-amplitude audio waveforms; zooming out is useful to distinguish high-amplitude audio waveforms.

■ **MIDI Zoom In and Out button.** This button changes the display of MIDI data on all MIDI-compatible tracks in the session by modifying the note range shown in the track (represented by the track's mini-keyboard). Zooming in shows a narrower range of notes, with each note appearing fatter; zooming out shows a broader range of notes, with each note appearing thinner.

Tip: The MIDI Zoom buttons do not affect tracks in Clips view.

■ **Horizontal Zoom In button.** This button changes the time display of all tracks in the session by enlarging the track Timeline, audio waveform views, and MIDI displays to show less time across the screen, with greater detail. This adjustment is useful for distinguishing precise edit points and magnifying the Edit window display to a very high resolution.

Shortcut: Click and drag on any one of the Zoom buttons for continuous zooming.

Shortcut: ALT-CLICK (Windows) or OPTION-CLICK (Mac) on any one of the Zoom buttons to return to the previous zoom magnification.

Storing and Recalling Zoom Presets

Directly beneath the Zoom buttons are five buttons numbered 1 through 5. These are the Zoom Preset buttons, which are used to store and recall commonly used zoom magnifications. Each Zoom Preset can be updated to store a zoom setting of your choice. Custom presets are saved with your session.

Zoom presets ———

Figure 7.25
Zoom Preset buttons 1 through 5

To store a zoom setting as a Zoom Preset, do the following:

1. Using either the **ZOOM** buttons or the **ZOOMER** tool, set the screen to the desired zoom display.

2. While pressing the **CTRL** key (Windows) or **COMMAND** key (Mac), click one of the five **ZOOM PRESET** buttons, or click and hold a button and select **SAVE ZOOM PRESET** from the pop-up menu.

To recall a Zoom Preset, click your mouse directly on the preset number you want to recall. The zoom setting will be instantly recalled.

Shortcut: You can also recall Zoom Presets 1 through 5 by pressing the START key (Windows) or the CONTROL key (Mac) followed by a numeral key (1 through 5) on your computer's alpha keyboard.

Adding Markers to Your Session

Markers can be used to bookmark locations in your session for quick recall. The following sections describe how to add and delete markers, how to use the Memory Locations window and other techniques to recall marker locations, and how to create selections using marker locations.

About Memory Locations

Pro Tools provides up to 999 memory locations for each session, which can be used to store and recall a variety of commonly used display and edit settings. Like Zoom Presets, memory locations can store horizontal and vertical screen magnification settings. However, memory locations can also do much more.

Memory locations come in two main varieties: markers and selections. Markers are used to store locations on the Timeline (playback locations), while selections are used to store Edit selections (edit locations). In this lesson, we will work only with markers.

In addition to storing a Timeline selection, a marker can store a variety of additional information, such as the current zoom setting, track height settings, track show/hide status, and more. Timeline locations and other settings stored with a marker memory location are reestablished when the memory location is later recalled.

Creating a Marker

Markers can be added to a session at any time. Often you will be able to set markers at specified points when playback is stopped. Other times, you might find it useful to add markers on the fly during playback or recording.

Adding Markers at Specified Points

To create a marker at a specified point, do the following:

1. If it is not already displayed, choose VIEW > RULERS > MARKERS to display the Marker Ruler.

2. Place the cursor or make a selection at the desired location in the track.

3. Click the ADD MARKER/MEMORY LOCATION button (plus sign) at the head of the Marker Ruler. The New Memory Location dialog box will appear.

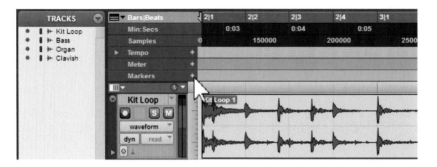

Figure 7.26
Adding a new marker using the Marker Ruler

4. Give the marker a descriptive name. You can also change the marker number, if desired.

Figure 7.27
The New Memory Location dialog box

5. In the Time Properties section of the dialog box, select **MARKER.**

6. In the Reference pop-up menu, choose one of the following two options:

- **Absolute.** This option sets the marker at a sample-based location on the Timeline. The marker will remain at a fixed location in time, regardless of session meter or tempo changes.

- **Bar|Beat.** This option sets the marker at a tick-based location on the Timeline. The marker will maintain its relative position with respect to the bars and beats in the session, adjusting its absolute location with session meter or tempo changes.

7. (Optional) Under General Properties, select any options you wish to associate with the marker. For basic marking, the optional selections can all remain unchecked.

8. Click **OK.** A small yellow marker symbol corresponding to the memory location will appear in the Marker Ruler at the selected location.

Figure 7.28
Absolute marker symbol on the Marker Ruler

Adding Markers during Playback and Recording

Memory locations can be added during real-time playback and recording in much the same way as when playback is stopped. When added this way, the marker stores the cursor position at the time that the operation is initiated.

To create a marker during playback (or recording), do the following:

1. If it is not already displayed, choose **VIEW > RULERS > MARKERS** to display the Marker Ruler.

2. Start playback (or record) from the desired starting position.

3. Click the **ADD MARKER/MEMORY LOCATION** button (plus sign) at the head of the Marker Ruler. The New Memory Location dialog box will appear.

4. Select the desired options (see Steps 4 through 7 in the previous section) and click **OK.**

Tip: You can also add markers on the fly by pressing ENTER on the numeric keypad during playback or recording.

The Memory Locations Window

The Memory Locations window can be used to view all markers and other memory locations that you have stored. To access the Memory Locations window, choose **WINDOW > MEMORY LOCATIONS.** The Memory Locations window will open.

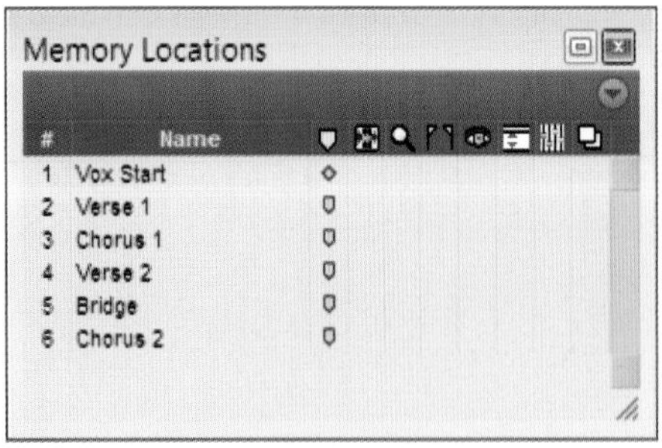

Figure 7.29
The Memory Locations window

Recalling a Marker Location

To recall a marker location, do one of the following:

■ In the Memory Locations window, click the entry for the desired marker location.

■ On the numeric keypad, type a period, followed by the marker location number (1 through 999), and another period.

■ Click the corresponding marker symbol in the Marker Ruler.

The marker location will be instantly recalled, and the playback cursor will be positioned at this spot.

Deleting a Marker Location

To delete a single marker that you no longer need, do the following:

1. Display the Memory Locations window (**WINDOW > MEMORY LOCATIONS**).

2. Click on the entry that you want to delete.

3. Click on the Memory Locations menu button and choose **CLEAR "MARKER NAME"** from the pop-up menu. The selected marker will be deleted.

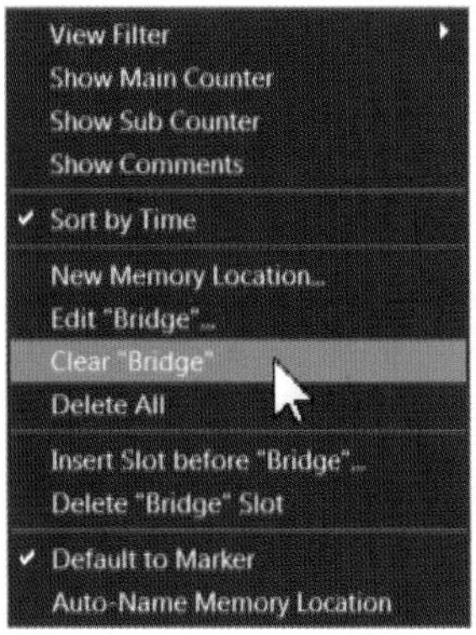

Figure 7.30
Removing the Bridge marker

Shortcut: ALT-CLICK **(Windows) or** OPTION-CLICK **(Mac) on any entry in the**
Memory Locations window (or in the Marker Ruler) to instantly delete it.

Creating a Selection Using Markers

You can easily select between two previously created markers. This can be handy
for quickly selecting song sections that you have marked, such as a verse, chorus,
bridge, or guitar solo, for example.

To make a selection between two marker locations, do the following:

1. Click the first marker to recall the stored location.

2. Press the **SHIFT** key and click the second marker. The area between the two
    markers will become selected.

Review/Discussion Questions

1. What does the Universe view display? How can you use this view to scroll
    the Edit window display? (See pages 176 and 177.)

2. How can you adjust a selection using the Timeline Selection In/Out Points?
    (See page 180.)

3. How can you make an Edit selection using the Grabber tool? (See page 181.)

4. Describe two ways to make an Edit selection using the Selector tool. How
    can the Selector tool be used to easily select an entire clip? (See page 181.)

5. How can you make a selection on adjacent tracks with the Selector tool?
    How can you make a selection on nonadjacent tracks? (See pages 183 and
    184.)

6. What does the Link Track and Edit Selection setting do? (See page 184.)

7. How does the Tab key affect the cursor position when working in a track?
    How does this behavior change when the Tab to Transients button is active
    in the Edit window? (See pages 186 and 187.)

8. How can the track height be adjusted for a track? How can all tracks be set to the same height? (See pages 189 and 190.)

9. Describe three ways to change the order of tracks in Pro Tools. (See page 191.)

10. Which button in the Edit window activates Zoom Toggle? What does the Zoom Toggle function do? (See page 193.)

11. What is the function of the buttons numbered 1 through 5 beneath the Zoom buttons? (See page 194.)

12. What are the two main types of memory locations provided in Pro Tools? How many memory locations can you add to a session? (See page 195.)

13. How can you add a marker at the current cursor location? How can you add markers on the fly during playback? (See pages 195 through 197.)

14. Describe three ways to recall a memory location. (See page 198.)

Configuring the Session and Adding Memory Locations

In this exercise tutorial, you will configure various settings for the session, set the session tempo, and use the Tab to Transients function to create memory locations. You will use these memory locations in the next exercise.

Duration: 10 to 15 Minutes   **Media: DrumLoop.wav, Guitar.wav, 10_01.wav, 10_03.wav**

Getting Started

You will start by opening the Pro Tools session you created in Exercise 4. If that session is not available, use the Ex04.ptxt session template in the Completed Exercises folder on the DVD.

To create the session:

1. Launch Pro Tools and open the session you created in Exercise 4.

2. Choose FILE > SAVE AS and name your session Exercise5-YourName.

Configuring the Session

In this part of the exercise, you will configure various settings in the Pro Tools Edit window toolbar, rearrange the track order, and set the session tempo.

To configure the session:

1. Enable the following options, as needed, by clicking the associated buttons in the Edit window toolbar (the buttons will be lit blue when enabled):

   - Tab to Transients
   - Link Timeline and Edit Selection
   - Link Track and Edit Selection

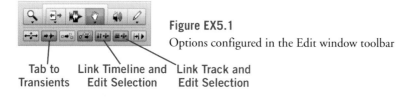

Figure EX5.1
Options configured in the Edit window toolbar

Tab to   Link Timeline and Link Track and
Transients   Edit Selection   Edit Selection

2. Click and drag on the track nameplate for the Guitar track to move it below the Drums track.

3. Click and drag on the track nameplate for the other tracks, as needed, to arrange your track order as follows, from top to bottom: Drums, Guitar, Vox1, Vox2, and the Master Fader.

4. Click on the **HORIZONTAL ZOOM IN** button in the toolbar to zoom in a few levels for a better view of the audio waveforms.

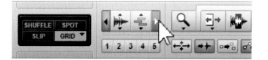

Figure EX5.2
Clicking on the Horizontal Zoom In button in the Edit window toolbar

5. Choose **VIEW > RULERS > TEMPO** to display the Tempo Ruler, if not already shown.

6. Double-click on the red Tempo event at the start of the Tempo Ruler. The Tempo Change dialog box will open.

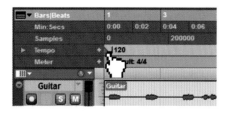

Figure EX5.3
Double-clicking on the red Tempo event on the Tempo Ruler

7. Change the session tempo in the dialog box to 91.72 BPM and click **OK**. The Tempo event will update to reflect the change.

Creating Memory Locations

In this part of the exercise, you will use the Tab to Transients function to locate the start of the performance on the Guitar and Drums tracks, and you will mark each point with a memory location.

To create the Drum Start memory location:

1. Choose VIEW > RULERS > MARKERS to display the Markers Ruler, if not already shown.

2. Select just the Drums track by clicking the track nameplate. The nameplate will be highlighted.

3. Press ENTER (Windows) or RETURN (Mac), if needed, to return the cursor to the start of the track.

4. Tab to the first transient on the track after the silence (around Bar 6) to locate the start of the drum pattern.

5. Click the plus sign (+) at the head of the Markers Ruler or press [ENTER] on the numeric keypad to display the New Memory Location dialog box.

6. In the dialog box, change the marker name from Location 1 to Drum Start and click **OK**. The new marker will appear on the Markers Ruler.

Figure EX5.4
New Memory Location dialog box configured for the Drum Start marker

To create the Guitar Start memory location:

1. Press ENTER (Windows) or RETURN (Mac) to place the cursor back at the start of the track.

2. Select the Guitar track by clicking on its nameplate.

3. Tab to the first transient on the track to locate the start of the guitar performance.

4. As before, click the plus sign (**+**) at the head of the Markers Ruler or press [**ENTER**] on the numeric keypad to display the New Memory Location dialog box.

5. Change the marker name from Location 2 to Guitar Start and click **OK**. The new marker will appear on the Markers Ruler.

6. Press **ENTER** (Windows) or **RETURN** (Mac) to place the cursor back at the start of the track.

Finishing Up

To complete this exercise tutorial, you will need to save your work and close the session. You will be reusing this session in Exercise 6, so it is important to save the work you've done.

1. Choose **FILE > SAVE** to save the session.

2. Choose **FILE > CLOSE SESSION** to close the session.

Basic Editing Techniques

This lesson covers the basics of editing audio and MIDI data in Pro Tools. It provides details on playback options, Edit modes, edit commands, and moving and trimming operations. It also introduces techniques for creating fades and for undoing edit actions.

Duration: 120 Minutes

GOALS

- Set options for scrolling and looping during playback

- Understand the Pro Tools Edit modes

- Recognize the difference between Absolute Grid mode and Relative Grid mode

- Configure Grid and Nudge values

- Use standard editing commands to modify your playlists

- Understand the effects of Edit modes on moving and trimming operations

- Create fade-in, fade-out, and crossfade effects on your tracks

Any time you add audio or MIDI data to the tracks in your session, you are likely to need to do some editing. Whether you need to adjust timing, smooth out a transition, or improve a performance, editing techniques will play a large part in transforming a session from a basic recording to a polished final product. The processes described in the following sections will help you make that transformation, enabling your recordings and compositions to sound their best.

Selecting Playback Options

To simplify your navigation and workflow, Pro Tools provides various playback options to choose from while working on your sessions. Two common options you will likely want to adjust from time to time include the scrolling options and the Loop Playback option.

Scrolling

As discussed in Lesson 3, Pro Tools offers various different scrolling options that determine how the contents of the Edit window are displayed during playback and recording. The available scrolling options include the following:

- **No Scrolling.** This option prevents the screen from following the position of the playback cursor. Use this option to keep the display located on an area that you are editing while playing back an area that starts or ends off screen.

- **After Playback.** This option scrolls the screen to the point where playback ends, centering the end point on the screen. Use this option to locate an area that needs editing by auditioning your tracks. By stopping playback when you hear something amiss, your screen will automatically be scrolled to the area needing attention.

- **Page Scrolling.** This option scrolls the screen one page at a time during playback. Use this option to view the contents of your tracks as they are played back.

Additional details on scrolling options are provided in Lesson 3.

Loop Playback

During editing, you will often want to listen to a selection repeatedly. Loop Playback allows you to repeat your selection continuously, looping from the end of the selection back to the start without interruption. This allows you to easily review the continuity of an edit or transition point.

To use Loop Playback, do the following:

1. Select the desired audio or MIDI data.

2. Choose **OPTIONS > LOOP PLAYBACK**. The Playback button in the Edit window and Transport window will change to show a loop arrow.

3. Click **PLAY** or press the **SPACE BAR** to start continuous looped playback.

Figure 8.1
Transport window in Loop Playback

You can adjust the start and end points of the loop during playback by modifying your selection, as discussed in Lesson 7. By dragging the corresponding In/Out Points in the Timeline Rulers, for example, you can resize your loop on either side. The loop will immediately play back from the start of the selection after you make an adjustment.

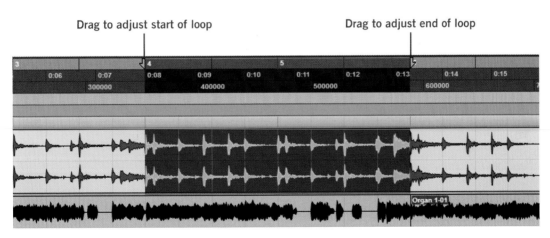

Figure 8.2
Area selected for Loop Playback

Note: Loop Playback requires a selection at least 0.5 seconds in length.

Using the Edit Modes

As you learned in Lesson 2, Pro Tools provides four Edit modes: Shuffle, Slip, Spot, and Grid. The Edit modes affect the movement and placement of audio and MIDI clips, the results of commands such as Copy and Paste, and the functions of the Edit tools. You will find each Edit mode useful for different purposes while editing your sessions.

- **Shuffle.** This mode allows you to shuffle the order of clips without adding space between them or having them overlap. Use Shuffle mode to rearrange adjacent parts in your session.

- **Slip.** This mode allows you to place a clip anywhere on a track without affecting the placement of other clips, leaving space between clips or over-lapping clips as desired. Use Slip mode to move or arrange the parts of your session freely.

- **Spot.** This mode allows you to specify exact locations using numerical values when moving, placing, or trimming clips. Use Spot mode to move the parts of your session to specific known destinations.

- **Grid.** This mode allows you to snap clips and MIDI notes to the nearest time increment on a grid, based on the currently selected Time Scale. Use Grid mode to fine-tune timing by aligning parts using defined timing intervals.

Pro Tools also provides a combo-mode feature called Snap to Grid. This feature allows you to make selections based on the Grid while editing in Shuffle, Slip, or Spot mode.

You can activate the desired Edit mode at any time by clicking on the corresponding mode button in the toolbar area of the Edit window. To activate Snap to Grid, SHIFT-CLICK on the Grid mode button when in any other mode.

Figure 8.3
The Edit mode buttons (Slip mode selected)

Shuffle, Slip, and Spot modes have only one option each and do not require any additional configuration before you use them. Grid mode provides two options to choose from, Absolute Grid and Relative Grid. The functions of both options are affected by the Grid configuration.

Shuffle Mode

In Shuffle mode, when you move or place clips on a track, their placement is constrained by other clips, and any edits you make to a clip will affect the placement of subsequent clips on the track. Clips being moved or placed will automatically snap to the end of the preceding clip, causing the two clips to butt up against each other. If a clip is inserted between two existing clips, all subsequent clips on the track will move to the right to make space for the inserted clip. Conversely, if a clip is removed from between two existing clips, the subsequent clips on the track will move to the left to fill the void.

You can "shuffle" the order of clips in this mode, but you cannot separate them from each other, or add space between clips, and you cannot make them overlap as in Slip mode. However, any space between existing clips is maintained when the clips move as a result of insertions, deletions, or edits made earlier in the track.

When using the Trim tool in Shuffle mode, changing a clip's start or end point will automatically move the subsequent clips by the amount added to or trimmed from the edited clip.

Tip: The placement and insertion of individual MIDI notes is not affected by Shuffle mode.

To activate Shuffle mode, click on the **Shuffle** button in the Edit window or press function key **F1**.

Slip Mode

In Slip mode, when you move, trim, cut, or paste clips, their placement is unconstrained by other clips on the track. Editing a clip has no effect on subsequent clips, unless the edit causes clips to overlap, in which case the underlying clip is trimmed out to accommodate the added material.

To activate Slip mode, click on the **Slip** button in the Edit window or press function key **F2**.

Spot Mode

In Spot mode, you can move or place clips within a track at precise locations by specifying the desired destination numerically. As in Slip mode, edit operations do not affect the placement of other clips on the track.

Spot mode allows you to specify a destination based on any time format. You can also use Spot mode to capture an incoming time code address or to spot a clip using its time stamps as reference points. This can be particularly useful when you are performing post-production tasks involving SMPTE frame locations.

When Spot mode is enabled, Pro Tools prompts you with a dialog box whenever a clip is dragged from the Clip List or a DigiBase browser or whenever you click on a clip with the Grabber or Trim tool. When placing or moving a clip, you specify a destination location for the clip's start, sync point, or end by entering a value in the Start, Sync Point, or End field in the dialog box, respectively. When trimming a clip, you specify the start or end points for the trim using the Start or End fields in the dialog box, respectively.

To activate Spot mode, click on the **SPOT** button in the Edit window or press function key **F3**.

Grid Mode

In Grid mode, you can make edits based on the timing interval defined by the Grid. (See the following "Configuring the Grid" section.) Selections and insertion points snap to Grid intervals, affecting cut, copy, and paste operations. Move and trim operations either align to the Grid or move in Grid increments relative to their origination point, depending on the option selected (Absolute or Relative).

■ In Absolute Grid mode, moving any clip snaps the clip start to the Grid; trimming a clip snaps the trimmed edge to the Grid. If a clip's start point falls between Grid lines, moving the clip will snap its start time to the nearest Grid line; trimming it will align the trimmed edge to the nearest Grid line. This mode is commonly used to ensure that clips start or end cleanly on the beat or on a subdivision of the beat.

■ In Relative Grid mode, clips are moved and trimmed by Grid units. If a clip's start point falls between Grid lines, the clip will move in Grid increments, preserving its offset from the Grid. Likewise, the Trim tool will trim in Grid increments, preserving the starting point or ending point offset. This mode is commonly used to move clips by bars or beats while maintaining any offset relative to the beat.

To activate Grid mode using the last-used option, click the **GRID** button in the Edit window or press function key **F4**. To change the Grid mode from the last-used option, click and hold the **GRID** button and select the desired option from the pop-up selector, or press **F4** a second time to toggle the mode.

Tip: You can temporarily suspend Grid mode and switch to Slip mode by holding down the CTRL key (Windows) or COMMAND key (Mac).

Snap To Grid

The Pro Tools Snap To Grid feature lets you make grid-based selections while working in Shuffle, Slip, or Spot mode. With Snap To Grid enabled, placing the Edit cursor and making Edit selections is constrained by the Grid, but any clip editing you perform is based on the other selected Edit mode.

For example, in Shuffle mode with Snap To Grid enabled, any selections you make on audio clips will snap to Grid boundaries; however, if you cut a selection of audio, any clips to the right of the edit will shuffle to the left as normal in Shuffle mode.

To enable Snap To Grid, do the following:

1. Activate the Edit mode you wish to work in (Shuffle, Slip, or Spot).

2. Shift-click on the **GRID** mode button or press **SHIFT+F4**.

Figure 8.4
Snap To Grid in Shuffle mode

Shortcut: Press F1+F4 to enable Snap To Grid and Shuffle mode, press F2+F4 to enable Snap To Grid and Slip mode, and press F3+F4 to enable Snap To Grid and Spot mode.

Configuring the Grid

Pro Tools allows you to set a timing Grid, based on an interval of your choosing, to help maintain the timing of clips, notes, events, and selections as you edit your session. The Grid settings affect edit operations in Grid mode. (See the preceding "Grid Mode" section.) The Grid can also be used for display only, allowing it to serve as a visual reference without affecting edit operations.

Grid boundaries can be based on frames, bar and beat values, minutes or seconds, or a specified number of samples.

To configure the Grid, do the following:

1. Click the **GRID VALUE** pop-up selector in the toolbar area of the Edit window.

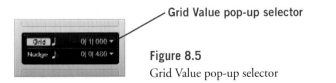

Grid Value pop-up selector

Figure 8.5
Grid Value pop-up selector

2. From the Grid Value pop-up menu, choose an appropriate TIME SCALE or choose CLIPS/MARKERS, which causes clips and selections to snap to existing clip boundaries and memory location markers whenever they are in close proximity. The menu will close after you make a selection.

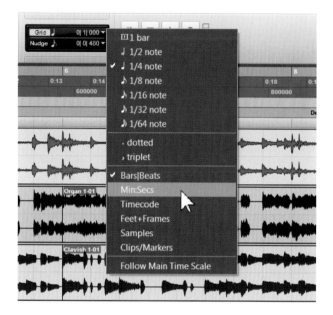

Figure 8.6
Selecting a Time Scale for the Grid

3. Click the GRID VALUE pop-up selector again to choose a corresponding Grid size; the options available will vary depending on the Time Scale selected in Step 2.

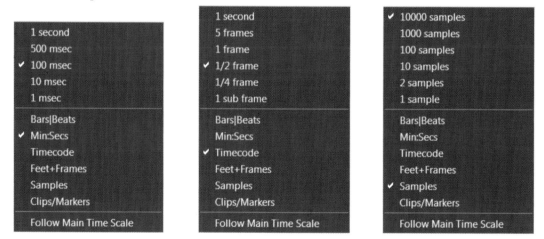

Figure 8.7
Grid-size options for various Time Scales

Tip: The Follow Main Time Scale option at the bottom of the Grid Value pop-up menu causes the grid to change automatically whenever the Main Time Scale is changed, using the Grid size last set for each Time Scale.

To maintain the Grid in a Time Scale that is different from your Main Time Scale, deselect this option.

Once you have set the Grid to an appropriate Time Scale and size, you have the option of displaying the Grid lines in the Edit window to serve as a visual reference. To display or hide Grid lines, click at the head of the currently selected main Timebase Ruler or click on the Grid indicator in the toolbar. The Grid lines will toggle on or off, and the Grid indicator light (green highlight) will toggle on or off, correspondingly.

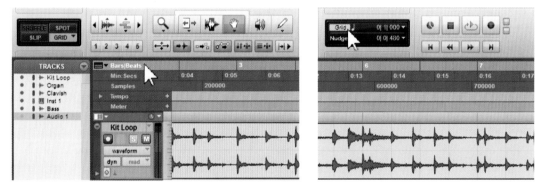

Figure 8.8
Click the current Timebase Ruler or Grid indicator to toggle the Grid-line display

Editing Clips

Pro Tools offers a variety of standard editing commands, such as Copy and Paste, as well as application-specific commands, such as Separate Clip and Heal Separation, that affect clips.

As discussed in Lesson 4, Pro Tools distinguishes between clips (portions of an audio file) and whole-file clips (entire parent audio files). The editing techniques described in this section apply to both types of clips, unless otherwise specified.

Standard Editing Commands

Like most commercial applications, Pro Tools offers standard Cut, Copy, Paste, and Clear (delete) commands. The Pro Tools Duplicate and Repeat commands also offer standard functionality similar to that found in other media applications.

Pro Tools performs each of these editing functions non-destructively, meaning that the operations do not alter your original audio files.

Each of these commands can be performed on a single track or on multiple tracks simultaneously, depending on the selection or the Clipboard contents. Edits can apply to the following material:

- Part of a clip or parts of multiple clips (selected with the Selector tool)

- A whole clip or multiple whole clips (selected with the Grabber tool)

Selections made for Cut, Copy, and Clear commands can cross multiple clip boundaries, can include entire clips or partial clips, and can even include silence, if desired.

The effects of Paste, Duplicate, and Repeat operations vary depending on the Edit mode being used:

- In Shuffle mode, all audio or MIDI data that falls after the inserted selection will be moved later in the track(s) by the length of the insertion.

- In Slip mode, all audio and MIDI data remains in place, so inserted material replaces any existing material for the length of the insertion.

When you use any of the editing commands on audio selections within a clip or clips, Pro Tools creates byproduct clips and automatically adds them to the Clip List.

The Cut Command

Using the Cut command, you can cut a selected range, clip, or series of clips from its current position and place the audio or MIDI data on the Clipboard to be pasted elsewhere.

To cut a selection and place the material on the Clipboard, do the following:

1. Make a selection of any length on a single track or multiple tracks.

2. Choose **EDIT > CUT**, or press **CTRL+X** (Windows) or **COMMAND+X** (Mac). The selected audio and/or MIDI data will be removed from the original location and copied to the Clipboard.

Note: When you cut or clear a selection in Shuffle mode, all audio to the right will slide over by the amount of time removed so that no gap remains.

The Copy Command

The Copy command is much like the Cut command, but instead of removing the selected range, it leaves the original and places a copy of it on the Clipboard so that you can paste it elsewhere.

To copy a selection, do the following:

1. Make a selection of any length on a single track or multiple tracks.

2. Choose **EDIT > COPY**, or press **CTRL+C** (Windows) or **COMMAND+C** (Mac). The selected audio and/or MIDI data will be copied to the Clipboard.

Note: When you place a selection on the computer's Clipboard using a Cut or Copy command, you replace any material previously stored on the Clipboard.

The Paste Command

Using the Paste command, you can insert the contents of the Clipboard into a location that you have chosen with the Selector. You can paste data only after something has been cut or copied to the Clipboard.

To use the Paste command, do the following:

1. Select the desired paste destination using one of the following methods:

   ● Place the cursor (insertion point) on the desired destination track or tracks at the location where you want the start of the paste to occur.

   ● Make a selection of any length on the desired destination track or tracks, with the beginning of the selection at the location where you want the start of the paste to occur.

Note: To paste on multiple tracks, you must make an insertion point or selection on each of the desired destination tracks.

2. Choose **EDIT > PASTE**, or press **CTRL+V** (Windows) or **COMMAND+V** (Mac). The material on the Clipboard will be pasted in, beginning at the selected start point.

Note: If the Clipboard contains material from multiple tracks, the data will be pasted in starting with the topmost track, and the selected destination tracks will be filled from top to bottom.

Tip: To paste data immediately after a clip, use the TAB key (with the Tab to Transient function turned off) to place the cursor exactly at the clip's end.

The Clear Command

The Clear command allows you to remove any selected clips or any selected range of audio or MIDI data without placing the deleted audio on the Clipboard.

To clear a selection, do the following:

1. Make a selection of any length on a single track or multiple tracks.

2. Choose EDIT > CLEAR, or press CTRL+B (Windows) or COMMAND+B (Mac). This command has the same result as using the Delete key on the keyboard.

The Duplicate Command

The Duplicate command copies a selection within a single clip, a selection that crosses multiple clip boundaries (including space), a whole-file clip, multiple clips, or any combination of these and places the selected audio or MIDI data immediately after the end of the selection. This command provides a handy way of quickly repeating a selection to extend a sound or create a simple looping effect—it is faster and more convenient than copying and pasting data to achieve the same result.

Tip: For advanced looping effects, use the clip looping features in Pro Tools.

In the Avid Learning Series   **Clip looping is covered in the Pro Tools 110 course.**

To duplicate audio or MIDI data, do the following:

1. Make a selection of any length and content on one or more tracks.

2. (Optional) Play the selection using Loop Playback to ensure that it plays smoothly in succession, without glitches. If the selection plays smoothly when it loops, you can duplicate it without creating an audible edit point.

3. Adjust the selection as needed to create a smooth loop transition. You might want to zoom in to position the start and end of the selection on a zero crossing (a point of no amplitude in a waveform).

4. After you are satisfied with the selection, choose EDIT > DUPLICATE or press CTRL+D (Windows) or COMMAND+D (Mac). The selection will be duplicated and pasted at the end of the selected area or clip.

The Repeat Command

The Repeat command is similar to Duplicate, but it allows you to specify the number of times the selected material will be duplicated.

To repeat a selection of audio or MIDI data multiple times, do the following:

1. Make a selection of any length and content on one or more tracks.

2. Choose **EDIT > REPEAT** or press **ALT+R** (Windows) or **OPTION+R** (Mac). The Repeat dialog box will open.

> Repeat
>
> Number Of Repeats: 1
>
> Cancel   OK

Figure 8.9
Repeat dialog box

3. Enter the desired number of repeat iterations and click **OK**. The selected material will be duplicated in succession immediately following the selection's end point, as specified in the Repeat dialog box.

Pro Tools–Specific Editing Commands

Pro Tools includes a number of editing commands that are specifically geared toward working with audio and MIDI clips. The following sections introduce commands for separating audio selections into two or more clips and for restoring clips that have been separated.

The Separate Clip Command

Separating a clip is the process of breaking a clip in two or separating a section of an original clip into a new clip.

You can separate a clip for one of several purposes:

■ To split a clip into two separate clips at the insertion point. Use this process to split the source clip into two new clips in the track, adding both to the Clip List.

■ To separate a selection from a parent clip or from the material on either side of the selection. Use this process to separate a selection from its source clip(s), creating new clips in the track and adding them to the Clip List.

■ To create multiple new clips from a selection, dividing the selection at Grid intervals or at transients. Use this process to automatically create clips based on a defined timing or based on audio events on the track.

 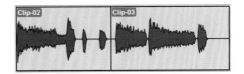

Figure 8.10
Separating a clip at the insertion point (before and after)

 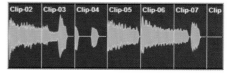

Figure 8.11
Separating a selection as a new clip (before and after)

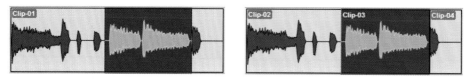

Figure 8.12
Separating a selection into new clips at Grid intervals (before and after)

When you separate clips, you create *byproduct* clips from the material remaining on either side of the selection. These new byproduct clips appear on the track and in the Clip List with new edit numbers appended to the ends of their names.

To separate a clip, do the following:

1. Make a selection of any length within a clip or across multiple clips, or place the cursor (insertion point) at the location where you want a split to occur.

2. Do one of the following:

   • To create a separation at the insertion point or selection boundaries, choose EDIT > SEPARATE CLIP > AT SELECTION or press CTRL+E (Windows) or COMMAND+E (Mac).

   • To create separations at each Grid boundary or transient, choose EDIT > SEPARATE CLIP > ON GRID or EDIT > SEPARATE CLIP > AT TRANSIENTS, respectively. The Pre-Separate Amount dialog box will open.

Pre-Separate Amount
0   mSec
Cancel   OK

Figure 8.13
The Pre-Separate Amount dialog box

3. Enter the pre-separate amount in the dialog box, if needed, and click **OK**. This specifies the amount of pad time Pro Tools will include in the new clips before each Grid boundary or transient point.

Pro Tools creates new clips based on the selection start and end points. If the **ON GRID** or **AT TRANSIENTS** option is chosen, Pro Tools will create additional clips within the selection at each Grid line or transient point. Pro Tools automatically names all resulting new clips by appending the next available edit number to the end of the original clip name.

Tip: To have Pro Tools display the Name dialog box for new clips created from a continuous selection, deselect the **AUTO-NAME SEPARATED CLIPS** option in the Editing tab of the Pro Tools Preferences.

The Heal Separation Command

If you've separated a clip and you later decide to undo the separation, you can repair the separations and restore the original unedited material using the Heal Separation command. The Heal Separation command gives you a way to repair separated clips, provided that the clips are contiguous and their relative start and end points haven't changed since the separation.

To heal a separation between two or more contiguous clips, do the following:

1. Create a selection across the separation points of the clips to repair.

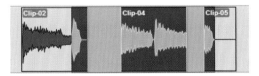

Figure 8.14
Selecting across separation points

2. Choose **EDIT > HEAL SEPARATION** or press **CTRL+H** (Windows) or **COMMAND+H** (Mac).

Figure 8.15
Selection after separations are healed

Moving and Trimming Clips

The following sections describe techniques for moving and trimming clips and discuss the effects of the Edit modes on these operations. The Nudge function is also introduced, along with the process for setting the Nudge value.

Using the Grabber Tool

The Grabber tool can be used to drag a clip from the Clip List or from an existing location on a Track Playlist. You can drag a clip to a different location within the same track or to a different track.

Figure 8.16
The Grabber tool selected in the Edit toolbar

Moving Clips in Slip Mode

In Slip mode, you can move clips freely within a track or onto other tracks using the Grabber tool. You can place clips so that they overlap or so that there is space between the clips on a track. When you play back the track, there will be silence in any open areas. Table 8.1 shows the results of moving clips in Slip mode.

Table 8.1   Rules for Moving Clips in Slip Mode

Slip Mode Action	Result
When clips partially overlap	The audio on top trims the audio underneath.
When a smaller clip is completely covered by a larger clip	The smaller clip is cleared from the track with no warning, although this action can be undone.
When a smaller clip is placed inside a larger one	The smaller clip will trim out the audio it covers, so that when it is dragged away, a hole (delete) results. The hole can be repaired using the Heal Separation command.

To move a clip in Slip mode, do the following:

1. Select the **Grabber** tool. The cursor will change into a hand.

2. Click on the clip and drag it to the desired destination. An outline of the clip will appear as you position it.

3. Release the mouse to position the clip.

Tip: As you drag clips, the Start, End, and Length Selection indicator boxes dynamically update to show you the result of the movement.

Moving Clips in Grid Mode

When using the Grabber tool in Grid mode, moving and dragging clips is constrained by the current Grid Value pop-up menu setting.

To move a clip in Grid mode, do the following:

1. Verify that the Grid Time Scale and size have been set as desired. (See the "Configuring the Grid" section earlier in this lesson.)

2. Select the **Grabber** tool. The cursor will change into a hand.

3. Click and drag the clip to the desired destination. An outline of the clip will appear on the track, snapping to each successive Grid line as you position the clip.

4. Release the mouse to position the clip.

Moving Clips in Shuffle Mode

In Shuffle mode, you can move clips within a track or onto another track, but their movement is constrained by other clips. When moved, clips automatically snap to each other like magnets. You can shuffle their order, but you cannot leave space between clips or overlap them.

To move a clip in Shuffle mode, do the following:

1. Select the **Grabber** tool. The cursor will change into a hand.

2. Drag a clip to the desired destination. The insertion point will snap between the start and end points of existing clips on the track as you position the clip.

3. Release the mouse to position the start of the clip at the insertion point. Adjacent clips reposition themselves as needed to accommodate the clip and to close up the space left at its point of origin.

Moving Clips in Spot Mode

Spotting is the process of placing clips at predetermined time locations within your tracks based on exact Time Scale units, such as Min:Secs, Bars|Beats, or SMPTE time code.

To move and place a clip in Spot mode, do the following:

1. Select the **Grabber** tool. The cursor will change into a hand.

2. Click on the desired clip or drag a clip from the Clip List. The Spot dialog box will appear.

Spot Dialog

Current Timecode:	00:00:00:00 ▼
Time Scale:	Bars Beats ▼
Start:	■| 2| 000
Sync Point:	3| 2| 000
End:	5| 1| 000
Duration:	1| 3| 000
☐ Use Subframes	
Original Time Stamp:	6| 2| 000 ▲
User Time Stamp:	2| 2| 000 ▲
Cancel	OK

Figure 8.17
The Spot dialog box

3. Choose the desired **TIME SCALE** from the Time Scale pop-up menu. (The menu selection defaults to the Main Time Scale of the session.)

4. Enter the new location in either the **START** or **END** field and click **OK**. (Other options for this dialog box are covered in later courses.) The clip's start or end point will align to the specified location.

Using the Trim Functions

Clips can be trimmed using either the Trim tool or the Trim command. The Trim functions allow you to shorten or lengthen clips as desired by trimming their heads or tails.

The Trim Tool

The Trim tool can be used to dynamically adjust the length of a clip. By trimming the head or tail of a clip, you can eliminate unwanted audio that precedes or follows any audio that you want to retain.

Figure 8.18
The Trim tool selected in the Edit toolbar

To trim a clip, do the following:

1. If needed, use the **ZOOMER** tool to zoom in on the area you want to trim.

2. Click the **TRIM** tool (standard).

3. Move the cursor over the audio clip you want to trim. The cursor will change to a left trim shape or a right trim shape on either side of the clip's midpoint.

Left Trim (from start)   Right Trim (from end)

Figure 8.19
Trim tool, as displayed on either side of the clip midpoint

4. Click the cursor on the left side to trim the clip head or on the right side to trim the clip tail; drag toward the center to shorten the clip or away from the center to extend the clip. As you drag, the clip outline will preview the trim effect.

5. Release the mouse button to accept the trim. The clip will update to display the new length.

Tip: To reverse the direction of the Trim tool so that you can trim in either direction without having to trim past the midpoint, press ALT (Windows) or OPTION (Mac) before trimming a clip.

The Trim Clip Command

The Trim Clip command in the Edit menu allows you trim a clip to the boundaries of a selection or to trim (clear) all audio in a clip to the left or right of the insertion point.

To use the Trim Clip command based on a selection within a clip, do the following:

1. Select the portion of a clip you want to retain.

Figure 8.20
Audio selected for trimming

2. Choose **EDIT > TRIM CLIP > TO SELECTION**. The portion of the clip outside of the selection will be deleted.

Figure 8.21
Selection after trimming

The Shuffle mode affects the Trim Clip operation in the same way that it affects the operation of the Trim tool; the trimmed audio moves on the Timeline so that the clip head retains its position, and any clips after the trimmed clip move by the amount of the trim.

Shortcut: You can also press CTRL+T (Windows) or COMMAND+T (Mac) to trim a clip to a selection.

To use the Trim Clip command to clear audio preceding or following the insertion point, do the following:

1. Position the insertion point within a clip where you want the clip to start or end.

2. Choose EDIT > TRIM CLIP > START TO INSERTION or EDIT >TRIM CLIP > END TO INSERTION to trim all audio before the insertion point or after the insertion point, respectively.

Using the Nudge Function

Pro Tools allows you to set an increment for adjusting the placement of clips and selections in small, precise amounts using the keyboard. The increment amount, or *Nudge value*, is set much like the Grid size. Nudging a clip is similar to moving a clip in Grid mode, in that the clip is moved incrementally by predefined units.

You can use the Nudge function in any of the four editing modes, although it's most commonly used in Slip, Shuffle, and Grid modes. Nudging will always move the selected clip or clips without moving adjacent clips, regardless of Edit mode.

Configuring the Nudge Value

The Nudge value can be based on frames, bar and beat values, a time measurement (in milliseconds), or a specified number of samples, depending on the Time Scale selected.

To configure the Nudge value, do the following:

1. Click the **NUDGE VALUE** pop-up selector in the toolbar area of the Edit window.

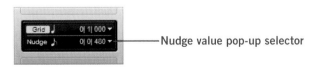

Figure 8.22
Nudge value pop-up selector

2. From the **NUDGE VALUE** pop-up menu, choose the desired Time Scale. The menu will close after you make a selection.

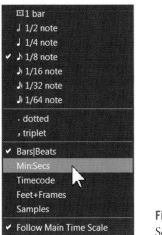

Figure 8.23
Selecting a Time Scale for the Nudge

3. Click the **NUDGE VALUE** pop-up selector again to choose a corresponding Nudge size; the options available will vary depending on the Time Scale selected in Step 2.

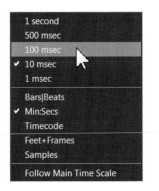

Figure 8.24
Selecting a Nudge size

Tip: The Follow Main Time Scale option at the bottom of the Nudge value pop-up menu enables the Nudge value to change automatically whenever the Main Time Scale is changed, adopting the last used value for that Time Scale.

To maintain the Nudge in a Time Scale that is different from your Main Time Scale, deselect this option.

Nudging Clips

To nudge a single clip or multiple clips, do the following:

1. Verify that the Nudge Time Scale and size have been set as desired. (See the preceding "Configuring the Nudge Value" section.)

2. With the GRABBER tool, select the clip or clips you want to nudge.

3. On the numeric keypad, press the PLUS key [+] to move the clip(s) later in the track or the MINUS key [−] to move the clip(s) earlier in the track. The clips will move incrementally by the Nudge value.

Tip: If you are using a laptop computer that does not have a numeric keypad, you can use the Function key (marked Fn) and the corresponding +/− keys to nudge regions.

Shortcut: You can manually enter a Nudge value by typing it directly into the Nudge display.

Nudging Selections

In addition to nudging clips, you can also nudge selections using the PLUS [+] and MINUS [−] keys on the numeric keypad.

To nudge a selection, do the following:

1. Make a selection on any track or tracks that does not encompass an entire clip.

2. On the numeric keypad, press the PLUS key [+] to move the selection later or the MINUS key [−] to move the selection earlier. The selection will move incrementally by the Nudge value.

Or

1. Make a selection on any track or tracks that includes one or more entire clips.

2. Hold the SHIFT key.

3. On the numeric keypad, press the PLUS key [+] to move the selection later or the MINUS key [−] to move the selection earlier. The selection will move incrementally by the Nudge value without affecting the underlying clips.

Adding the Shift Key to Freely Nudge any Selection

When a selection encompasses one or more entire clips, nudging will cause the underlying clip(s) to move with the selection. By holding Shift while nudging, you can nudge the selection independently, without affecting the underlying clip(s).

Creating Fade Effects

A *fade* is a steady volume ramp up or ramp down that Pro Tools can create on any clip boundary you desire. Fades have many different applications, from smoothing out an edit, to creating seamless clip overlaps, to building volume fade-ins and fade-outs for music and sound effects. This section covers the process of creating simple fade-ins, fades-outs, and crossfades for a variety of useful applications.

Fade-Ins and Fade-Outs

Fade-in and fade-out effects can be created at the beginning or ending of any audio clip, respectively, using a selection that touches or crosses the clip boundary.

Following are some basic guidelines for creating fades:

■ Make your selection to match the desired fade; the length of the fade is determined by the selection length.

■ Make a selection that touches or crosses an open clip boundary (in other words, a boundary that is not adjacent to another clip); boundaries between adjacent clips can be faded only with a crossfade. (See the "Crossfades" section that follows.)

■ To create a fade-in, touch or cross the beginning clip boundary; to create a fade-out, touch or cross an ending clip boundary.

■ Fade-ins always begin at the head boundary, and fade-outs always end at the tail boundary. Extending a selection into a blank area beyond a clip's boundaries will not change the fade length.

To create a fade, do the following:

1. Select the beginning or ending of a clip. (**SHIFT-CLICK** additional tracks to create fades on multiple tracks whose clips begin or end simultaneously.)

2. Choose **EDIT > FADES > CREATE** or press **CTRL+F** (Windows) or **COMMAND+F** (Mac). The corresponding Fade-In or Fade-Out dialog box will appear.

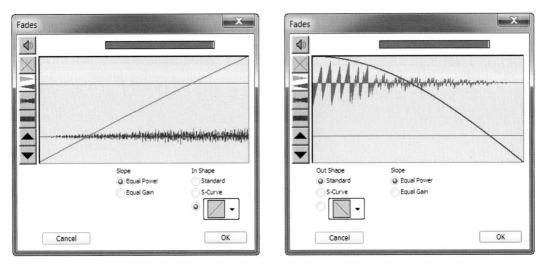

Figure 8.25
The Fade-In and Fade-Out dialog boxes

3. Choose the desired settings in the dialog box (see the "Fade Settings" section later in this lesson) and click **OK**. The fade will be appear in the Track Playlist at the head or tail of the source clip.

Figure 8.26
Fade-in at the head of a clip

Crossfades

Pro Tools allows you to create crossfades between any two adjacent audio clips that have sufficient underlying audio in their parent audio files. *Crossfading* is essentially the process of overlapping two audio sources and fading out the first source while simultaneously fading in the second source. Pro Tools achieves this effect by overlapping the underlying audio on either side of the boundary between the adjacent clips.

To define an area for a crossfade, you must make a selection across the end of an outgoing clip's file and the beginning of an incoming clip's file, and both clips must have sufficient underlying audio to extend across the length of the selection.

To create a crossfade between two adjacent clips, do the following:

1. Make a selection across the boundary between the clips.

Figure 8.27
Area for crossfade selected in the Edit window

2. Choose **EDIT > FADES > CREATE** or press **CTRL+F** (Windows) or **COMMAND+F** (Mac). The Fades dialog box will open.

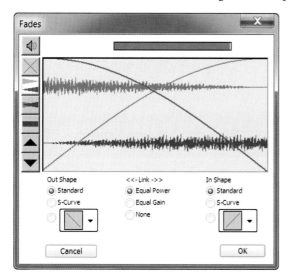

Figure 8.28
The Fades dialog box displaying a crossfade (mono track shown)

3. Choose the desired settings in the Fades dialog box (see the "Fade Settings" section that follows) and click **OK**. If sufficient underlying audio is available, the crossfade will appear in the Track Playlist between the source clips.

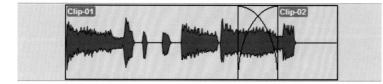

Figure 8.29
Crossfade rendered between clips

Tip: You can audition and view the resulting crossfade before generating it by clicking the corresponding icons on the left edge of the Fades dialog box.

If either or both source clips lack sufficient underlying audio to generate a cross-fade based on the selection boundaries, a warning will display after you click **OK** in the Fades dialog box to alert you that the attempted crossfade is invalid.

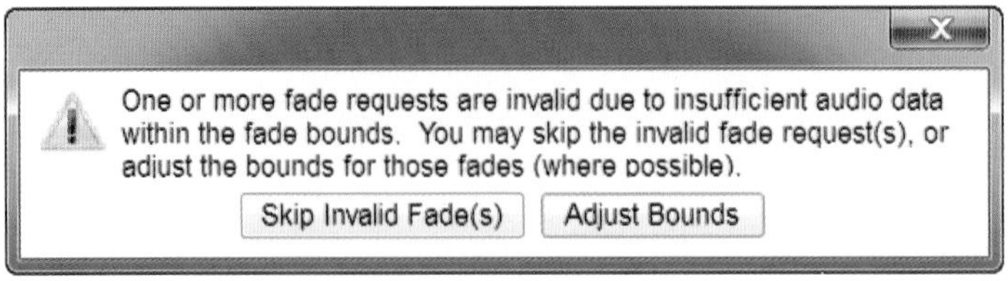

> ⚠ One or more fade requests are invalid due to insufficient audio data within the fade bounds. You may skip the invalid fade request(s), or adjust the bounds for those fades (where possible).
>
> [Skip Invalid Fade(s)]   [Adjust Bounds]

Figure 8.30
Invalid fade warning

Clicking the **ADJUST BOUNDS** button in this warning box will adjust the placement and length of the fade to fit the available audio from the incoming or outgoing clip. If insufficient audio is available to overlap the clips at all, no fade will be created.

Fade Settings

The Fades dialog box displays the fade-in shape in red and the fade-out shape in blue. Either shape can be changed by choosing from the seven presets in the Shape drop-down selectors or by choosing one of the two editable fade shapes using the radio buttons. The shape of each curve determines how the amplitude of a clip changes during the course of the fade.

Undoing Your Work

Often your editing tasks will involve performing a series of related steps to achieve a desired effect. Along the way, you might find that you want to go back to an earlier point, either to start over or to do a before-and-after comparison of the composition. Fortunately, Pro Tools provides rich undo options that give you the flexibility you need to work without worry.

Using Multi-Level Undo

Multi-level undo operations make it possible to revert to earlier stages of work during the editing process. This in turn enables you to experiment more freely, with the confidence of knowing that you can return to an earlier point if you are not satisfied with the results.

Pro Tools provides up to 32 levels of edit undo. All commands that are undoable are stored sequentially in a queue for undo/redo purposes. However, certain commands cause changes that are not undoable, and any of these events will clear the undo queue.

Some common actions that *cannot* be undone include the following:

- Deleting tracks
- Closing a session and/or quitting Pro Tools
- Clearing audio from the Clip List
- Destructive recording

The Pro Tools default settings provide the maximum of 32 levels of undo operation. If available memory for your system is running low, you can lower this setting to free up memory used by the undo queue. (Large undo queues require more RAM and can affect system performance if you have insufficient RAM.)

To change the number of levels of undo, follow these steps:

1. Choose **SETUP > PREFERENCES** and then click the **EDITING** tab.

2. At the bottom of the dialog box, enter the desired undo setting between 1 and 32 and click **OK**.

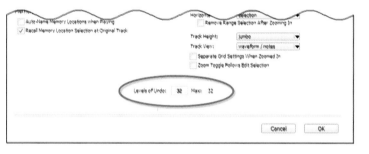

Figure 8.31

Levels of undo, as set in the Editing Preferences tab

Undoable actions are stored sequentially in the queue, with the most recent action at the front of the queue. Actions must be undone in reverse order; you cannot undo an individual action out of sequence.

To access the Undo command, choose **EDIT > UNDO** or press **CTRL+Z** (Windows) or **COMMAND+Z** (Mac). The Undo command in the Edit menu lists the action to be undone along with the command name.

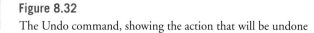

Figure 8.32

The Undo command, showing the action that will be undone

To perform multiple undo operations, repeat the above process as needed, up to the limit set on the Editing Preferences page.

If you undo an action that you want to keep, you can reinstate the action using the Redo command. To access the Redo command, choose **EDIT > REDO** or press **CTRL+SHIFT+Z** (Windows) or **COMMAND+SHIFT+Z** (Mac). Like the Undo command, the Redo command lists the action that it will affect.

Undo History

The Undo History window displays the undo queue, showing up to the last 32 actions that can be undone. You can use this window to view the recent actions taken and the sequence of those actions, as well as any actions recently undone. The Undo History window allows you to instantly return to any previous state from the actions listed. The Undo History can also show the creation time of each action, enabling you to revert to the state a session held at a particular time.

To show the Undo History window, choose **WINDOW > UNDO HISTORY**. The Undo History window displays undoable operations in bold and operations that have already been undone in italics.

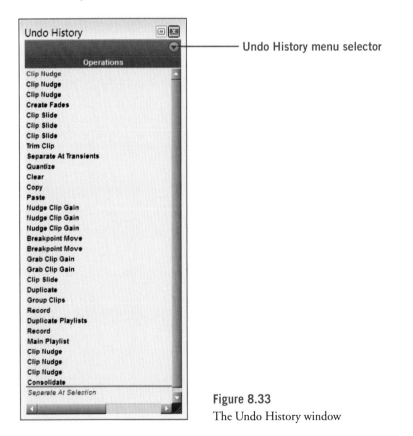

Undo History menu selector

Figure 8.33
The Undo History window

The following actions can be performed using the Undo History window:

- **Multiple simultaneous undos.** To undo multiple operations in the Undo History window, click on the last bold operation that you want to undo in the list. The selected operation and all operations performed after it will be undone; the undone operations will display in italics.

- **Multiple simultaneous redos.** To redo multiple operations in the Undo History window, click the latest italicized operation that you want to redo in the list. The selected operation and all operations that precede it will be redone; the redone operations will again display in bold.

- **Undo all.** To undo all the operations in the undo queue, click the UNDO HISTORY MENU selector and choose UNDO ALL from the pop-up menu.

- **Redo all.** To redo all the operations in the redo queue, click the UNDO HISTORY MENU selector and choose REDO ALL.

- **Clear the queue.** To clear the undo queue, click the UNDO HISTORY MENU selector and choose CLEAR UNDO QUEUE. When you select this option, a dialog box opens, verifying the action; click YES to complete the command.

When the number of operations in the Undo History exceeds 32 or the limit set in the Edit Preferences, the operations at the top of the list are removed. The operation next in line to be pushed out of the queue is shown in red.

Restore Last Selection

Pro Tools provides a separate command that enables you to restore your last Edit or Timeline selection in the event that you accidentally lose the selection or find that you need to reuse a selection you had made previously.

To restore the last selection, choose EDIT > RESTORE LAST SELECTION or press CTRL+ALT+Z (Windows) or COMMAND+OPTION+Z (Mac).

Revert to Saved

If you need to undo changes that are not available in the Undo History, you can use the Revert to Saved command to restore the last saved version of your session. Reverting to the last saved version has the same effect as closing the session without saving changes and then reopening it.

To revert to the last saved version of your session, do the following:

1. Choose FILE > REVERT TO SAVED. A dialog box will prompt you to verify that you want to revert the session.

Figure 8.34
Revert to Saved dialog box

2. Click **REVERT** to continue.

Review/Discussion Questions

1. What does the Loop Playback option do? What is the minimum loop length required for loop playback? (See pages 206 and 207.)

2. What happens when you delete a clip from between two existing clips in Shuffle mode? What happens when you do the same thing in Slip mode? (See page 209.)

3. What happens when you move a clip whose start point falls between Grid lines in Absolute Grid mode? What happens when you do the same thing in Relative Grid mode? (See page 210.)

4. How can you configure the size of the Grid increments used in Grid mode? How can you display or hide the Grid lines in the Edit window? (See pages 211 through 213.)

5. Name some standard editing commands provided in Pro Tools. (See page 213.)

6. What are some operations that the Separate Clip command can be used for? (See page 217.)

7. What happens when you click on a clip with the Grabber tool in Spot mode? (See page 221.)

8. What is the Trim tool used for? What modifier can be used to reverse the direction of the Trim tool? (See pages 222 and 223.)

9. What is the Nudge value used for? In what Edit modes can the Nudge function be used? (See page 224.)

10. What keys are used to nudge a clip or selection earlier or later on a track? (See page 226.)

11. How would you go about creating a fade-out at the end of a clip? How would you go about creating a crossfade between two adjacent clips? (See pages 227 through 229.)

12. How many levels of operations can you undo in Pro Tools? What are some operations that cannot be undone? (See pages 230 and 231.)

13. How can you display the Undo History window? What are some actions available in this window? (See pages 232 and 233.)

14. What option can you use to undo changes that are not available in the Undo History window? (See page 233.)

Editing Audio

In this exercise tutorial, you will begin editing the audio files that you previously imported using the memory locations you created in Exercise 5.

Duration: 10 to 15 Minutes   **Media: DrumLoop.wav, Guitar.wav, 10_01.wav, 10_03.wav**

Getting Started

You will start by opening the Pro Tools session you created in Exercise 5. If that session is not available, use the Ex05.ptxt session template in the Completed Exercises folder on the DVD. After saving the session for this exercise, you will configure the session for the editing work you will be doing.

To create the session:

1. Launch Pro Tools and open the session you created in Exercise 5.

2. Choose **FILE > SAVE AS** and name your session Exercise6-YourName.

To configure the session:

1. Click on the **GRID** mode button on the left side of the Edit window toolbar to place the session into Grid mode. The Grid button will be lit blue when active.

Figure EX6.1
Enabling Grid mode in the Edit window

2. Click on the GRID VALUE pop-up selector in the toolbar and set the Grid to 0|2|000 (1/2 note). (Make sure the Main Timescale is still set to Bars|Beats.)

Figure EX6.2
Clicking the Grid Value pop-up selector in the Edit window

3. Click the MUTE button (M) on the Vox1 and Vox2 tracks to temporarily silence these tracks while working with the other tracks.

Editing the Drums and Guitar

In this part of the exercise, you will remove the silence from the beginning of the DrumLoop and Guitar clips. You will also trim the drum pattern to make it shorter and add a fade-out effect at the end. Lastly, you will extend the guitar pattern by duplicating a portion of it and then trim out the last clip so that it ends naturally.

To remove silence before the drum pattern:

1. Select the Drums track by clicking on its nameplate.

2. Recall the Drum Start memory location (Location 1) by pressing .[1]. (period, 1, period) on the numeric keypad.

3. Choose EDIT > TRIM CLIP > START TO INSERTION to remove the silence before the start of the drum pattern.

4. Using the Grabber tool, click and drag on the trimmed clip to place it at the session start.

To shorten the drum pattern:

1. Select the Trim tool in the toolbar (next to the magnifying glass icon). The tool will be lit blue when active.

Figure EX6.3
Enabling the Trim tool in the Edit window

2. Position the Trim tool near Bar 10 on the Drums track. A left-bracket icon will appear over the DrumLoop clip, indicating left-trim mode.

3. Press and hold the **ALT** key (Windows) or **OPTION** key (Mac) to reverse the tool direction (for right-trim mode); then click to trim the tail of the clip to 10|1|000.

4. Switch to the Selector tool and make a one-bar selection at the end of the DrumLoop clip (from 9|1|000 to 10|1|000).

Figure EX6.4
Enabling the Selector tool in the Edit window

5. Choose **EDIT > FADES > CREATE** to open the Fades dialog box.

6. Click **OK** to accept the default fade shape; then press **ENTER** (Windows) or **RETURN** (Mac) to deselect the fade and return the insertion point to the song start.

To remove silence before the guitar pattern:

1. Click on the **SHUFFLE** mode button on the left side of the toolbar to place the session into Shuffle mode.

2. Select the Guitar track by clicking on its nameplate.

3. While holding Shift, recall the Guitar Start memory location (Location 2) by pressing **.[2].** (period, 2, period) on the numeric keypad. The area from the song start to the Guitar Start memory location will be selected.

4. Press **BACKSPACE** (Windows) or **DELETE** (Mac) to clear the selected audio. The remaining audio will shuffle over, leaving no blank space on the track.

To extend the guitar pattern:

1. Place the session back into Grid mode.

2. Using the Selector tool, make a selection on the Guitar track from 3|1|000 to 5|1|000.

3. Choose **EDIT > REPEAT** to open the Repeat dialog box.

4. Enter **2** for the Number of Repeats and click **OK**. The selection will be duplicated two times, and two new clips will appear selected on the track.

5. Disable the Tab to Transients button in the toolbar area of the Edit window (under the Trim tool). The button will be gray when disabled.

6. With the repeated clips still selected, press **TAB** twice to advance the edit cursor past the new clips.

7. Press **SHIFT+TAB** once to select the remainder of the audio on the Guitar track; then clear the selection by pressing **BACKSPACE** (Windows) or **DELETE** (Mac).

8. Using the Trim tool, extend the end of the last clip on the Guitar track by one bar so that it ends with the DrumLoop clip. (Click inside the clip and drag to the right.)

Finishing Up

Before wrapping up this exercise tutorial, take a moment to listen to the work you've completed up to this point. Then be sure to save your work before closing the session. Once again, you will be reusing this session in the next exercise, so it is important to save the work you've done.

1. Press **ENTER** (Windows) or **RETURN** (Mac) followed by **SPACE BAR** to begin playback from the session start and hear the results of your edits. Press **SPACE BAR** a second time to stop playback.

2. When finished, save and close the session.

Basic Mixing Techniques

This lesson covers basic mixing techniques and processes as they are performed in a Pro Tools environment. It includes discussions of mixer terminology, Mix window configuration (including configuring inserts, sends, and returns), basic automation, and real-time plug-ins.

Duration: 90 Minutes

GOALS

- Recognize common mixer terminology
- Configure inserts and send-and-return paths to add signal processing to your tracks
- Configure the Inserts and Sends views in the Mix window
- Record and edit basic automation for your mix
- Add plug-ins to your tracks for internal effects processing and sound shaping

In this lesson, we focus on using Pro Tools' mix functions to route signals, set levels, and add effects when creating a session mix and preparing for mixdown. For the purposes of this course, we will limit our focus to standard stereo mixing. Other mixing options, such as mixing for surround sound, are covered in advanced courses.

Basic Mixer Terminology

The fundamental job of any audio mixer is to route incoming and outgoing audio via the mixer's inputs and outputs. Additional signal routing and processing can be achieved using the mixer's inserts and send and return functions. These terms are defined in the following sections as they apply to general audio mixing; specific Pro Tools applications of these concepts are described in "The Pro Tools Mix Window" section later in this lesson.

Inputs

The term *input* refers to an audio signal traveling into an audio hardware device, such as a mixer or an audio interface.

The inputs available from within the Mix window in the Pro Tools software vary depending on the Pro Tools system and hardware interface you are using.

Outputs

The term *output* refers to an audio signal traveling out of an audio hardware device, such as a mixer or an audio interface.

The outputs available from within the Mix window in Pro Tools also vary depending on the Pro Tools system and hardware interface you are using.

Inserts

Most mixers have a feature known as a *channel insert*. A channel insert is an audio patch point that allows either a plug-in insert or a hardware signal processor to be inserted directly into the signal path of the audio channel.

Pro Tools provides 10 insert positions per track, allowing you to process a track's signal through multiple software plug-ins and/or external effects loops in series.

Sends and Returns

The term *send* refers to a signal path carrying a mix output of one or more Audio tracks routed for parallel processing. The send may route to an external receiving device, such as an external reverb or digital delay, or to an internal processor, such as a software plug-in. Sends can be *pre-fader*, meaning the send level is independent of the channel's fader level, or *post-fader*, meaning the send level is affected by the channel's fader level. Pro Tools allows you to set sends to pre- or post-fader, as needed.

When using a send for external processing, the sent signal is received on the input of an external device, some type of effect or processing is added to the signal, and then the signal is returned to the original sending device through an *auxiliary input* or *auxiliary return*. When using a send for internal processing, effects are added by a plug-in applied to the send signal; the processed signal is added to the mix through an auxiliary input channel.

The return inputs provide level and pan controls, allowing precise control over how the reintroduced signal combines with other audio in the system.

The Pro Tools Mix Window

Many of Pro Tools' mixing operations and functions are performed using the Mix window. The Mix window in Pro Tools is similar to a standard mixing console. If you are acquainted with mixing console functions, the Pro Tools Mix window will be familiar territory. This window offers a variety of display options, many of which can also be customized.

The Mix window can be displayed or hidden as needed. To toggle the Mix window display on or off, choose **WINDOW > MIX**. If the Mix window is already open but is inactive (such as when it is hidden behind another window), this command will make it active, bringing it to the front of the display.

Tip: Press CTRL+= (Windows) or COMMAND+= (Mac) to toggle between the Mix and Edit windows.

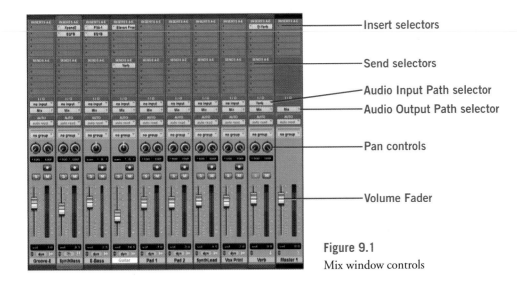

Insert selectors

Send selectors

Audio Input Path selector
Audio Output Path selector

Pan controls

Volume Fader

Figure 9.1
Mix window controls

Configuring the Mix Window

The Mix window includes several component parts, a number of which can be selectively turned on and off as needed. Among the parts of the Mix window that you will use to create a session mix are Track Volume Faders, Pan controls, I/O selectors, and Insert and Send selectors.

Tip: The Input and Output selectors (I/O selectors) include Audio Input Path selectors and Audio Output Path selectors, as well as MIDI Input selectors and MIDI Output selectors (MIDI and Instrument tracks only).

To create a session mix, you will set the Volume Faders and Pan controls for each track to achieve an appropriate blend of audio levels and the desired positioning of sounds within the stereo field. You can make changes in real time during playback/ mixdown either by manually adjusting the controls or by using automation. (See the "Basic Automation" section later in this lesson.)

The Input selectors and Output selectors are used to route signals to and from your tracks. Often the primary I/O routing for your mix will already be set as needed, based on the routing you used during recording and editing operations. However, your mix might call for new or different input and output settings for certain tracks; use these selectors to configure your I/O as needed. See the following "Input and Output Selectors" section for more detail.

Mixing also often involves using inserts and sends to add various types of signal processing to the audio on a session's tracks. Use the Insert and Send selectors in the Mix window to achieve these operations. See the "Inserts and Sends Views" section later in this lesson for more detail.

Input and Output Selectors

The Mix window always displays the main Input and Output selectors for each track in the session. Though much of your signal routing might have been set up during the recording and editing stages of your project, it is always a good idea to double-check the I/O settings when you begin mixing.

Input Paths

For tracks that are playing back material from their own Edit Playlist, no input routing is necessary. Tracks that are receiving input from other sources will need to have their inputs set accordingly.

When modifying or setting up tracks for mixing, pay particular attention to the Audio Input Path selector settings for the following types of tracks:

■ Auxiliary Input tracks

■ Instrument tracks

■ Audio tracks used for internal mixdown or bounce destinations

For Auxiliary Input tracks and Instrument tracks, the Audio Input Path selector is often used to route audio from an available input source connection on the system. For internal mixdown on Audio tracks, the Input Path selector is often used to route audio from an internal bus. (See Lesson 10, "Finishing Your Work," for more information on setting up an internal mixdown.)

The following diagram shows how the Audio Input Path selector for an Auxiliary Input track corresponds to the input connectors of an Mbox 2 used to route live input from a synthesizer.

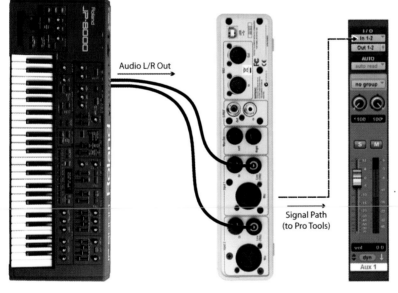

Figure 9.2
Common signal flow using an Auxiliary Input track for live input with an Mbox 2

Output Paths

Pro Tools gives you the flexibility to route the output of each track to any output channel or bus. For the purposes of creating a stereo mix, however, you will generally select the main stereo outputs of your audio interface.

To set up your mix, verify that the Audio Output Path selectors for the tracks in your session are set to the main outputs of your audio interface, as appropriate, so that the audio from each track is included in the stereo mix. Exceptions would include the following:

■ Tracks that you don't want to include in the mix

■ MIDI tracks feeding an outboard device

■ Tracks sent to a bus to create a sub-mix

If needed, use the Audio Output Path selector to remove a track from the stereo mix and/or to select any of the other available outputs. The following diagram shows how the Audio Output Path selector on an Aux Input track corresponds to the output connectors of an Mbox 2.

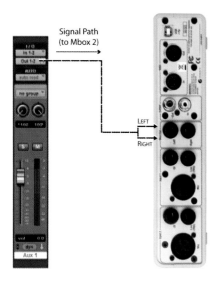

Figure 9.3

Signal flow from an Auxiliary Input track to stereo (left and right) monitor outputs on an Mbox 2

Inserts and Sends Views

The Mix window has independent view areas for the track inserts and the track sends. These view areas can each be toggled on or off in the Mix window.

■ **Inserts view.** The two Inserts view areas (Inserts A–E and Inserts F–J) allow you to access and view the 10 track Insert selectors. (Five are displayed in each view area.)

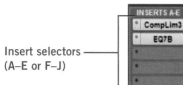

Insert selectors (A–E or F–J)

Figure 9.4

Inserts view area

- **Sends view.** The two Sends view areas (Sends A–E and Sends F–J) allow you to access and view the 10 track Send selectors. (Five are displayed in each view area.)

Send selectors ———
(A–E or F–J)

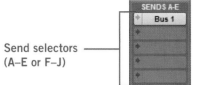

Figure 9.5
Sends view area

To toggle the display of an Inserts or Sends view area in the Mix window, choose VIEW > MIX WINDOW VIEWS and click an option in the submenu to select or deselect it.

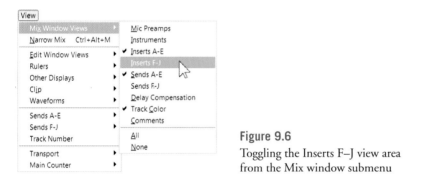

Figure 9.6
Toggling the Inserts F–J view area from the Mix window submenu

The two Sends view areas can be further customized to display their sends in one of two ways.

- **Assignments.** Shows the status of all five track Send selectors simultaneously. Each send that has been assigned will display the send assignment.

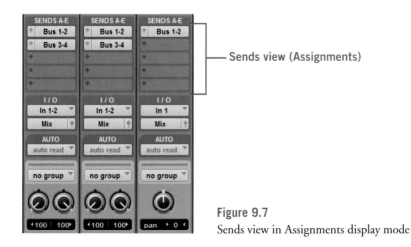

Sends view (Assignments)

Figure 9.7
Sends view in Assignments display mode

■ **Single Send.** Shows only one Send selector at a time across all tracks. On any tracks that have that send assigned, the Sends view will display the assignment and send level controls. In Single Send display mode, each Sends view area can be set to display any one of its five Send selectors.

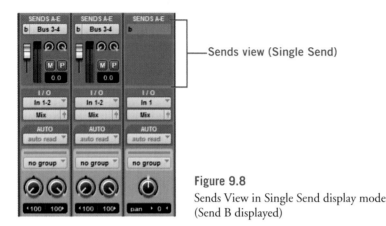

Sends view (Single Send)

Figure 9.8
Sends View in Single Send display mode
(Send B displayed)

To toggle between Send Assignments view and Single Send view, choose **VIEW > SENDS A–E** or **VIEW > SENDS F–J** and select the desired display mode from the submenu. The corresponding Sends view will be displayed using the chosen mode.

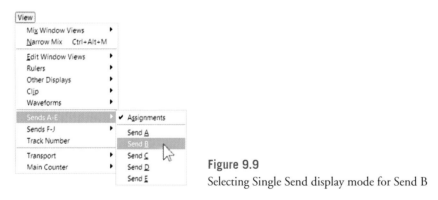

Figure 9.9
Selecting Single Send display mode for Send B

Tip: The Inserts and Sends view areas are available in both the Mix and Edit windows and can be shown or hidden independently in each window.

Configuring Inserts

With an Inserts view area displayed in the Mix window, you can insert a processor on any track. To add an insert processor, click on the Insert selector and choose a plug-in option or an I/O option from the pop-up menu. Plug-ins provide software-based signal processing, while I/O routing lets you use an external hardware device.

Plug-In Insert

Plug-in inserts can route audio through a software add-on from within the channel strip in the Mix window.

Choose a plug-in insert to add a software signal processor, such as the1-band EQ III plug-in, directly into the signal path of the channel.

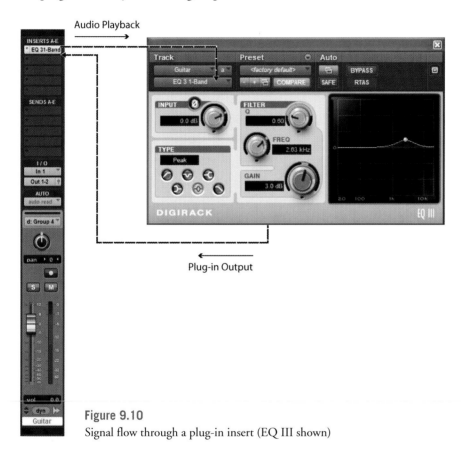

Figure 9.10
Signal flow through a plug-in insert (EQ III shown)

Hardware I/O Insert

Hardware I/O inserts can route audio through an external device connected to parallel inputs and outputs of an audio interface. This option requires an audio interface with available hardware inputs and outputs for line-level signals, such as a 003 interface.

AVID

In the Avid Learning Series   Hardware inserts are covered in the Pro Tools 110 course.

Configuring Sends and Returns

Sends are used to route a track's signal to a secondary path for parallel processing (internal or external) without interrupting the signal flow through the originating track. To add the processed signal back into the mix, it is usually returned via an Auxiliary Input.

To route a send to an external device, choose INTERFACE from the Send selector and select the appropriate output(s) on your audio interface. Connect these outputs to the external device and return the processed signal from the device to available inputs on your audio interface. This signal is the return, which then must be routed to the Audio Input of an Auxiliary Input track.

To route a send to an internal processor, such as a plug-in on an Auxiliary Input, choose BUS from the Send selector and select the appropriate bus for routing the signal. Busses can also be used to create sub-mixes that are returned via an Auxiliary Input.

Basic Automation

For a very simple mix, you can probably set your Track Volume Faders, Pan Sliders, and other controls and leave them unchanged from the start of the mix to the end. Most mixes are more complex, though, and require dynamic changes during the course of playback. Pro Tools allows you to record and edit these changes, automating various controls on your tracks. The automatable controls include volume, pan, mute, and real-time plug-in controls, depending on the track type.

Tracks in Pro Tools use automation modes to determine how automation is used on the track. You can set the automation mode for each track independently using a pop-up menu. The following sections discuss three of these modes, Write, Read, and Off, to illustrate the basic automation functions that Pro Tools offers.

Recording Automation (Write Mode)

By setting automation on a track to Write mode, you can record the changes you make to the controls on the track in real time. The basic steps for recording automation in Write mode are as follows:

1. Enable the automation type that you want to record, such as volume or pan, as follows:

    a. Choose WINDOW > AUTOMATION. The Automation window will open.

    b. Verify that the automation type is write-enabled (armed) for the session. Many automatable controls are armed by default.

c. If needed, click on an automation type to toggle its state (armed versus suspended).

Figure 9.11
Toggling an automation type in the Automation Enable window

Tip: The buttons in the Automation Enable window toggle between red to indicate *enabled* automation types and dark gray to indicate *suspended* automation types.

2. Put the track in automation writing mode by choosing **WRITE** from the Automation Mode selector.

Figure 9.12
Automation Mode selector in the Edit window and Mix window

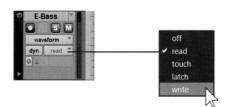

Figure 9.13
Selecting Write mode from the Automation Mode selector pop-up menu

3. Begin playback to start automation recording, and adjust controls as needed. Pro Tools will record all adjustments performed on enabled controls.

If you are not satisfied with the automation, you can repeat these steps to write new automation over the previous data.

Viewing and Editing Breakpoint Automation

Each Pro Tools track contains a single automation playlist for each automatable parameter. The automation playlist can be displayed in the Edit window, providing a convenient way to view the recorded automation changes over time. While visible, the automation playlist can also be edited and refined using Edit tools, such as the Grabber.

To display the automation playlist, do the following:

1. Click on the **Track View selector** in the Edit window.

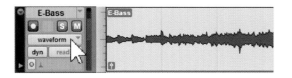

Figure 9.14
Track View selector

2. Select the automation playlist that you want to display from the **Track View** pop-up menu. The automation graph line will be displayed, superimposed on the track audio or MIDI data.

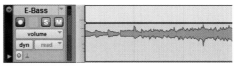

Figure 9.15
Showing the Volume automation Track view

Pro Tools also allows you to view automation playlists by clicking on the **Show/Hide Automation Lanes** button (triangle) at the head of a track. The Volume automation lane will be displayed beneath the parent track. Additional automation lanes can be displayed by clicking the plus sign (+) at the head of the Volume automation lane.

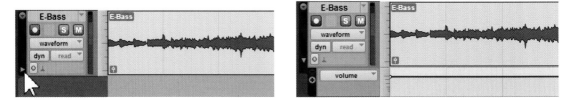

Figure 9.16
Showing Volume automation in an automation lane

You can edit an automation playlist by adding, moving, or deleting breakpoints using the Grabber tool. To edit a playlist with the Grabber tool, do any of the following:

- Click on the automation graph line to add a breakpoint.

- Click and drag an existing breakpoint to adjust its position.

- **Alt-click** (Windows) or **Option-click** (Mac) on an existing breakpoint to remove it.

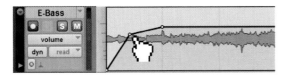

Figure 9.17
Editing the Volume playlist using the Grabber tool

Automation playlists can also be edited using other Edit tools. Additional information on using and editing automation is provided in advanced courses.

Playing Back Automation (Read Mode)

The default automation mode for a track is Read mode. In this mode, the automation playlist is used to play the automation data that has been recorded or written for a track. Automation is not recorded in Read mode, but the automation playlist can be edited with the Edit tools.

To return to Read mode when a different mode has been activated, click the **Automaton Mode selector** and choose **Read**.

Tip: Use Read mode to play back automation without running the risk of recording over any of it.

Turning Automation Off

The Off mode turns off automation for all automatable parameters on the track, such as the following:

- Volume

- Pan

- Mute

- Send volume, pan, and mute

- Plug-in controls

- MIDI volume, pan, and mute

In Off mode, automation is not recorded during playback, and existing automation data for all parameters is ignored. To turn off automation, click the **AUTOMATION MODE SELECTOR** and choose **OFF**.

Real-Time Plug-Ins

As you learned in earlier lessons, plug-ins can be used to add functionality to a Pro Tools session, such as a metronome click or a virtual instrument. Plug-ins are independent software programs that function as add-ons to Pro Tools. Plug-ins exist for a multitude of sound-processing applications—from synthesis to effects processing to sonic modeling of hardware processors, amplifiers, and microphones.

Pro Tools provides two main categories of plug-ins:

- Real-time processing, provided by Native and DSP plug-ins
- File-based processing (non-real-time), provided by AudioSuite plug-ins

In the Avid Learning Series   Details on using AudioSuite plug-ins are provided in the Pro Tools 110 course.

The following sections explain the basic concepts behind real-time plug-ins.

Real-Time Plug-In Features

Real-time plug-ins are available as track inserts in Pro Tools. When you add a real-time plug-in to a track, it processes the audio or MIDI data non-destructively and in real time—you instantly hear its effect on the track while playing back audio.

As discussed in Lesson 1, Pro Tools supports two formats of real-time plug-ins: *DSP* and *Native*. The difference between the formats lies in how your system provides processing power for the plug-in. Both types of plug-ins function as track inserts, are applied to audio during playback, and process audio non-destructively in real time.

DSP Plug-Ins (Pro Tools|HD and Pro Tools|HDX Hardware Only)

DSP plug-ins are designed for use on systems with Pro Tools|HD or Pro Tools|HDX hardware and rely on the processing power of the respective DSP cards.

Native Plug-Ins (All Pro Tools Systems)

Native plug-ins rely on the processing power of the host computer. This format is supported on all Pro Tools systems.

The more powerful your computer, the greater the number and variety of Native plug-ins that you can use simultaneously. You can increase the number of Native plug-ins your system can support by increasing the Hardware Buffer Size and CPU Usage Limit. See Lesson 2 for details on adjusting these parameters.

Real-Time Plug-In Formats

Plug-ins can be used in mono, multi-mono, or multi-channel formats. (For the purposes of this book, discussion of multi-channel formats will be limited to stereo configurations.) The plug-in format(s) available depend on the plug-in selected and the format of the track (mono or stereo). You should generally use multi-channel plug-ins for stereo tracks, if possible; if no multi-channel version is available, use a multi-mono version.

- **Mono plug-ins.** Plug-ins in this format are designed for use on mono tracks. Some mono plug-ins can generate stereo output from a mono channel.

- **Multi-mono plug-ins.** Plug-ins in this format can be used on stereo tracks or multi-channel surround tracks. Multi-mono plug-ins analyze and process each channel independently. Controls for all channels are linked by default so that adjustments are made to all channels in tandem. The controls can be unlinked for specialized purposes, allowing you to adjust channels independently.

- **Multi-channel plug-ins.** Plug-ins in this format are designed for use on stereo or multi-channel surround tracks. Controls for all channels are always linked together in multi-channel plug-ins.

Plug-Ins Provided with Pro Tools

Pro Tools comes bundled with a variety of additional software packages that extend its functionality. The plug-in extras bundled with Pro Tools include the Avid Pro Tools plug-ins listed in Appendix A and the Avid Creative Collection plug-ins listed in Appendix B. Among these, you will find dynamics processors, EQs, reverbs, delays, flangers, choruses, and a variety of other special effects.

Two commonly used types of processing for Audio tracks are dynamics processing (such as compressors and gates) and equalizers (such as graphic and parametric EQs). Pro Tools 10 provides a variety of options for adding dynamics and EQ processing to a track. The following plug-ins are available in Native format for real-time, non-destructive processing on any Pro Tools 10 system:

- Avid EQ III

- Avid Dynamics III

- Avid Channel Strip

EQ III

The Avid EQ III is an equalizer plug-in for adjusting the frequency spectrum of audio material in Pro Tools. This plug-in can be added to a track in a 1-band, 4-band, or 7-band parametric EQ configuration.

To add the EQ III plug-in to a Pro Tools track, do one of the following:

- For a mono track, click on an **INSERT SELECTOR** and choose **PLUG-IN > EQ > 1-BAND EQ 3 (MONO)** (or choose the 4- or 7-Band EQ 3, as appropriate). The EQ III plug-in window will open.

- For a stereo track, click on an **INSERT SELECTOR** and choose **MULTI-MONO PLUG-IN > EQ > 1-BAND EQ 3 (MONO)** (or choose the 4- or 7-Band EQ 3, as appropriate). The multi-mono EQ III plug-in window will open.

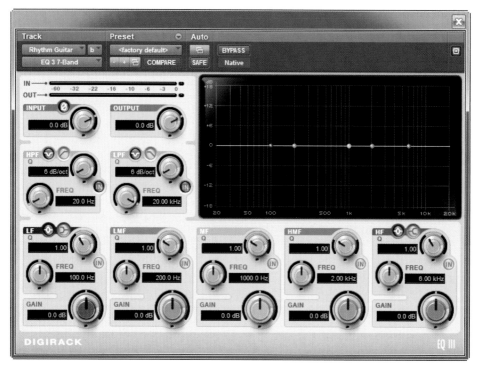

Figure 9.18
The EQ III 7-band equalizer plug-in window

Dynamics III

The Avid Dynamics III plug-in provides a suite of dynamics processing plug-ins, including a Compressor/Limiter, an Expander/Gate, and a De-Esser.

The Compressor/Limiter plug-in can be used to control dynamic levels, using standard attack, release, threshold, and ratio controls. The Expander/Gate plug-in can be added to a track to eliminate unwanted background noise by fine-tuning the ratio, attack, hold, release, and range. The De-Esser can be used to reduce sibilants, using frequency and range controls.

To add a Dynamics III plug-in to a Pro Tools track, do one of the following:

- For a mono track, click on an **INSERT SELECTOR** and choose **PLUG-IN > DYNAMICS > COMPRESSOR/LIMITER DYN 3 (MONO)** (or choose the De-Esser or Expander/Gate Dyn 3, as appropriate). The selected Dynamics III plug-in window will open.

- For a stereo track, click on an **INSERT SELECTOR** and choose **PLUG-IN > MULTI-CHANNEL PLUG-IN > DYNAMICS > COMPRESSOR/LIMITER DYN 3 (STEREO)** (or choose the De-Esser or Expander/Gate Dyn 3, as appropriate). The selected Dynamics III plug-in window will open.

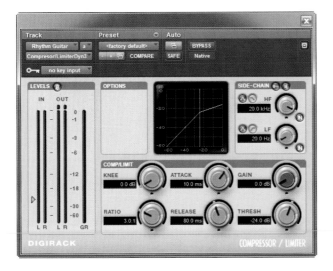

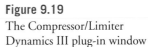

Figure 9.19
The Compressor/Limiter Dynamics III plug-in window

Avid Channel Strip

The Avid Channel Strip is a new plug-in that is included with Pro Tools 10. This plug-in combines EQ, Dynamics, Filter, and Gain effects processing in a single user interface. The Avid Channel Strip processing algorithms are based on the award-winning Euphonix System 5 console channel strip effects. In addition to standard knob and fader controls, Channel Strip also provides a graph of the gain transfer curve for the Expander/Gate and Compressor/Limiter effects, and a Frequency Graph display that shows the response curve for the current EQ settings.

To add the Channel Strip plug-in to a Pro Tools track, do one of the following:

- For a mono track, click on an **INSERT SELECTOR** and choose **PLUG-IN > EQ > CHANNEL STRIP (MONO)** or **PLUG-IN > DYNAMICS > CHANNEL STRIP (MONO)**. A mono version of the Avid Channel Strip plug-in will open.

- For a stereo track, click on an **INSERT SELECTOR** and choose **PLUG-IN > MULTI-CHANNEL PLUG-IN > EQ > CHANNEL STRIP (STEREO)** or **PLUG-IN > MULTI-CHANNEL PLUG-IN > DYNAMICS > CHANNEL STRIP (STEREO)**. A stereo version of the Avid Channel Strip plug-in will open.

Figure 9.20

The Avid Channel Strip plug-in window

Review/Discussion Questions

1. What term is used to describe an audio patch point that applies a signal processor directly into the signal path on a track? How many of these patch points does Pro Tools provide on each track? (See page 242.)

2. What term is used to describe a signal path carrying a mix output of one or more tracks routed for parallel processing? How can this signal be returned to the sending device? (See pages 242 and 243.)

3. What menu would you use to display or hide the Mix window? What keyboard shortcut can you use to toggle between the Mix and Edit windows? (See page 243.)

4. How can you toggle the display of an Inserts or Sends view area in the Mix window? (See page 247.)

5. What are the two ways that Sends can be displayed in the Mix window? Which display shows only one Send selector at a time across all tracks? (See pages 247 and 248.)

6. Which Pro Tools automation mode discussed in this lesson records changes to track controls in real time when playing back the session? (See page 250.)

7. What track control can you use to display an automation playlist? What window are automation playlists displayed in? (See page 252.)

8. What tool can you use to add, move, or delete automation breakpoints? What modifier can you use to delete a breakpoint by clicking on it? (See page 253.)

9. Which Pro Tools automation mode can you use to play back automation that has been recorded, without the risk of recording over it? (See page 253.)

10. What is the difference between Read mode and Off mode? Will Off mode allow you to play back existing automation on the track? (See pages 253 and 254.)

11. What two types of plug-ins provide real-time processing? What type provides non-real-time processing? (See page 254.)

12. What real-time plug-in format requires Pro Tools|HD or Pro Tools|HDX hardware? What real-time plug-in format can be used on all Pro Tools systems? (See page 254.)

13. What plug-in options are available for EQ and dynamics processing? (See pages 255 through 257.)

14. What types of processors does the Avid Channel Strip provide? (See page 257.)

Arranging Audio and Creating Shared Effects

In this exercise tutorial, you will arrange the audio on the vocal tracks and set up a shared effect using a reverb plug-in on an Aux Input track.

Duration: 10 to 15 Minutes   **Media: DrumLoop.wav, Guitar.wav, 10_01.wav, 10_03.wav**

Getting Started

You will start by opening the Pro Tools session you created in Exercise 6. If that session is not available, use the Ex06.ptxt session template in the Completed Exercises folder on the DVD.

To create the session:

1. Launch Pro Tools and open the session you created in Exercise 6.

2. Choose FILE > SAVE AS and name your session Exercise7-YourName.

Arranging the Vocal Tracks

In this part of the exercise, you will modify the clips that you placed on the Vox1 and Vox2 tracks using various editing operations to arrange the vocals in repeating patterns.

To arrange audio on the Vox1 track:

1. Unmute the Vox1 track and play through the beginning of the session to get familiar with the clip on the track.

2. Using the Grabber tool, select the clip and choose EDIT > REPEAT; set the Number of Repeats to **3** and click **OK**.

3. Make sure you are in Grid mode and set the Grid to 0|0|480 (1/8 note).

4. If needed, use the Horizontal Zoom In button (or another zoom method) to zoom in sufficiently; you should be able to see the waveform change shape with each word.

5. Using the Selector tool, select the word "Time" in the second clip (2|2|000 to 2|2|480).

6. Choose **EDIT > CUT** or press **CTRL+X** (Windows) or **COMMAND+X** (Mac). The selected word will be removed and placed on your computer's Clipboard.

7. Place the insertion point at the second 1/8 note in Bar 4 (4|1|480) on the Vox1 track and choose **EDIT > PASTE**. The word "Time" will be pasted in as a new clip on the track.

8. Press **ENTER** (Windows) or **RETURN** (Mac) followed by the spacebar to listen to your edits.

To arrange audio on the Vox2 track:

1. Unmute the Vox2 track and place the session into Spot mode.

2. With the Grabber tool, click on the 10_03 clip on the Vox2 track to select it. The Spot dialog box will open.

3. In the dialog box, enter **5|1|000** as the Start location for the clip and click **OK**. The clip will move to start at Bar 5 and will remain selected. Play through the selection to get familiar with the clip.

4. Choose **EDIT > COPY** or press **CTRL+C** (Windows) or **COMMAND+C** (Mac) to copy the clip to the Clipboard.

5. Using the Edit Selection Start field in the Edit window, enter a start time of **7|1|000** and press **ENTER** to move the insertion point to that location.

Figure EX7.1
Setting the start time in the Edit window

6. Choose **EDIT > PASTE** or press **CTRL+V** (Windows) or **COMMAND+V** (Mac). A copy of the clip will appear on the track at the selected location.

7. Place the session into Grid mode, keeping the Grid set to 0|0|480 (1/8 note).

8. With the Selector tool, select the first three 1/8 notes in the second region (7|1|000 to 7|2|480), corresponding to the words, "Baby you got me."

9. Choose EDIT > COPY or press CTRL+C (Windows) or COMMAND+C (Mac) to copy the selection to the Clipboard.

10. Next, make a selection from 7|2|480 to 8|1|000, corresponding to the words "making circles," and press BACKSPACE (Windows) or DELETE (Mac) to remove that portion of the clip.

11. Click with the Selector tool at Bar 7, Beat 3 (7|3|000) and choose EDIT > PASTE or press CTRL+V (Windows) or COMMAND+V (Mac). The portion of the clip you copied in Step 4 will appear on the track at the selected location.

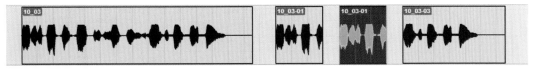

Figure EX7.2
Arrangement of clips on the Vox2 track

12. Press ENTER (Windows) or RETURN (Mac) followed by the SPACE BAR to listen to your edits. When finished, press the SPACE BAR again to stop playback.

Creating a Reverb Effect

In this part of the exercise, you will create an Aux Input track to function as the reverb return, assign the D-Verb plug-in on the track, and create sends from the Vox1 and Vox2 tracks to the reverb effect.

To create a reverb return:

1. Select the Vox2 track by clicking on its nameplate in the Edit window.

2. Choose TRACK > NEW and create a new stereo Aux Input track. A new track named Aux 1 will appear below the Vox2 track.

3. Double-click on the track nameplate for the Aux 1 track and rename it Reverb.

4. Choose WINDOW > MIX or press CTRL+= (Windows) or COMMAND+= (Mac) to switch to the Mix window.

To assign a plug-in and configure sends:

1. Click on the AUDIO INPUT PATH SELECTOR for the Reverb track (the first selector under the I/O label) and select BUS > BUS 1-2 (STEREO).

Figure EX7.3
Audio Input Path selector set
to Bus 1-2 on the Reverb track

2. Click on Insert Selector A for the Reverb track (first selector under the Inserts A-E label) and choose **MULTICHANNEL PLUG-IN > REVERB > D-VERB (STEREO)**. The D-Verb plug-in window will open.

3. In the plug-in window, select Hall and Large for Algorithm and Size, respectively. Close the plug-in window when you're finished.

4. Click on Send Selector A on the Vox1 track (first selector under the Sends A-E label) and select **BUS > BUS 1-2 (STEREO)**. The Send window will open.

5. **ALT-CLICK** (Windows) or **OPTION-CLICK** (Mac) on the Send fader to set it to 0.0 dB. Close the Send window when finished.

6. Repeat the above process on the Vox2 track.

Finishing Up

Before wrapping up this exercise tutorial, take a moment to listen to the work you've completed up to this point and adjust the mix as needed. Be sure to save your work before closing the session, as you will be reusing this session in the next exercise.

1. Press **ENTER** (Windows) or **RETURN** (Mac) followed by the **SPACE BAR** to begin playback from the session start and hear the effect of the reverb return. Adjust the mix as desired to blend the tracks and the reverb effect, while keeping the effect pronounced.

2. When you're finished, press the **SPACE BAR** a second time to stop playback.

3. Save and close the session to complete the exercise.

Finishing Your Work

This lesson covers processes that you can use to create copies of your work in various formats. It describes how to create a session backup, how to mix down tracks for use within or outside of Pro Tools, and how to share your completed mix by burning an audio CD or posting a bounce to SoundCloud.

Duration: 60 Minutes

GOALS

- Understand the purpose of the Save Copy In command and recognize situations in which you should use it
- Create a copy of your session for use on a different Pro Tools system
- Create a mixdown of tracks in your session by bouncing to tracks or bouncing to disk
- Select appropriate options for your bounced files when bouncing to disk
- Add your bounced files to your iTunes library or SoundCloud account
- Create an audio CD of your bounced files to share your results with others

After completing any significant recording, editing, or mixing work, it is wise to safeguard your work by creating a backup copy. You might also need to convert your session for subsequent work on another system or bounce your tracks to share your results as a completed mix. The sections in this lesson provide details on the processes you can use to create a finished copy of your work at any milestone point in your project's lifecycle.

Backing Up Your Session

Creating backups of your sessions is critical for archival and disaster recovery purposes. Because Pro Tools sessions are stored electronically, you typically will have no physical media housing your work other than a hard drive. As a result, it is possible to accidentally lose your work by deleting or overwriting files, having a file become corrupt, contracting a virus, or having a drive fail.

To protect yourself against these problems, it is a good idea to create regular session backups. Some of the best protection measures include creating multiple copies of your files, using a separate drive for backup copies, and storing backup copies offsite to protect against disasters such as fire or flood. The more valuable your sessions, the more robust your backup plans should be. At a minimum, you should create a backup session upon completing any work that would be difficult or time-consuming to re-create, especially if the recording has significant value or importance to you or your clients.

Saving a Session Copy

To create a session backup, you can save a copy of your session and all related files using the Save Copy In command. Unlike the Save As command, which creates a copy of the Pro Tools session file only, the Save Copy In command can be used to save all files used in the session, allowing you to create a self-contained duplicate session folder in a separate location, such as on another drive.

The Save Copy In command saves a copy of your current session without closing the original session, meaning that as you continue to work, any subsequent changes are saved in the original and do not affect the copy.

Tip: One key difference between the Save As command and the Save Copy In command is their effect on the open session. After a Save As operation, the open session will be the *renamed copy* that you created. By contrast, after a Save Copy In operation, the *original session* will remain open, not the copy.

When using the Save Copy In command, you have a number of options available that allow you to convert and consolidate session information as you are saving. Some of the more useful applications of the Save Copy In command are as follows:

■ It allows you to back up an entire Pro Tools session and all of its associated files without leaving the original session.

■ It allows multiple versions of a session to be saved at various stages of a project. Later, these versions can be used as a basis of comparison or to easily revert to an earlier stage of the project.

■ It allows sessions to be saved using a different resolution (16-bit or 24-bit), sample rate (up to the maximum rate supported by your system), and/or file format (AIFF or WAV) from the original. This allows complete flexibility and compatibility with other Pro Tools systems.

■ It allows all session audio files, video files, and plug-in settings to be copied into a single folder.

■ It allows a current Pro Tools session to be saved as an earlier version so that it can be opened on older Pro Tools systems.

To use this saving option, do the following:

1. Choose FILE > SAVE COPY IN. A special Save dialog box will open, allowing you to specify format options for the session copy.

Figure 10.1
The Save Session Copy dialog box

2. In the Session Format drop-down menu, choose from among the available format options as needed to maintain compatibility with an earlier Pro Tools version.

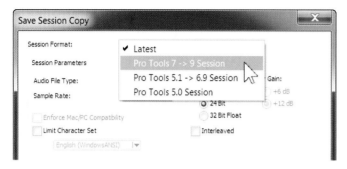

Figure 10.2
Selecting an earlier Pro Tools version

3. In the Session Parameters section of the dialog box, choose a desired audio file type, sample rate, and bit depth, and select or deselect the Interleaved option, as desired (Pro Tools 10 only). These parameters default to the settings of your current session and can be changed as needed.

Tip: If you choose the Pro Tools 5.1 -> 6.9 Session option in Step 2 and either the AIFF or WAV file format in Step 3, the Enforce PC/Mac Compatibility check box will become available. Enabling this option ensures that the session and its associated files will be compatible with supported Mac and Windows Pro Tools systems.

4. In the Items to Copy section of the dialog box, enable additional options as desired:

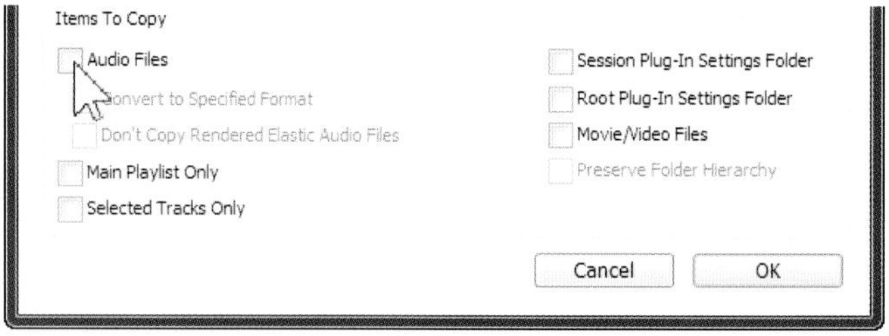

Figure 10.3
Optional items that can be copied with the session

- **Audio Files.** If you are changing the sample rate of the session, this option will be selected automatically; otherwise, you can choose whether to copy all associated audio files for the session using this option.

- **Convert to Specified Format.** If your session contains files in a format different from the specified Audio File Type, you can choose to convert the file format for the copied files. For example, if you select BWF (.WAV) format for the Audio File Type and your session includes AIFF files, you can choose to convert the AIFF files to BWF (.WAV) by checking the box.

- **Don't Copy Rendered Elastic Files.** Rendered Elastic Audio files will not be copied if no audio files are copied. (The option will be grayed out.) If the Audio Files option is selected, rendered Elastic Audio files can be excluded by selecting this check box.

- **Main Playlist Only.** This option allows you to exclude alternate playlists in the copied session.

- **Selected Tracks Only.** This option allows you to include only selected tracks in the copied session. To use this option, select the desired tracks before choosing FILE > SAVE COPY IN.

- **Session Plug-In Settings Folder.** This option copies the session's Plug-In Settings folder, if present, to the new session location.

- **Root Plug-In Settings Folder.** This option copies the contents of the root-level Plug-In Settings folder to a folder in the new session named Place in Root Settings Folder. These files will need to be moved to the root-level Plug-In Settings folder on the destination system.

AVI ▶
In the Avid Learning Series   The location options for plug-in settings files are discussed in advanced Pro Tools courses.

- **Movie/Video Files.** This option copies movie or video files (if present in the session) to the new session location.

6. Click SAVE when you are finished selecting all of the options you want. The new session and optional files will be saved into the directory location you selected.

Sharing a Session between Systems

After completing your editing work on a session, you might want to save and convert your session data for use on a different Pro Tools system. The Save Copy In command can be used to ensure the compatibility of your session. See the preceding "Saving a Session Copy" section.

Creating a Stereo Mixdown

Mixing down is the process of recording the output from multiple tracks to a stereo or multi-channel format. This process is also often referred to as *bouncing*, which can be done for the entire mix or to combine selected tracks to free up resources or reduce track count. Mixdown is often the last phase of music production, but in Pro Tools mixdown can be done any time you want to bounce tracks or create a completed mix for use outside of your session.

The most common mixdown technique in Pro Tools is to bounce to a stereo mix. You can record your mix to Audio tracks within your session or create an external recording using the Bounce to Disk command. Once you have created a stereo mix, you can play back the results outside of Pro Tools and share your composition with others by burning the file onto a CD or posting it to your SoundCloud account.

Tip: Pro Tools with Complete Production Toolkit and Pro Tools HD also provide multi-channel mixdown and bouncing options for use in surround-sound applications.

Considerations for Bouncing Audio

Most digital audio workstations provide functions for mixing down or bouncing tracks; however, not all systems approach the process the same way. When performing a bounce with Pro Tools, it is important to recognize that the bounce will be performed in real time and will capture all audible information in your mix just as you hear it during playback.

The following principles apply to bouncing in Pro Tools:

- **Pro Tools bounces all audible tracks in real time.** When you play back your session, all tracks that you hear are included in the bounce. Any tracks that are muted will not be included. If you have soloed any tracks, only those soloed elements will be present in the bounce.

- **Pro Tools bounces tracks based on the output path.** All source tracks for the bounce must be assigned to the same output path. Any audio not assigned to that common output path will not be represented in the bounce file.

- **Pro Tools does not require extra voices to bounce to disk.** You can use all available voices in your system when using the Bounce to Disk command, without requiring extra voiced tracks for recording the bounced file.

■ **The bounced file will be a "flattened" version of your session.** Inserts, sends, and external effects are applied permanently to the bounced tracks, so make sure that you set levels carefully before bouncing tracks. Listen closely to ensure that everything sounds as it should. Pay close attention to levels, being sure to avoid clipping.

■ **Pro Tools bounces tracks based on Timeline selections.** If you have made a selection on the Timeline (or on a track with Timeline and Edit selections linked), Pro Tools will bounce all audible tracks for the length of the selection only. If no selection is present in any track, Pro Tools will bounce the audible tracks in your session from the start of the session or from the playback cursor position to the end of the longest track in the session.

■ **Bounced material is automatically time-stamped.** You can drag a bounced file into a track and place it at the same location as the original material using Spot mode.

Bouncing to Tracks

To create a stereo mixdown (or a sub-mix) within Pro Tools, you can record any or all of your session tracks to an available stereo Audio track. This technique lets you add live input to the mix, adjusting volume, pan, mute, and other controls in real time during the mixdown process. Recording to tracks requires that you have an available voiced track for each channel that you will be recording. For a stereo mix using Pro Tools, this simply means that you will need a stereo Audio track or two mono Audio tracks available.

Tip: Bouncing tracks in a large session using Pro Tools HD might require that you consider voice allocation. Voicing considerations are covered in advanced courses.

The typical process for creating a stereo mixdown within a session is to combine the audio output of selected tracks using an internal bus and to record the resulting mix onto a separate stereo Audio track.

To create a stereo mixdown using this method, do the following:

1. Create a stereo mix from the source tracks as described in Lesson 9, using appropriate settings for volume, panning, inserts, sends, plug-ins, and automation.

2. Set the output for each track you want to include to the same unused stereo bus. These tracks will be the source playback tracks for the bus bounce.

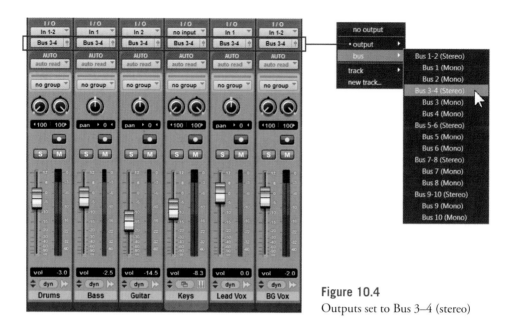

Figure 10.4
Outputs set to Bus 3–4 (stereo)

3. Create a stereo Audio track and record-enable the track. This track will be the destination track for the bus bounce.

4. Set the inputs for the stereo track to correspond to the stereo output bus you selected in Step 2, and set the output for the track to your main output path (typically analog outputs 1–2).

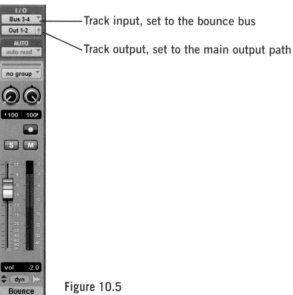

—— Track input, set to the bounce bus

—— Track output, set to the main output path

Figure 10.5
Stereo Audio track set up for an internal bounce

5. Do one of the following:

   ● Make a selection (to manually set the start and end times for the bounce).

   ● Place the playback cursor at the beginning of the session or at the desired start point.

6. In the Transport window, click the **RECORD** button followed by the **PLAY** button to begin recording the bounce.

7. During recording, perform any desired "live" mixing, such as Volume Fader adjustments and panning changes.

8. Allow recording to continue until playback stops automatically (if recording from a selection) or until you reach the desired end point. To stop the recording manually, click the **STOP** button in the Transport window or press the **SPACE BAR**.

Tip: After the recording is complete, you should see the waveform for your combined source tracks on the destination tracks. If no waveform is present, check the settings for your source outputs and record inputs and verify that the faders are set to an audible level.

9. Disarm the record-enabled track and rename the recorded clip, if desired.

Once you have combined multiple tracks into a single stereo track, you can continue with more recording or editing, using the stereo track in place of any original tracks to free up resources. You can also use the stereo track as part of a Bounce to Disk operation to create a completed audio mix.

Bouncing to Disk

The Bounce to Disk command allows you to mix your entire session directly to a hard drive in the same way a mixdown would occur with a traditional studio setup. This can be useful when you want to work with the mixed recording outside of Pro Tools, such as when you are posting song files to the Internet or burning them to CD. The Bounce to Disk function also provides more robust control than you have when bouncing to tracks, enabling you to set the bit depth, file format, and sample rate for the resulting bounced file.

The Bounce to Disk command combines the outputs of all currently audible tracks routed to a common output or output pair to create a new audio file on a selected hard drive or other supported volume. The newly bounced file can be automatically imported into the session at the completion of the bounce, if desired.

To bounce all currently audible tracks, do the following:

1. Adjust track output levels and finalize an automated mix. Any inserts or effects settings that are active on your tracks will be permanently written to the bounced audio files.

2. Make sure that all of the tracks you want to include in the bounce are audible. If you want to create a sub-mix of tracks, solo only those tracks. Conversely, if you want to mix down all tracks in your session, make sure no tracks are soloed or muted.

3. Assign the output of each track you want to include in your bounce to the same output pair by clicking the **AUDIO OUTPUT PATH SELECTOR** and choosing the corresponding output from the pop-up menu.

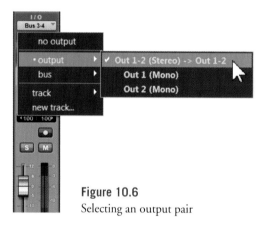

Figure 10.6
Selecting an output pair

4. Choose **FILE > BOUNCE TO > DISK**. The Bounce dialog box will appear.

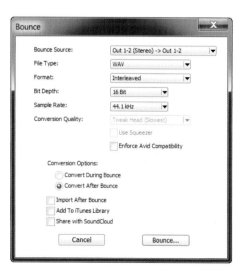

Figure 10.7
The Bounce dialog box

5. Select the output pair that you used in Step 3 from the **Bounce Source** drop-down list.

6. Choose the desired file type for your bounce file from the **File Type** pop-up menu. Available options include the following:

- **WAV.** This is the default file format for Windows- and Mac-based Pro Tools systems and is supported by many other Windows and Mac applications.

- **AIFF.** This file format is primarily used on Mac systems. Use the AIFF format if you plan to import the bounced audio into other Mac applications.

- **MP3.** This file format is used for streaming audio on the Internet, personal computers, and portable devices. Use this file format when you want to play back bounced files using MP3-compatible applications and devices.

- **QuickTime.** This is a file format for multimedia developed by Apple. Use the QuickTime format if you plan to use your audio in multimedia applications that support QuickTime, such as Adobe Premiere, Final Cut Pro, or Macromedia Director.

- **Windows Media (Windows systems only).** Microsoft's Windows Media Audio-9 file format is used for creating high-quality digital media files for streaming and download-and-play applications on PCs, set-top boxes, and portable devices. The WMA-9 file format supports 16- and 24-bit audio files, sample rates up to 96 kHz, multi-channel audio from stereo through 7.1 surround, lossless encoding, and file sizes that are roughly one-half the size of an equivalent MP3 file.

- **MXF.** MXF (*Material Exchange Format*) is a media file format that includes both video and audio files and is designed for the interchange of audio-visual material with associated data and metadata. This option requires **Enforce Avid Compatibility** to be checked.

7. Choose the **Multiple mono** or **Interleaved** file format for your stereo bounce from the **Format** pop-up menu.

Figure 10.8
Selecting a format for the bounced file

- **Multiple Mono.** This option creates split stereo files from the stereo bus path. Mono files will be created for the left and right channels, with .L and .R suffixes appended to the file names, respectively. Use this file format if you want to import the bounced audio back into an older Pro Tools session without conversion. This option is not available for use with MP3 or Windows Media file types.

Tip: The Multiple Mono format can also be used for multi-channel mixes. Multi-channel mixdown is covered in advanced courses.

- **Interleaved.** Choose this option to create a single interleaved stereo file from the stereo bus path. This file format is directly compatible with most applications that process stereo files for commercial use, including all Apple software applications and Roxio's Toast software application.

Tip: A third option, the Mono (Summed) format, provides a single audio file that is a summed mono mix of the bus path. Choose this option if you need to create a composite mix of mono tracks. All panning information will be disregarded.

8. Choose the desired bit depth for the bounced file(s) from the BIT DEPTH pop-up menu. You can choose 8-, 16-, or 24-Bit, or 32-Bit Float resolution.

- **8 Bit.** Use this option to minimize file size for recordings that do not require rich dynamic resolution. Eight-bit files are often used in multi-media applications.

- **16 Bit.** This is the standard resolution for compact discs. Use this option if you plan to burn your bounce to CD without further processing.

- **24 Bit.** This setting provides a higher dynamic resolution. Use this option when you want to create a bounce that retains high resolution, such as a final mix that is ready to master.

- **32 Bit Float.** This setting provides the highest dynamic resolution; however, 32-bit floating-point files also require a third more disk space than 24-bit files.

9. Choose the desired sample rate for the bounce files from the SAMPLE RATE pop-up menu. Higher sampling rates will provide better audio fidelity but will also increase the size of the resulting file(s).

Tip: If you plan to burn your bounced audio directly to CD without further processing, choose 44.1 kHz as the sample rate for the bounce.

Tip: The standard sample rate for compact discs is 44.1 kHz; the standard rate for professional and DVD video is 48 kHz. Selecting a multiple of the standard sample rate for the destination media will simplify the final sample rate conversion (44.1, 88.2, or 176.4 kHz for CD audio; 48, 96, or 192 kHz for DVD audio).

10. If the sample rate for your bounce differs from your session's sample rate, the Conversion Quality pop-up list will become available. Select the **CONVERSION QUALITY** setting based on the project needs. Higher settings require longer rendering times. The Good choice is adequate for general-purpose bounces.

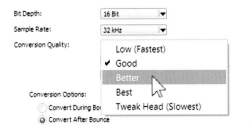

Figure 10.9
The Conversion Quality pop-up list

11. Choose from the two conversion options, if applicable.

   ● **Convert During Bounce.** This option converts file type, sample rate, and bit depth during the bounce process. This option generally takes less time, but it might not maintain plug-in automation accuracy. This option is best for bounces that do not involve plug-in automation.

   ● **Convert After Bounce.** This option converts file type, sample rate, and bit depth after bouncing is complete. This option is more time-consuming than Convert During Bounce, but it offers the highest level of plug-in automation accuracy possible.

12. To automatically import the newly bounced files into the Clip List of your session, select the **IMPORT AFTER BOUNCE** option.

Note: The Import After Bounce option is available only if the target sample rate for the bounce file matches the sample rate of your session.

13. To automatically add your bounced file to your iTunes library or upload it to SoundCloud, select the **ADD TO ITUNES LIBRARY** and/or **SHARE WITH SOUNDCLOUD** options. (See "Adding a Bounce File to Your iTunes Library" and "Sharing a Bounce File on SoundCloud" for details on these options.)

14. After confirming your settings, click the **Bounce** button. A Save dialog box will prompt you to name the new audio file and will allow you to navigate to the desired location to store the file.

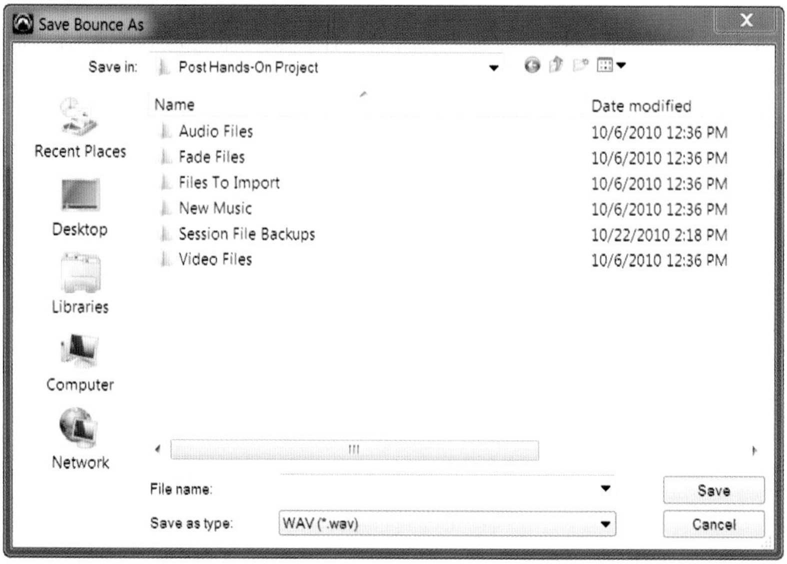

Figure 10.10
The Save Bounce As dialog box

15. Select a destination for the new audio file, enter a name, and click **Save**. The audio will play back as Pro Tools processes your bounce, and a countdown window will appear, displaying the time remaining for your bounce to complete.

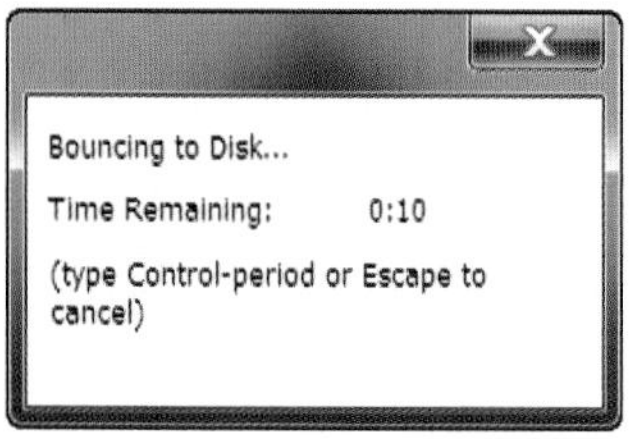

Figure 10.11
The Bounce to Disk countdown window

Note: You will not hear the bounce file play back in real time if you are not monitoring the bounce source.

Tip: If you did not select the Import After Bounce option, you can import the bounced files to your session later using the Import Audio command.

Adding a Bounce File to Your iTunes Library

If you plan to add your completed mix to an audio CD, one of your options is to use iTunes software to burn the CD. Pro Tools 10 lets you bounce your mix directly to your iTunes library to simplify this process. To add a bounce to your iTunes library, you can use the new Add to iTunes Library option in the Bounce to Disk dialog box.

Tip: If iTunes is not already installed on your system, you can download a copy from the Apple website at www.apple.com/itunes.

To add a bounce file to your iTunes library, do the following:

1. Choose FILE > BOUNCE TO > DISK.

2. In the Bounce to Disk dialog box, set the Bounce Source to a mono or stereo path.

3. Set the Format to INTERLEAVED and configure other options as desired.

4. Enable the ADD TO ITUNES LIBRARY option.

5. Click BOUNCE. The bounce process will proceed as described above, and a copy of your bounced file will automatically be imported into iTunes the next time you launch the iTunes application.

Figure 10.12
The Add to iTunes Library option in the Bounce to Disk dialog box

Note: If iTunes is not installed on your computer, the Add to iTunes Library option does not do anything.

Sharing a Bounce File on SoundCloud

SoundCloud is a social networking site built around the concept of shared audio files. By posting songs on SoundCloud, you can share your creations on the web with friends, family, coworkers, and more. Your SoundCloud files can be published to other social networking sites and services, such as Facebook and Twitter, or embedded in blogs or websites.

The SoundCloud player allows you and your listeners to view your audio in a waveform display and to add timed comments to the track. Comment markers appear on the waveform, and the comment text displays on playback.

Figure 10.13
An audio file shared on SoundCloud

Tip: For more information on SoundCloud, visit their website at
http://soundcloud.com.

Pro Tools users with a SoundCloud account can upload audio files from their system into their account and share them with others publicly or privately. Pro Tools 10 lets you post your mix directly to your SoundCloud account during the bounce process, saving you the bother of uploading the file after creating a bounce.

To add a bounce file to your SoundCloud account, do the following:

1. Choose FILE > BOUNCE TO > DISK.

2. In the Bounce to Disk dialog box, set the Bounce Source to a mono or stereo path.

3. Set the Format to INTERLEAVED and configure other options as desired.

4. Enable the SHARE WITH SOUNDCLOUD option.

5. Click BOUNCE. The bounce process will proceed as described above, after which the SHARE WITH SOUNDCLOUD dialog box will display.

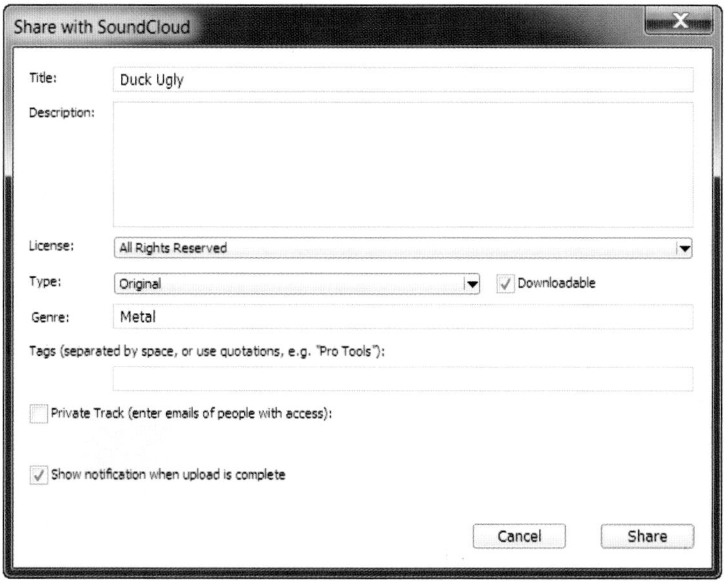

Figure 10.14
The Share with SoundCloud dialog box

6. Configure the Share with SoundCloud dialog box as appropriate for your mix:

- **Title.** Type the title for your song or composition.

- **Description.** Provide a description for the track.

- **License.** Select an appropriate license option, such as All Rights Reserved.

- **Type (optional).** Select a track type as appropriate, such as Original or Remix.

- **Downloadable.** Select (check) this option to allow listeners to download a copy of your song from SoundCloud; leave it unchecked to allow listeners to stream online playback only.

- **Genre (optional).** Add a description of the genre for the track, such as Hip Hop or Rock.

- **Tags (optional).** Type any tags you want associated with your track; tags help other SoundCloud users find your tracks when searching for audio with certain characteristics.

- **Private Track.** Enable this option to keep your track private; when enabled, you have the option of adding email addresses for users with whom you want to share your track. (SoundCloud will notify them when the track is posted.) You can also share private tracks from SoundCloud at any time by logging into your account.

Note: If you do not select the Private Track option, all SoundCloud users will be
able to discover and comment on your track.

● **Notify Me.** Enable this option to have SoundCloud notify you once your
mix has been posted; the notification will include a URL link to the posted
file on SoundCloud.

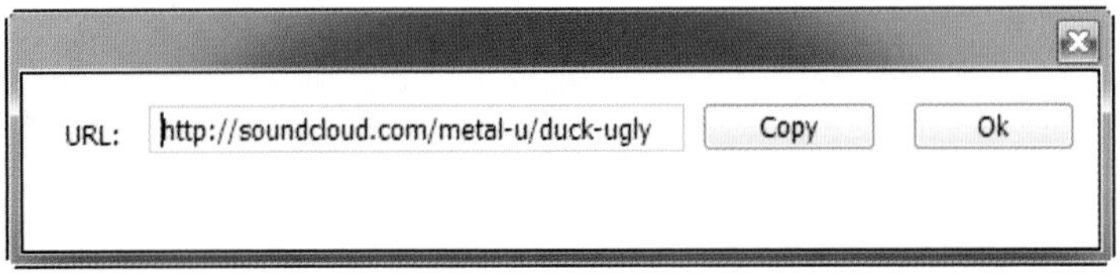

Figure 10.15
Upload notification

Creating a SoundCloud Account and Logging In

To use the Share with SoundCloud option in Pro Tools, you will need to have a SoundCloud
account and to log into your account through Pro Tools. You can create an account by visiting
https://soundcloud.com/signup or by using the login dialog box in Pro Tools. (Basic accounts
are free.)

To create an account or to log in to an existing account from Pro Tools, choose **SETUP >
LOGIN TO SOUNDCLOUD**. A dialog box will appear, allowing you to enter your login name
and password or to sign up for an account.

If you are not already logged in when you perform your bounce, Pro Tools will prompt you
with the same dialog box.

Burning Songs to CD from iTunes

Both PCs and Macs enable you to create audio CDs from your bounced mix using
software included with your computer or software purchased from a third-party
developer. You can copy one or more bounced files to create tracks on either
compact disc–recordable (CD-R) or compact disc–rewritable (CD-RW) media.

This section provides an overview of the typical process of burning audio CDs on
Windows and Mac operating systems using iTunes. The exact steps may vary,
depending on the operating system and iTunes version you use.

Tip: **CD-R discs provide a universal format that can be played on most CD players;
CD-RW discs can typically be played only by using a CD-ROM drive.**

Note: **When creating an audio CD using CD-R or CD-RW media, you must copy all tracks at the same time. You cannot add subsequent tracks after you have burned the disc. (CD-RW discs allow you erase the disc and start over, however.)**

Apple's iTunes software allows you to create audio CDs on both Windows and Mac computers. To create an audio CD from iTunes, your computer must have the iTunes software installed and an available CD recorder (burner) installed or attached.

By default, iTunes burns CDs in a universal format that can be used on Windows or Mac computers and in any standard CD player.

To burn an audio CD of your bounced files using iTunes, do the following:

1. Add your files to iTunes during a Bounce to Disk, as described earlier in this lesson, or drag existing audio files from Windows or the Mac Finder into iTunes.

2. Select the desired files in iTunes and choose FILE > NEW PLAYLIST FROM SELECTED. iTunes will create a new untitled playlist containing the selected files.

3. Name the playlist for easy identification.

4. Insert a blank CD into the optical drive of your computer.

5. If a dialog box appears prompting you for the action you want to take, select CREATE A CD USING ITUNES (Windows) or OPEN ITUNES (Mac).

6. In iTunes, a dialog box will display, providing directions for burning items on the CD; review the directions and click OK.

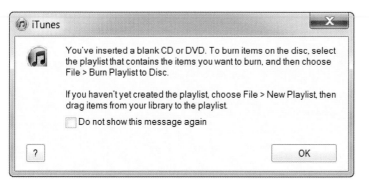

Figure 10.16
Directions for burning a CD from iTunes

7. With your playlist selected, choose FILE > BURN PLAYLIST TO DISC from the iTunes menus. A Burn Settings dialog box will open.

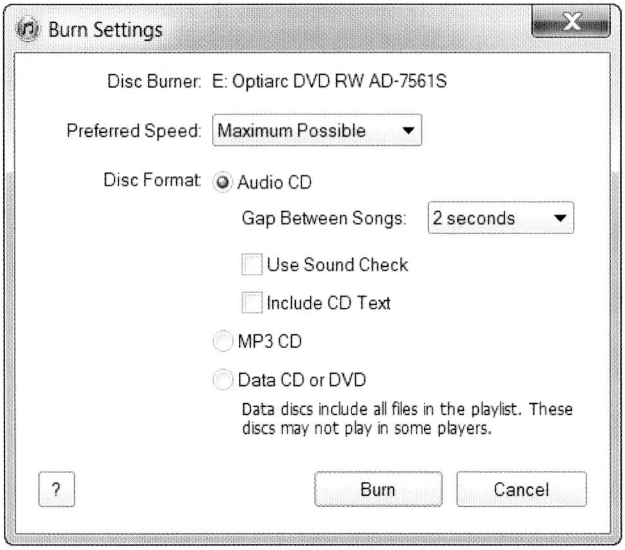

Figure 10.17
Burn Settings dialog box

8. In the Burn Settings dialog box, ensure that AUDIO CD is listed for the Disc Format setting. You can also modify the Gap Between Songs setting when burning multiple files to specify the amount of silence to include between tracks.

9. When you are ready, click the BURN button. The files in the playlist will be burned to the disc.

When burning is complete, you can eject the CD to share your recording with friends, band mates, and others.

Tip: The process for burning a CD can vary depending on the version of iTunes you are using. See the iTunes documentation for further details.

Review/Discussion Questions

1. Why is it important to back up your Pro Tools sessions? What are some ways in which your Pro Tools work can be lost accidentally? (See page 266.)

2. How is the Save Copy In command different from the Save As command, in terms of the files that are saved? (See page 266.)

3. Which session will be open after completing a Save Copy In operation: the original or the copy? How is this different from the Save As operation? (See page 266.)

4. What command can you use to save a session with a different sample rate or bit depth? (See page 267.)

5. What is the mixdown process used for? What Pro Tools command allows you to create an external recording of your session as a stereo mix? (See page 270.)

6. What are some considerations for bouncing audio in Pro Tools? How is the bounce affected by soloed or muted tracks? How is it affected by the Timeline selection? (See pages 270 and 271.)

7. What is meant by the term "bounce to tracks?" What is the typical process for creating a stereo bounce to tracks within a session? (See page 271.)

8. What command lets you mix your entire session directly to a hard drive? What file types are supported for the bounce file with this command? (See pages 273 and 275.)

9. What bit depth should you use when bouncing a session to disk if you plan to burn the file to CD without further processing? What sample rate should you use? (See page 276.)

10. How can you add audio files to iTunes for use in burning a CD? (See page 279.)

11. What are some of the options available when sharing a bounce file with SoundCloud? (See pages 281 and 282.)

12. What are some media options for burning your songs to CD after completing a bounce to disk? What are the differences between the writable CD formats? (See page 282.)

Recording Automation and Creating a Stereo Bounce

In this exercise tutorial, you will toggle the reverb effect on and off using Mute automation on the Reverb track and bounce the mix to a stereo file.

Duration: 15 to 20 Minutes   **Media: DrumLoop.wav, Guitar.wav, 10_01.wav, 10_03.wav**

Getting Started

You will start by opening the Pro Tools session you created in Exercise 7. If that session is not available, use the Ex07.ptxt session template in the Completed Exercises folder on the DVD.

To create the session:

1. Launch Pro Tools and open the session you created in Exercise 7.

2. Choose FILE > SAVE AS and name your session Exercise8-YourName.

Recording Automation

In this part of the exercise, you will enable mute automation for the session and place the Reverb track into Write automation mode. You will then record automation during playback, toggling the mute state on and off for the Reverb track.

To prepare the track for automation:

1. Press CTRL+= (Windows) or COMMAND+= (Mac) to activate the Edit window.

2. Choose WINDOW > AUTOMATION to open the Automation window.

3. If needed, click on the **MUTE** button in the Automation window to enable mute automation for the session. The button will be lit red when enabled.

Figure EX8.1
Mute automation enabled in the Automation window

4. Close the Automation window when finished.

5. Click the **MUTE** button (**M**) on the Reverb track to mute it at the session start.

6. Using the track's Automation Mode selector, put the Reverb track into Write automation mode.

Figure EX8.2
Automation Mode selector on the Reverb track set to Write mode

7. Press **ENTER** (Windows) or **RETURN** (Mac) to return to the session start.

In the next set of steps, you will be muting/unmuting the track on the fly during playback. Estimate the timing visually and by ear—your timing does not need to be precise.

To record mute automation:

1. Begin playback, keeping the track muted for Bars 1 and 2.

2. As the playback cursor crosses Bar 3 Beat 1, **UNMUTE** the Reverb track. You will hear the reverb effect kick in.

3. At Bar 5 Beat 1, **MUTE** the Reverb track again. The reverb effect will be silenced.

4. At Bar 7 Beat 1, **UNMUTE** the Reverb track. The reverb effect will be audible again.

5. Allow playback to continue through the end of the vocals and then press the **SPACE BAR** to stop playback. If needed, you can place the track back into Write mode and try the automation pass again.

6. When finished, set the **AUTOMATION MODE** selector for the Reverb track back to Read mode.

Bouncing to Disk

In this part of the exercise, you will use the Bounce to Disk function to create a stereo file from your session mix.

To bounce the session to a stereo file:

1. Using the Grabber tool, click on the DrumLoop clip on the Drums track to create a selection from 1|1|000 to 10|1|000.

2. Choose FILE > BOUNCE TO > DISK to open the Bounce dialog box.

3. Select the following options for your bounce:
   - File Type: WAV
   - Format: Interleaved
   - Bit Depth: 16 Bit
   - Sample Rate: 44.1 kHz

4. Leave the other options set to their defaults and click the BOUNCE button. A save dialog box will appear.

5. Name the file YourName-Exercise8.wav and save it to an appropriate location on your system. (Note that bounces save in your session's Audio Files folder by default; you may want to navigate up one level, at a minimum, to save it inside your session folder.)

Finishing Up

Congratulations! Over the course of these exercises, you have created a session from scratch, imported and edited audio, added effects, recorded automation, and bounced the result to a stereo file.

1. When your bounce completes, save your session and quit Pro Tools.

2. Verify the location of your bounced file. In classroom settings, your instructor may require that you copy this file and/or your session folder to a CD-R, flash drive, or shared network location to turn in.

For more hands-on experience, see the Music Hands-On Project and the Post Hands-On Project in Section III of this book.

Hands-On Projects

OVERVIEW

Part III of this course includes two projects that allow you to work with pre-recorded sessions to experiment with Audio, MIDI, and Video files. Throughout this part, you will apply many of the concepts that you learned in Parts I and II of this book. The goal of the projects is to illustrate the concepts discussed earlier in the book using straightforward, practical workflows. The projects also include examples of more advanced functionality to broaden your understanding of Pro Tools in the music and post-production environments.

COMPONENTS

OVERVIEW   Project Introduction and Setup

PROJECT 1   Music Hands-On Project

PROJECT 2   Post Hands-On Project

Project Introduction and Setup

The following pages describe the two hands-on projects included in this course and provide setup instructions for the work you will be doing. Included is a description of Pro Tools system requirements and instructions for installing the media files from the DVD for use in the projects.

Getting to Know the Projects

The projects that you will complete are real-world sessions provided in incomplete form. This part of the coursework includes two projects, one from a music production workflow and one from a video post-production workflow. While these projects remain focused on the core set of Pro Tools functions described in the first two parts of the book, you will find that the workflows occasionally introduce concepts that have not been covered. (These concepts are discussed in later courses.)

Project 1

Project 1, the Music Hands-On Project, is a one-minute segment of a song by Ballet Mechanique. The session consists of 10 tracks in rough form. To complete this project, you will add Audio and Instrument tracks, add drums using the Xpand![2] and Boom plug-ins, import audio and MIDI, and add loops and effects processing to polish the mix.

Project 2

Project 2, the Post Hands-On Project, is a 45-second commercial spot for Glad Trash Bags consisting of 20 tracks in rough form. To complete this project, you will import video footage as a QuickTime movie, import additional music and sound effects files, make various improvements and enhancements to the audio, replace the music bed, and add effects processing to polish the mix.

Pro Tools System Requirements

To complete these projects, you will need a qualified audio interface and computer with Pro Tools 10 software installed. Many parts of the projects can be completed using earlier Pro Tools versions with slight modifications in various steps; however, to complete the projects as written, you will need current software. Some menu commands, preference options, dialog boxes, and user interface features may vary or be unavailable on older systems.

Tip: Project write-ups for earlier versions of Pro Tools are included as PDF files on the DVD supplied with this book.

Installing Project Session Files

Before you begin work on the projects, you will need to install the project files on an available hard drive. The project files are provided on the DVD and include session templates, audio files, MIDI files, and other media files that you will need to complete the projects.

System Requirements for Project Sessions

The projects are designed to be completed using Pro Tools 10 software with a qualified audio interface. Users running Pro Tools 10 software using built-in audio on Mac computers (Core Audio) or third-party audio interfaces that support Core Audio (Mac) or ASIO (Windows) drivers should be able to complete the projects as written; however, the projects have not been tested with these configurations. The projects can also be completed using any current Pro Tools system with Pro Tools HD 10 software, although certain steps may vary slightly.

See Lesson 1 for a description of qualified interfaces or check the Avid website for qualified products (www.avid.com/compatibility).

You will need space available on your destination drive for the session files and related media. If possible, select a hard drive that is separate from your system drive to use as the destination for the session files.

The minimum recommended disk space for completing both projects is 1 GB:

- 250 MB for the Music project session files
- 500 MB for the Post project session files
- 250 MB available for recording and additional processing

To check the available space on your selected drive, do the following:

- In Windows, click on the **START** icon in the lower left and select **COMPUTER** to view information about the available drives.
- On a Mac, click on the selected drive icon from the desktop and choose **FILE > GET INFO** to display the Information window for the drive.

Installation Instructions for Session Files

To install the project session files and related media, copy the materials from the DVD to your selected hard drive:

1. Insert the DVD and open it to view the included files and folders.

2. Open the **HANDS-ON PROJECTS** folder.

3. Copy the **MUSIC HANDS-ON PROJECT** and the **POST HANDS-ON PROJECT** folders from the DVD to your selected hard drive.

4. Close the DVD window when finished copying.

Music Hands-On Project

In this project, you will complete a one-minute song snippet. To complete this project, you will add Audio and Instrument tracks, add drums using the Xpand!^{2} and Boom plug-ins, import audio and MIDI, and add loops and effects processing to polish the mix.

Duration: 90 Minutes

The media files for this project are provided courtesy of Eric Kuehnl of Ballet Mechanique:

WRITTEN BY: Eric Kuehnl and Zack Vieira

PERFORMED AND PRODUCED BY: Ballet Mechanique ©2008

Note: The audio files provided for this project are strictly for use to complete the exercises contained herein. No rights are granted to use the files or any portion thereof in any commercial or non-commercial production or performance.

Powering Up

To get started on this project, you will need to power up your system. It is important to power up properly to avoid problems that could possibly damage your equipment.

When using audio equipment, you should power up components in the order that the audio signal flows through them. The general process for powering up a Pro Tools 10.0 system is as follows (see your system documentation for powering up a system with HD or HDX hardware):

1. Power up external hard drives, if used.

2. Verify connections and power up audio/MIDI interfaces.

3. Start the computer.

4. Power up your monitoring system, if applicable.

5. Launch Pro Tools.

Refer to Lesson 2 for more details on powering up your system.

Opening the Music Project

In this section of the hands-on project, you will open the project and prepare your session for the work you will be doing.

The session you will use for this project was saved in a special format called a *session template*. When you open the session template, Pro Tools will create a new session based on the template, leaving the original template file unchanged. All existing tracks and audio files used in the template file will be duplicated in your new session.

Locate and Open the Session Template

Pro Tools provides a number of ways to open a session or session template. You can navigate to the session folder in your computer's Explorer or Finder window and double-click on the session or template file to open it. You can also locate and open the session or template file from the Workspace browser.

Locate and open the Music session template:

1. From the desktop, navigate to your copy of the session template using an Explorer window (Windows) or a Finder window (Mac). The template file is named *Music Project PT10.ptxt*.

Or

Locate the session template using the Workspace browser:

a. Choose WINDOW > WORKSPACE.

b. Click the FIND icon (magnifying glass) to activate a search.

c. Type **Music Project PT10** in the Name field.

d. Select SESSION FILE TEMPLATE from the Kind pop-up menu.

e. Click the SEARCH button. After a few moments the session template will display in the lower area of the Workspace browser.

2. Double-click on the template file to open it.

3. In the resulting New Session dialog box, select the defaults for the audio file type (.wav), bit depth (24 bit), and sample rate (44.1 kHz) and click **OK**.

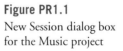

Figure PR1.1
New Session dialog box
for the Music project

4. Select a save location for the new session, rename the session if desired (for example, add a dash and your initials at the end of the file name), and click **SAVE**.

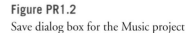

Figure PR1.2
Save dialog box for the Music project

Refer to Lesson 3 for additional information on locating and opening sessions.

Orient the Session Windows

When the session opens, you will see the Edit window displayed on your screen. You will use this window for much of the arranging and editing you do in this project. You will also use the Mix window, the Transport window, and the Score Editor window. As you work, you may need to reposition and resize the windows to maximize your efficiency.

You can use the following steps to create a basic starting point, or you can position and size the windows as you go.

Set a starting position and size for the windows:

1. If you used the Workspace browser to open the session, bring it to the front and close it. (Choose **WINDOW > WORKSPACE** or press **ALT+;** (Windows) or **OPTION+;** (Mac) to view the Workspace browser; then repeat the action to close the window.)

2. Open both the Mix window (**WINDOW > MIX**) and the Transport window (**WINDOW > TRANSPORT**).

3. Press **CTRL+=** (Windows) or **COMMAND+=** (Mac) to toggle to the Edit window and bring it to the front.

4. Choose **WINDOW > ARRANGE > CASCADE** to arrange the Mix and Edit windows in a cascading fashion. (Alternatively, you can maximize each window as you open them for full-screen views.)

5. Position the Transport window where it will least interfere with your work. Try the top or bottom of the screen. Figure PR1.3 shows the window layout after positioning the Transport window.

The 10 tracks in the session are displayed horizontally (left to right) in the Mix window and vertically (top to bottom) in the Edit window. From time to time, you might need to scroll each window and/or reposition the Transport window to view and work with a particular track.

Set the Preferences

This project requires certain Preference settings. Before continuing, you will need to verify the Zoom Toggle Preference settings for your session. You will also need to ensure that the Preference for Timeline Insertion/Play Start Marker Follows Playback is off. Although you can change this setting in the Preferences dialog box, Pro Tools also makes it available via a button in the Edit window.

Tip: Some of the Preferences settings on older systems may vary. Users on systems prior to Pro Tools 8.0 should use those settings that are applicable.

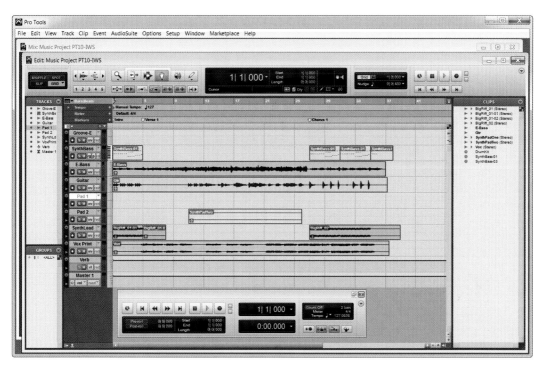

Figure PR1.3
Session windows oriented for the start of the project

Check Preferences settings:

1. Choose **SETUP > PREFERENCES**. The Preferences dialog box will open.

2. Click on the **EDITING** tab.

3. In the **ZOOM TOGGLE** section of the Editing tab, select the following settings:

   • Verify that both **VERTICAL MIDI ZOOM** and **HORIZONTAL ZOOM** are set to Selection.

   • Verify that **REMOVE RANGE SELECTION AFTER ZOOMING IN** is unchecked.

   • Set **TRACK HEIGHT** to Jumbo.

   • Set **TRACK VIEW** to Waveform/Notes.

   • Verify that **ZOOM TOGGLE FOLLOWS EDIT SELECTION** is unchecked.

Figure PR1.4
Preference settings under the Editing tab

4. Click **OK** to close the Preferences dialog box.

- Verify that the **INSERTION FOLLOWS PLAYBACK** button is off (unlit) in the Edit window toolbar.

Figure PR1.5
Insertion Follows Playback button in the Edit window

Connect Monitoring Devices

If you have a monitoring system connected to the left and right outputs of your audio interface, you will use that to listen to the session playback. If you do not have a monitoring system, you can listen to the session playback using headphones on a compatible interface. If your interface has an available headphone jack, plug in your headphones and test the playback level.

Creating New Tracks

In this section of the project, you will create the new tracks needed for the session. Additional details on the commands and processes used in this section can be found in Lesson 3.

Create and Name Tracks

You will need to create two new tracks for the session. Both tracks will play back MIDI information using virtual instruments. When creating tracks, you will select the track type and format, based on how each track will be used. In this case, the tracks will be used for stereo virtual instruments, so you will create two stereo Instrument tracks.

Create new Instrument tracks:

1. If needed, activate the Edit window by clicking on it or choosing WINDOW > EDIT.

2. Choose TRACK > NEW. The New Tracks dialog box will open, displaying Mono, Audio Track, and Samples as default selections from left to right.

3. Type the number **2** into the number field. This will create two tracks.

4. Click on the TRACK FORMAT pop-up menu and choose STEREO.

5. Click on the TRACK TYPE pop-up menu and choose INSTRUMENT TRACK.

6. Click CREATE. The new tracks will be added to the session.

Figure PR1.6
Creating the new tracks for your session

Name and reposition your new tracks:

1. Double-click on the nameplate of the first Instrument track (Inst 1) to open the Track Name dialog box.

2. Type **DRUMS** in the Name the Track field.

3. Add comments to help identify the track function, such as "Instrument – Xpand2."

Figure PR1.7
Naming the Drums track

4. Click the **NEXT** button. You will see Inst 2 displayed.

5. Type **BOOM** in the Name the Track field and add comments, such as "Instrument – Boom."

6. Click **OK**. The tracks will display with their new names.

7. With both tracks still selected, click on the nameplate of the Drums track and drag the tracks to the top of the Tracks display area in the Edit window (above the Groove-E track).

Figure PR1.8
New tracks positioned at the top of the Edit window

Save Your Session

After making any significant changes to a session, it is a good idea to save. Doing so will minimize any rework that you have to do in the event that something disrupts your progress (such as a power outage).

Save your work:

1. Choose FILE > SAVE to save your progress up to this point.

Working with MIDI Data

For this section of the project, you will add the Xpand!^{2} and Boom virtual instrument plug-ins to your Instrument tracks, add a MIDI clip from the Clip List, and create MIDI data using a variety of Edit tools.

Add a Virtual Instrument

In the previous section, you created an Instrument track and named it Drums. Now, you will add a virtual instrument to this track using the Xpand!^{2} plug-in. This will allow the Instrument track to play back audio based on MIDI data.

Insert Xpand!^{2} onto the Drums track:

1. Choose WINDOW > MIX or press CTRL+= (Windows) or COMMAND+= (Mac) to bring the Mix window forward and make it active.

2. In the Mix window, click on INSERT SELECTOR A on the Drums track.

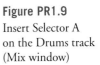

Figure PR1.9

Insert Selector A on the Drums track (Mix window)

3. Choose MULTICHANNEL PLUG-IN > INSTRUMENT > XPAND2 (STEREO) from the pop-up list. The Xpand!² plug-in window will appear on screen.

4. Click on the LIBRARIAN MENU (currently set to <factory default>) and choose 26 DRUMS > +02 POP KIT.

Figure PR1.10
Selecting a drum kit for the Xpand!² plug-in

5. Click on the CLOSE button in the upper-right corner (Windows) or upper-left corner (Mac) of the Xpand!² window to close the plug-in window.

Drag in a MIDI Clip

The session's Clip List includes a MIDI clip containing a previously recorded MIDI drum performance for this song. You will now bring it onto the Drums track.

Drag the DrumKit clip onto the Drums track:

1. Toggle back to the Edit window by choosing **WINDOW > EDIT** or pressing **CTRL+=** (Windows) or **COMMAND+=** (Mac).

2. With the **GRABBER** tool, select the DrumKit clip in the Clip List.

3. Drag the DrumKit clip from the Clip List onto the Drums track. Position the clip to start at the beginning of the session (1|1|000).

4. Solo the Drums track by clicking on the track's **SOLO** button (labeled "S") in the Edit window under the track name.

Shortcut: You can also toggle Solo mode on and off for any track containing the Edit cursor by pressing SHIFT+S on the computer's QWERTY keyboard.

5. Press the **SPACE BAR** to audition the MIDI drums. Press the **SPACE BAR** a second time to stop playback.

6. If necessary, adjust the clip placement to ensure that it begins at 1|1|000.

7. Unsolo the Drums track.

Add another Virtual Instrument

In the previous section, you added an Xpand![2] virtual instrument plug-in to the Drums track. Now, you will add a Boom virtual instrument plug-in to the Boom track.

Insert Boom onto the Boom track:

1. Choose **WINDOW > MIX** or press **CTRL+=** (Windows) or **COMMAND+=** (Mac) to again activate the Mix window.

2. Click on **INSERT SELECTOR A** on the Boom track.

3. Choose **MULTICHANNEL PLUG-IN > INSTRUMENT > BOOM (STEREO)** from the pop-up list. The Boom plug-in window will appear on screen.

Figure PR1.11
The Boom instrument plug-in

4. Click on the LIBRARIAN MENU and choose **086-100 > STANDART BEAT 090**.

5. Click on the CLOSE button in the upper-right corner (Windows) or upper-left corner (Mac) of the Boom window to close the plug-in window.

Create a MIDI Clip

Pro Tools provides a variety of ways to create MIDI data. In this section, you will use the Pencil tool to trigger playback of the Boom virtual instrument.

Draw MIDI data to control pattern playback of Boom:

1. Press CTRL+= (Windows) or COMMAND+= (Mac) to toggle back to the Edit window.

2. Click on the TRACK VIEW SELECTOR of the Boom track and choose NOTES from the pop-up menu.

Figure PR1.12
Clicking on the Track View selector and selecting Notes view

3. With the **Pencil** tool, draw a note beginning at 13|1|000 and extending to 36|1|000. You may need to trim the note to get the perfect length.

Tip: MIDI notes in the range of C3 through D#4 each trigger a different pattern in Boom. Click and hold the note to audition the current pattern; drag the note up or down to select a different pattern.

4. Press the **SPACE BAR** to audition the Boom drum pattern with your session. Press the **SPACE BAR** a second time to stop playback. If needed, adjust the note position to change the pattern and audition again until you're happy with the playback.

Edit MIDI Performance

Next you need to edit the SynthBass track to help it stand out more. To do this, you will edit the velocities of the MIDI events on SynthBass track. Because this track contains a single clip repeated multiple times, you can use a Pro Tools feature called *mirrored MIDI editing* to make the change. Any changes made to the one MIDI clip will be reflected in all of the other instances of the clip.

Verify the Part A assignment for Xpand![2]:

1. Press **CTRL+=** (Windows) or **COMMAND+=** (Mac) to toggle to the Mix window.

2. Locate the SynthBass track in the Mix window and click on the Xpand![2] plug-in on Insert A to open the plug-in window.

3. Verify that Part A displays the 022 Synth Basses > Hybrid Thump Bass part.

Figure PR1.13
Part A assignment in the Xpand!² plug-in

4. If needed, click on the Part A display and select 022 Synth Basses > Hybrid Thump Bass from the pop-up menu.

Figure PR1.14
Assigning Part A, if not previously assigned

5. Click on the **CLOSE** button in the upper-right corner (Windows) or upper-left corner (Mac) of the Xpand!² window to close the plug-in window.

6. Press **CTRL+=** (Windows) or **COMMAND+=** (Mac) to toggle back to the Edit window.

View the MIDI velocity stalks on the SynthBass track:

1. Locate the SynthBass track in the Edit window.

2. With the **GRABBER** tool, select the first SynthBass clip on the track.

3. Press **E** on your keyboard to activate Zoom Toggle. The selection will expand, filling the available space in the window, and the track will change to Notes view.

4. Click on the **TRACK VIEW SELECTOR** for the SynthBass track and choose **VELOCITY** from the pop-up menu. (Alternatively, you can display the Velocity controller lane for the track by clicking the Show/Hide Lanes button [triangle] at the head of the track.)

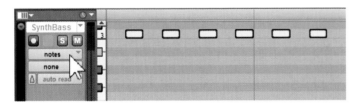

Figure PR1.15
Track View selector on the SynthBass track

The Velocity view displays velocity stalks associated with each MIDI note, representing the velocity value for that note. (The longer the stalk, the higher the velocity value.)

Edit the velocities for the first clip:

1. Enable Loop Playback mode by choosing **OPTIONS > LOOP PLAYBACK**.

2. Press the **SPACE BAR** to play back the selection and allow it to continue playing throughout this section.

3. Click the **MIRRORED MIDI EDITING** button at the top of the Edit window to enable mirrored MIDI editing. The button will turn blue when active.

Figure PR1.16
Click the Mirrored MIDI Editing button to enable it.

4. With the **GRABBER** tool, click any open area of the track to deselect all of the notes in the clip.

5. With the **GRABBER** tool still active, click on the diamond at the top of the second velocity stalk so that it becomes selected. The diamond will turn white, and the corresponding note will become highlighted.

6. Press and hold the **SHIFT** key while clicking on alternating velocity stalks so that every other velocity stalk is selected.

7. With alternating stalks selected, click any selected velocity stalk and drag it upward. This will increase the velocity of all highlighted notes, allowing the synth bass to cut through the mix.

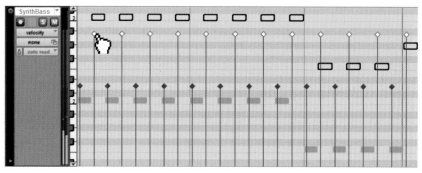

Figure PR1.17
Raising velocity stalks of selected notes

8. When you are satisfied with the result, stop playback.

9. Press **E** on your keyboard to return the session to its previous view and click the **MIRRORED MIDI EDITING** button a second time to disable mirrored MIDI editing.

Notice that the velocity changes that you made are reflected in subsequent occurrences of the SynthBass clip.

Save Work in Progress

Earlier, you created a copy of the session using the Save As command. As you complete each main portion of the project, you should save your work in progress. To do this, you will use the **SAVE** command from the File menu. This will not create a copy of your session; rather, it will save your changes to the existing session that is currently open.

Save your work:

1. Choose **FILE > SAVE** to save your progress up to this point.

Working with Audio Data

In the next section of the project, you will use a variety of techniques to manipulate audio clips.

Import an Audio File to a Track

As you've already seen, the Workspace browser is a great resource for locating, opening, and importing all sorts of media files. For this part of the project, you will use the Workspace browser to import an audio file containing an electronic loop for the song.

Locate the Groove-E audio file with the Workspace browser:

1. Choose **WINDOW > WORKSPACE** to open the Workspace browser.

Shortcut: You can also press ALT+; (Windows) or OPTION+; (Mac) to toggle the Workspace browser open and closed.

2. Click the **FIND** button (magnifying glass), if it's not already active, to reveal the search fields or click **RESET** to clear the previous search.

3. Type **Groove-E** in the Name field.

4. Select **AUDIO FILE** from the Kind pop-up menu.

Figure PR1.18
Selecting the file type from the Kind pop-up menu

5. Click **SEARCH**. After a moment, the Groove-E file will appear in the lower pane of the Workspace browser.

Drag the audio file to the Groove-E Audio track:

1. Reposition the Workspace browser, if necessary, so you can see both the Groove-E track in the Edit window and the Groove-E audio file in the Workspace browser.

2. Drag the **GROOVE-E** audio file from the Workspace browser onto the Groove-E track in the Edit window.

3. Use the **GRABBER** tool to drag the Groove-E file to start at 13|1|000.

Tip: Use the Bars|Beats Ruler as a reference while positioning the Groove-E file.

4. Close the Workspace browser to reduce on-screen clutter.

Use Clip Looping

Now that you've imported the audio file, it's time to clean it up and loop it.

Clean up the audio file using the Trim tool:

1. Solo the Groove-E track.

2. With the **TRIM** tool, trim the end of the clip to 17|1|000. This will make the clip exactly four bars long.

3. With the **GRABBER** tool, select the clip.

4. With Loop Playback enabled, press the **SPACE BAR** to audition the clip and ensure that it loops smoothly.

5. Press the **SPACE BAR** again to stop playback and take the track out of Solo mode.

Loop the clip:

1. With the Groove-E clip still selected, choose **CLIP > LOOP**. The Clip Looping dialog box will appear on screen.

2. Select the **LOOP LENGTH** option and type **24|0|000** in the corresponding field to extend the loop to 24 bars.

Figure PR1.19
The Clip Looping dialog box

3. Click **OK**.

The clip will now display a looped arrow at the bottom, indicating that it is a looped clip. It has been extended out to 24 bars in length.

Import a Clip Group to a Track

For this part of the project, we'll return to the Workspace browser to import a clip group. A clip group can be thought of as simply a collection of individual clips grouped together to look and act as a single, larger clip.

Locate the SynthPads clip group with the Workspace browser:

1. Choose **WINDOW > WORKSPACE** to open the Workspace browser.

2. Click the **FIND** button (magnifying glass) if it's not already active or click **RESET** to clear the previous search.

3. Type **SynthPads** in the Name field.

4. Select **CLIP GROUP FILE** from the Kind pop-up menu.

5. Click **SEARCH**. After a moment, the SynthPads clip group file will appear in the lower pane of the Workspace browser.

Drag the clip group to the Pad 1 and Pad 2 Audio tracks:

1. Reposition the Workspace browser, if necessary, so you can see both the Pad 1 and Pad 2 tracks in the Edit window and the SynthPads clip group in the Workspace browser.

2. Drag the SynthPads file from the Workspace browser onto the Pad tracks in the Edit window.

3. Use the **GRABBER** tool to drag the SynthPads file to the session start.

4. Close the Workspace browser to reduce on-screen clutter.

Insert Time

For this part of the project, we're going to add a four-bar intro to the song.

Select the location to insert time at the beginning of the song:

1. Press **ENTER** (Windows) or **RETURN** (Mac) to set the Edit Selection Start to 1|1|000.

2. In the Edit Selection Length field at the top of the Edit window, enter **4|0|000**:

- Click in the first field to activate it and type **4**. The remaining fields will zero out.

- Press **ENTER** (Windows) or **RETURN** (Mac) to confirm the entry.

Figure PR1.20
Entering the Edit Selection Length values

You now have a four-bar selection spanning from Bar 1 to Bar 5.

Use the Insert Time operation to add the selected amount of time:

1. Choose **EVENT > TIME OPERATIONS > INSERT TIME**. The Time Operations window will appear on screen.

2. Verify that the Start, End, and Length times are correct. The values should be the following:

- **START:** 1|1|000

- **END:** 5|1|000

- **LENGTH:** 4|0|000

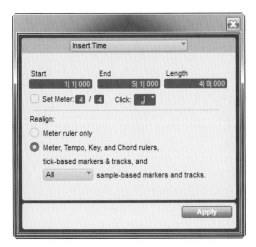

Figure PR1.21
The Time Operations window

3. Click **APPLY**. Four bars will be inserted into the session.

4. Close the Time Operations window.

Edit the SynthLead track:

1. If necessary, scroll the Edit window so that the SynthLead track is visible on screen.

2. Click the **SPOT** button in the upper-left corner of the Edit window to activate Spot mode.

3. While holding down **ALT** (Windows) or **OPTION** (Mac), use the **GRABBER** tool to click in the BigRiff_02 clip at the end of the track. The Spot dialog box will open.

4. Set the Time Scale to **BARS|BEATS**.

5. In the Start field, type **1|1|000** and click **OK**. A copy of the clip will move to the beginning of the session.

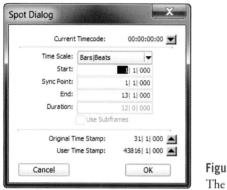

Figure PR1.22
The Spot dialog box

6. Click the **GRID** button to reactivate Grid mode.

Listen to the edit:

1. Press **ENTER** (Windows) or **RETURN** (Mac) to go to the beginning of the session.

2. Press the **SPACE BAR** to begin playback.

You should now hear a four-bar intro featuring only the SynthLead track.

Save Work in Progress

You have now imported the additional audio files and completed the editing tasks needed for the session. You should take this opportunity to save your work.

Save your work:

1. Choose **FILE > SAVE** to save your progress up to this point.

Mixing in Pro Tools

Now that the editing is complete, you will use some of the mixing features in Pro Tools to add real-time processing to the project and blend the sound elements together. You will complete this work using the Mix window.

Add EQ

The bass guitar track has a little too much low end, making it difficult to blend with the drums and synth bass. To fix the problem, you will use the EQ III plug-in to roll off some of the low end.

Insert the 1-Band EQ III plug-in on the E-Bass track:

1. Choose **WINDOW > MIX** or press **CTRL+=** (Windows) or **COMMAND+=** (Mac) to activate the Mix window.

2. Click on **INSERT SELECTOR B** of the E-Bass track and choose **PLUG-IN > EQ > EQ 3 1-BAND (MONO)** from the pop-up menu. The 1-Band EQ III plug-in window will appear.

3. In the 1-Band EQ III plug-in window, select the **HIGH-PASS** filter type.

Figure PR1.23
Using the High-Pass filter in the EQ III plug-in window

Adjust the EQ to roll off the low end:

1. Solo the E-Bass track by clicking on the **SOLO (S)** button just above the Volume Fader in the Mix window.

2. Open the Memory Locations window (**WINDOW > MEMORY LOCATIONS**) and click on **VERSE 1** to place the insertion point at the beginning of the first verse.

Tip: If needed, you can resize the Memory Locations window by clicking on any window border and dragging with the double-headed arrow.

3. Press the **SPACE BAR** to initiate playback.

4. In the 1-Band EQ III plug-in window, drag the gray ball to the left or right until you hear the desired reduction in low frequencies when playing back (try around 80 to 120 Hz).

5. Unsolo the E-Bass track and press the **SPACE BAR** to stop playback.

6. Close the EQ III plug-in window to reduce on-screen clutter.

Enhance the Guitar

In this part of the project, you will use the Eleven Free plug-in to add guitar amp and speaker cabinet emulation to the Guitar track.

Insert the Eleven Free plug-in on the Guitar track:

1. Click on **INSERT SELECTOR A** of the Guitar track and choose **PLUG-IN > HARMONIC > ELEVEN FREE (MONO)** from the pop-up menu. The Eleven Free plug-in window will appear.

2. In the Eleven Free plug-in window, select the **DC MODERN OVERDRIVE** amp and the **4x12 GREEN 25W** cabinet by clicking on the **AMP TYPE** and **CABINET TYPE** display screens, respectively, and selecting models for each from the pop-up menus.

Figure PR1.24
Selecting an amp type in the Eleven Free plug-in

Adjust the Eleven Free settings:

1. Solo the Guitar track by clicking on the **SOLO (S)** button just above the Volume Fader in the Mix window.

2. Click on **INTRO** in the Memory Locations window to place the insertion point at the beginning of the intro.

3. Press the **SPACE BAR** to initiate playback.

4. In the Eleven Free plug-in window, adjust the **GAIN** setting to achieve a rich, distorted lead sound (try around 10).

5. Adjust the other Eleven Free settings to taste.

6. Unsolo the Guitar track and press the **SPACE BAR** to stop playback.

7. Close the Eleven Free plug-in window and the Memory Locations window to reduce on-screen clutter.

Add Reverb

Next, you will add some reverb to the Guitar track to help it fit into the rest of the mix. This project already includes an Auxiliary track that was previously set up with its input assigned to Bus 1 (Verb) and a D-Verb plug-in configured. Additionally, Send A on the Guitar track has been assigned to Bus 1 (Verb). Therefore, all you will need to do is increase the level of the send on the Guitar track to add reverb to the mix.

Increase the Send A level on the Guitar track:

1. Click on **SEND ASSIGNMENT A** on the Guitar track. The Send A window will appear.

2. Click the **SOLO (S)** button in the Send A window to solo the Guitar track.

3. Press the **SPACE BAR** to begin playback.

4. While listening to the track, raise the level on the Send Fader to introduce reverb. (Try between –10 and –6 dB.)

   The reverb will play back while the Guitar track is soloed because the Reverb track is set to Solo Safe mode. Solo Safe mode is commonly used on Auxiliary tracks to prevent them from being muted when another track is soloed.

Tip: You can place a track in Solo Safe mode by CTRL-CLICKING (Windows) or COMMAND-CLICKING (Mac) on the Solo button in the Edit or Mix window.

Figure PR1.25
The Send A window

AVI►
In the Avid Learning Series   More information on Solo Safe mode can be found in the Pro Tools 110 course.

5. When you are satisfied with the results, press the **SPACE BAR** to stop playback.

6. Press the **SOLO (S)** button to take the track out of Solo mode and then close the Send A window.

Save Work in Progress

Before continuing with work on your session mix, you should take this opportunity to save your work.

Save your work:

1. Choose **FILE > SAVE** to save your progress up to this point.

Mix the Project

The project is now ready for mixing to blend all of the tracks together. You will use the Volume Faders and Pan Sliders to create a stereo mix.

Getting Started

To get started, you will determine the contribution of each track to the overall mix by soloing each track individually. Tracks such as the Verb track only process audio that passes through them and cannot be isolated by soloing. Such tracks can be muted and unmuted to identify their contribution to the mix.

Balance the main tracks:

1. Click the **RETURN TO ZERO** button in the Transport window to place the insertion point at the beginning of the Timeline.

Figure PR1.26
Transport window

2. Press the **SPACE BAR** to begin playback.

3. Solo each Audio and Instrument track for a few moments by clicking the Solo button above the Volume Fader in the Mix window.

   a. Consider how the track contributes to the overall mix and make adjustments as needed using the Volume Fader.

   b. When you are satisfied with the results, take the track out of Solo mode and move on to the next track.

4. Use the Pan knobs on the mono tracks to give some stereo separation to your mix. Offset panning to the left or right, using your discretion, to help distinguish each track in the mix.

5. When you are finished, press the **SPACE BAR** again to stop playback.

Adjust the effects tracks:

1. Press the SPACE BAR to begin playback.

2. Toggle Mute on and off for the Verb track to determine the track's contribution to the mix.

3. Make adjustments to the effects track levels as desired.

4. When you are finished, press the SPACE BAR again to stop playback.

Completing the Mix

Complete this portion of the project using your discretion, experimenting until you are happy with the results.

Save Work in Progress

You have now created a complete mix for your project. You should take this opportunity to save your work.

Save your work:

1. Choose FILE > SAVE to save your progress up to this point.

Finishing Your Work

For this part of the project, you will use the Score Editor to print a score for the SynthBass track. You will then create a stereo bounce of your session mix. Lastly, you will archive your work. This process will allow you to create a backup of your work without consuming excess disk space with unnecessary files.

Print the Score

It is often useful to create a score of a finished session. This might be used as a reference for live performance of the song. It could also be sent for copyright submission or to a publisher for licensing.

Open the Score Editor and modify the score setup:

1. Press ENTER (Windows) or RETURN (Mac) to ensure that the insertion point is located at the beginning of the Timeline.

2. Choose WINDOW > SCORE EDITOR to open the Score Editor window.

Figure PR1.27
Score Editor window

3. Right-click in the Score Editor and select **SCORE SETUP** or choose **FILE > SCORE SETUP** to open the Score Setup window.

4. In the Score Setup window, enter a title for the composition in the Title field and enter your name in the Composer field.

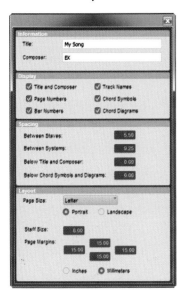

Figure PR1.28
Score Setup window

5. Close the Score Setup window.

Determine which tracks will be included in the score:

1. If it is not already visible, display the Track List by clicking the Show/Hide Track List button at the bottom left of the Score Editor.

2. Show or hide tracks as desired by clicking on the **TRACK SHOW/HIDE** icon to the left of each track name in the Track List. The icon will turn light gray to indicate a hidden track.

    For this project, hide the Drums and Boom tracks, so that only the SynthBass track is shown in the Score Editor.

Figure PR1.29
Track List after hiding the Drums and Boom tracks

Configure the staff and print the score:

1. Right-click in the Score Editor and select **NOTATION DISPLAY TRACK SETTINGS** from the pop-up menu or double-click on a **CLEF** symbol on the SynthBass track. The Notation Display Track Settings dialog box will open.

2. With the track set to SynthBass, click on the **CLEF** pop-up menu and change it from Grand Staff to Bass Clef.

Figure PR1.30
Setting the clef for the SynthBass track

3. Close the dialog box.

4. Right-click in the Score Editor again and choose **PRINT SCORE** or choose **FILE > PRINT SCORE**. The Print dialog box will open.

5. Configure the Print dialog settings as desired and click **PRINT** to print the score.

6. When you are finished, close the Score Editor window.

Add Maxim

Next, you will add a Maxim plug-in to the Master Fader. Maxim is a type of plug-in commonly referred to as an *ultra-maximizer*. The purpose of this type of plug-in is to maximize the overall level of the mix, while simultaneously limiting peaks to prevent clipping. The end result is a mix that sounds louder while preserving the overall quality of the mix.

Tip: Maxim performs "look-ahead" analysis, anticipating peaks in audio material and preserving attack transients during reduction. This makes Maxim more transparent and maintains the character of the original audio signal without clipping or distortion.

Insert the Maxim plug-in on the Master Fader:

1. In the Mix window, click on **INSERT SELECTOR A** of the Master 1 track and choose **MULTICHANNEL PLUG-IN > DYNAMICS > MAXIM (STEREO)**. The Maxim plug-in window will appear.

2. In the Maxim plug-in window, be sure that the Dither **ON** button is disabled (unlit). (You will insert a separate dither plug-in later.)

Figure PR1.31
The Maxim plug-in window

Adjust the Maxim settings to make the mix louder:

1. Open the Memory Locations window (WINDOW > MEMORY LOCATIONS) and click on CHORUS 1 to place the insertion point at the beginning of the chorus.

2. Press the SPACE BAR to initiate playback.

3. In the Maxim plug-in window, set the CEILING slider to –0.1 dB. This sets the maximum allowable level for the limiting function of Maxim.

4. While listening to the mix, adjust the THRESHOLD slider to achieve the desired volume. Adjusting the slider down increases the volume. A good starting point is around –3.0 dB.

5. When you're happy with the overall level of the mix, press the space bar to stop playback.

6. Close the Maxim window and the Memory Locations window to reduce on-screen clutter.

Add Dither

Next, you will make an external bounce of the finished project. The purpose of the bounce is to produce a CD-quality stereo audio file that you can burn to an audio CD from iTunes. For this, you will need to create a 16-bit audio file from your 24-bit session. To do so, you will need to add dither to the Master Fader. Dithering helps preserve the quality of audio during bit reduction, preventing quantization errors and LSB clipping.

Tip: As a rule of thumb, you should always add dither when bouncing to a lower bit depth.

Add dither to the Master Fader:

1. In the Mix window, click on INSERT SELECTOR B of the Master 1 track and choose MULTICHANNEL PLUG-IN > DITHER > POWR DITHER (STEREO). The POWr Dither plug-in window will appear on screen.

2. Choose the following settings in the POWr Dither plug-in window:

   - 16 bit
   - Noise Shaping Type 3

Figure PR1.32
The POWr Dither plug-in

3. Close the POWr Dither plug-in window.

Dither will now be added to your mix during playback.

Bounce the Song

For this part of the project, you will use the Bounce to Disk command to make a stereo file from your session and add it to your iTunes library.

Make a 16-bit stereo bounce of your session:

1. Choose **WINDOW > EDIT** or press **CTRL+=** (Windows) or **COMMAND+=** (Mac) to activate the Edit window.

2. With the **SELECTOR** tool, click anywhere in the session.

3. Press **ENTER** (Windows) or **RETURN** (Mac) to place the insertion point at the start of the session.

4. Press **CTRL+SHIFT+ENTER** (Windows) or **OPTION+SHIFT+RETURN** (Mac) to make a selection extending to the end of the session.

5. Choose **FILE > BOUNCE TO > DISK**. The Bounce dialog box will appear on screen.

6. Select the following settings in the Bounce dialog box:

   - **FILE TYPE:** WAV

   - **FORMAT:** Interleaved

   - **BIT DEPTH:** 16 bit

   - **SAMPLE RATE:** 44.1 kHz

   - **CONVERT AFTER BOUNCE:** Selected

   - **ADD TO ITUNES LIBRARY:** Checked (if you do not have iTunes installed, this option will not do anything)

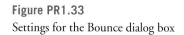

Figure PR1.33
Settings for the Bounce dialog box

7. Click **BOUNCE**. The Save Bounce As dialog box will appear on screen.

8. Select a location for the audio file and enter a name for the bounce.

9. Click **SAVE**. You will hear playback begin as Pro Tools creates a 16-bit
    stereo mix of your session. When the bounce completes, iTunes will
    launch, and your bounced file will appear in the iTunes music library.

Archive Your Work

Now that your project is complete, you will need to back it up for storage. On a
real-world project, you might also need to deliver the session to the client. Because
many files are associated with a session, something could get lost if the archival
process isn't completed properly. Fortunately, Pro Tools can help ensure that you
keep the files you need and remove the files you do not.

Note: The archival process will permanently remove any audio that is not currently
       being used in the session. This could limit your creative possibilities, should
       you need to revise some aspect of the session in the future. Perform this
       process only *after* the project is complete.

Remove Unused Material

To save disk space, you will first remove any audio files and clips that are no longer being used by the session. To remove unused audio files and clips, complete the following steps:

1. Click on the CLIP LIST POP-UP menu and choose SELECT > UNUSED. All of the clips that are not included on a Track Playlist will be selected.

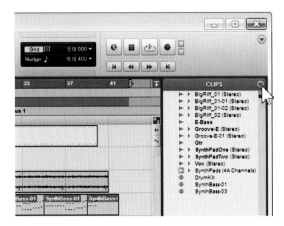

Figure PR1.34
Click the Clip List pop-up menu to select unused clips.

2. Click on the CLIP LIST POP-UP menu a second time and choose CLEAR. The Clear Clips dialog box will appear on screen.

3. Click REMOVE in the Clear Clips dialog box to remove the clips from your session. The audio files will be removed from the session without being deleted from the drive. If you later find that you need an audio file that has been removed, you can re-import it into your session.

Collect Session Files in a New Location

To save a copy of your session and all associated files, do the following:

1. Choose FILE > SAVE COPY IN. The Save Session Copy dialog box will appear on screen.

2. In the ITEMS TO COPY area, place a check next to ALL AUDIO FILES.

3. Click the OK button. A Save dialog box will appear.

4. Choose a directory to store the session copy and name the copy of the session. For backup and archive purposes, it is best to save to a drive other than the one used for the current session.

5. Click the SAVE button. Pro Tools will begin processing the save, copying the session file along with all of the audio files into the directory you chose.

6. Choose **FILE > CLOSE SESSION** to close the original session. If you are prompted to save, choose **OK** or **SAVE** to save your changes in the original session. (It will be saved with the unused material removed.)

Compact Your Session

You have one more step to complete your archive: compacting. Most clips in a session reference only a part of a larger audio recording. Because the copied session is now complete, it is safe to compact the session. Compacting is the process of removing the audio from a file that is not used by any clip. Hence, only the used portions of the audio files remain, reducing the amount of disk space being consumed.

To compact your project's audio files, do the following:

1. From the File menu, choose **OPEN SESSION**.

2. Navigate to the copy of your project that you created in the previous section; select the session file and click **OPEN**. A dialog box may appear, indicating that the original disk allocation cannot be used; click **NO** to avoid saving a report.

3. When the session opens, click on the **CLIP LIST POP-UP** menu and choose **SELECT > ALL**. All of the clips in the Clip List will be selected.

4. Click on the **CLIP LIST POP-UP** menu a second time and choose **COMPACT**. The Compact dialog box will appear on screen with a description of the compacting process.

5. Click **COMPACT** to compact the audio files. Pro Tools will begin modifying the files.

6. When you are finished, save your work by choosing **FILE > SAVE** and close your session by choosing **FILE > CLOSE SESSION**.

This concludes the Music Hands-On Project.

Post Hands-On Project

In this project, you will work with a 45-second commercial spot consisting of 20 tracks in rough form. To complete the project, you will import video footage as a QuickTime movie, import additional music and sound effects files, make various improvements and enhancements to the audio, and add effects processing to polish the mix.

Duration: 90 Minutes

The media files for this project are provided courtesy of Robert Campbell at One Union Recording:

- **CHIEF CREATIVE OFFICER:** Lisa Bennett
- **DIRECTOR OF PRODUCTION:** Frank Brooks
- **CREATIVE DIRECTOR:** Mike Andrews
- **COPYWRITER:** Brett Landry
- **ART DIRECTOR:** Dave Cuccinello
- **PRODUCER:** Bryan Holt
- **CLIENT:** Glad Trash Bags

Note: The audio and video files provided for this project are to be used only to complete the exercises contained herein. No rights are granted to use the files or any portion thereof in any commercial or non-commercial production or video.

Powering Up

To get started on this project, you will need to power up your system. It is important to power up properly to avoid problems that could possibly damage your equipment.

When using audio equipment, you should power up components in the order that the audio signal flows through them. The general process for powering up a Pro Tools system is as follows (see your system documentation for powering up a system with HD or HDX hardware):

1. Power up external hard drives, if used.

2. Verify connections and power up audio/MIDI interfaces.

3. Start the computer.

4. Power up your monitoring system, if applicable.

5. Launch Pro Tools.

Refer to Lesson 2 for more details on powering up your system.

Opening the Post Project

In this section of the hands-on project, you will open the Post project and prepare your session for the work you will be doing.

The session you will use for this project was saved in a special format called a *session template*. When you open the session template, Pro Tools will create a new session based on the template, leaving the original template file unchanged. All existing tracks and audio files used in the template file will be duplicated in your new session.

Locate and Open the Session

Pro Tools provides a number of ways to open a session or session template. You can navigate to the session folder in your Explorer or Finder window and double-click on the session or template file to open it. You can also locate and open the session or template file from the Workspace browser.

Locate and open the Post session template:

1. From the desktop, navigate to your copy of the session using an Explorer window (Windows) or a Finder window (Mac).

   - Or -

Locate the session using the Workspace browser:

a. Choose **WINDOW > WORKSPACE**.

b. Click the **FIND** icon (magnifying glass) to activate a search.

c. Type **Post Project PT10** in the Name field.

d. Select **SESSION FILE TEMPLATE** from the Kind pop-up menu.

e. Click the **SEARCH** button. After a few moments the session will display in the lower (green and white) area of the Workspace browser.

2. Double-click on the template file to open it.

3. In the resulting New Session dialog box, accept the default settings for file type (.wav), bit depth (24 bit), and sample rate (48 kHz) and click **OK**.

Figure PR2.1
New Session dialog box for the Post project

4. Select a save location for the new session, rename the session if desired (for example, add a dash and your initials at the end of the file name), and click **SAVE**.

Refer to Lesson 3 for additional information on locating and opening sessions.

Orient the Session Windows

When the session opens, you will see the Edit window displayed on your screen. You will use the Edit window for much of the recording and editing you do in this project. You will also be using the Mix window throughout the project. As you work, you will want to reposition and resize the windows to maximize your efficiency.

You can use the following steps at this point to create a basic starting point, or you can position and size the windows as you go.

Set a starting position and size for the windows:

1. Choose **WINDOW > MIX** to open the Mix window.

2. Press **CTRL+=** (Windows) or **COMMAND+=** (Mac) to toggle to the Edit window and bring it to the front.

3. Choose **WINDOW > ARRANGE > CASCADE** to arrange the Mix and Edit windows in a cascading fashion. (Alternatively, you can maximize each window for full-screen views.)

The 20 tracks in the session are displayed horizontally (left to right) in the Mix window and vertically (top to bottom) in the Edit window. From time to time, you might need to scroll each window and/or reposition the open windows to view and work with a particular track.

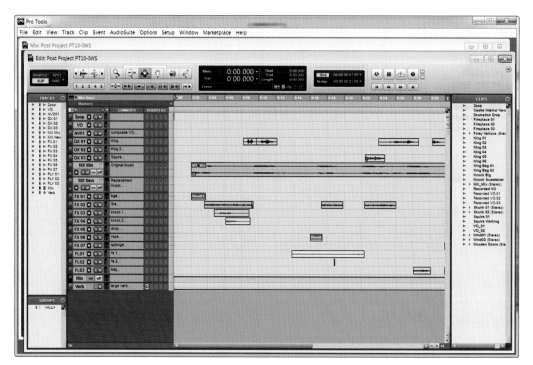

Figure PR2.2
Session windows oriented for the start of the project

Set the Preferences

For this project, you will need to configure certain Preference settings that affect the placement of the insertion point/selection during operation. Before continuing, make sure the following Preferences are set accordingly.

Tip: Some of the Preferences settings on older systems may vary. Users on systems prior to Pro Tools 8.0 should use those settings that are applicable.

Check Preferences settings:

1. Choose SETUP > PREFERENCES. The Preferences window will open.

2. Click on the OPERATION tab.

   ● Verify that TIMELINE INSERTION/PLAY START MARKER FOLLOWS PLAYBACK is unchecked.

   ● Verify that EDIT INSERTION FOLLOWS SCRUB/SHUTTLE is checked.

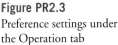

Figure PR2.3
Preference settings under the Operation tab

3. Click on the EDITING tab.

   ● Verify that EDIT SELECTION FOLLOWS CLIP LIST SELECTION is checked.

4. In the Zoom Toggle section of the Editing tab, select the following settings:

   ● Set both VERTICAL MIDI ZOOM and HORIZONTAL ZOOM to Selection.

   ● Verify that REMOVE RANGE SELECTION AFTER ZOOMING IN is unchecked.

   ● Set TRACK HEIGHT to Jumbo.

   ● Set TRACK VIEW to Waveform / Notes.

   ● Verify that ZOOM TOGGLE FOLLOWS EDIT SELECTION is unchecked.

Figure PR2.4
Preference settings under the Editing tab

5. Click **OK** to close the Preferences window.

Connect Monitoring Devices

If you have a monitoring system connected to the left and right outputs of your audio interface, you will use that to listen to the session playback. If you do not have a monitoring system, you can listen to the session playback using headphones on compatible audio interfaces. If your interface has an available headphone jack, plug in your headphones and test the playback level.

Creating New Tracks

In this section of the project, you will create a new track needed for the session. Additional details on the commands and processes used in this section can be found in Lesson 3.

Create and Name a Track

For this project, you will need to create one new track that you will use to edit a sound effect. When creating tracks, you should always select the track type and format based on how the tracks will be used. In this case, you will need to edit a stereo sound effect, so a stereo Audio track will be appropriate.

Create a stereo Audio track:

1. Click on the **FX 07** track nameplate toward the bottom of the Edit window to select the track. This will ensure that your new track will appear directly below FX 07, keeping all of the FX tracks together.

Tip: Pro Tools always places new tracks below the lowest selected track in the session. If no tracks are selected, Pro Tools places the new track(s) at the bottom of the session.

2. Choose **TRACK > NEW**. The New Tracks dialog box will open, displaying Mono, Audio Track, and Samples as default selections from left to right.

3. Click on the **TRACK FORMAT** selector and choose **STEREO** from the pop-up menu.

Figure PR2.5
Click the Track Format selector to create a stereo track

4. Click **CREATE** in the New Tracks dialog box. A new stereo track will be added to the session, beneath the FX 07 track.

5. Double-click on the track name (**AUDIO 1**) to open the Track Name dialog box.

6. Type **FX 08** in the Track Name field and add comments to help identify the track function, such as "Skunk FX."

7. Click **OK**. The track will display with its new name.

Figure PR2.6
Renaming the Audio track

Save Your Session

After making any significant changes to a session, it is a good idea to save your work. That way, if something should disrupt your progress (such as a power outage), you will not have to redo any of your work.

Save your work:

1. Choose FILE > SAVE to save your progress up to this point.

For more information on Save options, see Lessons 3 and 10.

Importing Media

Pro Tools provides many ways to import media into your session. (Refer to Lesson 5 for detailed information regarding importing media.) For this project, you will import a movie and background music using the Import command, and you will import sound effects using the Workspace browser.

Import a Movie

In this section, you will import a QuickTime movie and enhance it with music and sound effects.

Import GiftBasket.mov into your session:

1. Choose FILE > IMPORT > VIDEO. A dialog box will open on screen, prompting you to choose a video file.

2. Navigate to the VIDEO FILES folder (found within the Post Hands-On Project folder that you copied earlier).

Select Video File To Import:

Look in: Video Files

Recent Places

Desktop

GiftBasket.mov

Libraries

Computer

Network

File name:

Files of type: All Files (*.*)

Open

Cancel

Figure PR2.7
Dialog box for importing a video file

3. Select **GiftBasket.mov** and click **Open**. The Video Import Options dialog box will appear.

4. Uncheck the **Import Audio from File** option in the dialog box, if it is selected.

5. Select **Session Start** in the Location menu and click **OK**. The movie will be imported into your session and will open in a Video window. A Video track will also display at the top of the Edit window.

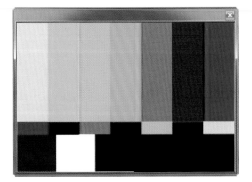

Figure PR2.8
The Video window as displayed after importing GiftBasket.mov

Tip: If you find that the Video window consumes too much space on screen, you can resize it. Click and drag near any edge to resize the window.

View the movie clip (optional):

1. Press ENTER (Windows) or RETURN (Mac) to move the insertion point to the beginning of the Timeline.

2. Press the SPACE BAR to begin playback. The movie clip will play back in time with the audio in the session.

3. When the clip ends, press the SPACE BAR again to stop playback. The insertion point will return to the beginning of the Timeline.

Figure PR2.9
The Video window during playback

Import Files to the Clip List

Next, you will need to import some additional music files into your session and place them in the Clip List for later use.

Import music audio files to the Clip List:

1. Choose FILE > IMPORT > AUDIO.

2. In the Import Audio dialog box, navigate to the NEW MUSIC folder (found within the Post Hands-On Project folder that you copied earlier).

3. Select the four NEW MUSIC files (click on the first and then Shift-click on the last to select them all) and click the ADD FILES button (ADD button on Mac). The files will be added to the Clips to Import area of the dialog box.

Figure PR2.10
The Import Audio dialog box as it appears after clicking Add Files

4. Click **Done**. The Audio Import Options dialog box will appear.

5. In the dialog box, select **Clip List** for the destination and click **OK**. The clips New Music 1 (Stereo) and New Music 2 (Stereo) will be imported and will display in your Clip List.

Import Files from the Workspace Browser

For this part of the project, you will use the Workspace browser to import a clip group containing sound effects. A clip group is simply a collection of individual clips grouped together to look and act as a single, larger clip.

In the Avid
Learning Series
Clip groups are covered in greater detail in the Pro Tools 110 course.

All of the sound effects have already been edited outside of the current session and grouped together as a single clip group. You will need to drag the clip group from the Workspace browser onto a stereo Audio track; the clip group will automatically be imported into your session.

Locate the clip group file called "Skunk Group" with the Workspace browser:

1. Choose WINDOW > WORKSPACE to open the Workspace browser. Reposition/resize the windows as necessary so that the Workspace browser is not obscured by the Video window.

Shortcut: You can also press ALT+; (Windows) or OPTION+; (Mac) to toggle the Workspace browser open and closed.

2. Click the FIND button (magnifying glass), if it is not already active, to reveal the search fields or click RESET to clear the previous search.

3. Type **Skunk Group** in the NAME field.

4. Select CLIP GROUP FILE from the Kind pop-up menu. Make sure that a check appears next to the disk volume that contains the Post Hands-On Project folder.

5. Click SEARCH. After a moment, the Skunk Group file will appear in the lower pane of the Workspace browser.

Drag the clip group to the FX 08 stereo Audio track:

1. Reposition the Workspace browser, if necessary, so you can see both the FX 08 track in the Edit window and the Skunk Group file in the Workspace browser.

2. Drag the SKUNK GROUP file onto the FX 08 track in the Edit window.

3. If necessary, use the GRABBER tool to drag the Skunk Group to the start of the session.

4. Close the Workspace browser to minimize on-screen clutter.

Audition the changes (optional):

1. If necessary, press ENTER (Windows) or RETURN (Mac) to move the insertion point to the beginning of the Timeline.

2. Press the SPACE BAR to begin playback. The movie clip will play back with the existing audio and newly added effects.

3. When the clip ends, press the SPACE BAR again to stop playback. The insertion point will return to the beginning of the Timeline.

Save Work in Progress

Now that you have imported the movie and audio files for the project, you should take the opportunity to save your work.

Save your work:

1. Choose FILE > SAVE to save your progress up to this point.

Editing in Pro Tools

Next, you will do some editing on your project. In the following sections, you will use the Zoomer, Trim, and Scrubber tools to modify the project so that it sounds more complete.

Review the Project

Before you begin editing this project, you should familiarize yourself with the progression of the movie. To do so, you can navigate along the Timeline to get a feel for the movie's transitional points.

Because Pro Tools provides a nonlinear editing environment, you can instantly jump to any point on the Timeline at any time. You can use the Selector tool to click at different points within the project and use the Video window to view the action based on the location of the playback cursor.

Experiment with the Selector tool to update the Video window:

■ Click on various parts of the Video track with the SELECTOR tool to get a rough idea where the main action transitions fall on the Timeline. Use the SPACE BAR to control playback.

■ Experiment with making selections on the Video track and the Audio tracks; try to select a scene from beginning to end and play it back.

Tip: The Video window will always reflect the start time of a Timeline selection. When you are making a selection based on the Video track, you may find it useful to locate the end point first and select backward to the start.

Add Sound Effects

The session is still missing some sound effects. During this part of the project, you will use various editing techniques to add the missing material. Refer to Lesson 6 as needed for details on editing techniques.

Add Wind

The first sound effect that you will add occurs at the point in the movie when the squire walks through the castle. You will need to add the sound of wind to match the action using the Wind02 sound effect in your Clip List.

Place the Wind02 clip onto the FX 01 track and spot it to the proper location:

1. Identify the FX 01 track on screen and make sure it is visible.

2. Select the **WIND02** clip in the Clip List (Edit window). If necessary, use the scroll bar to scroll the list until the clip is visible.

3. Drag the **WIND02** clip from the Clip List to any open space on the FX 01 track.

4. Click the **SPOT** button in the upper-left corner of the Edit window to activate Spot mode. (You might have to reposition the Video window first.)

5. With the **GRABBER** tool, click on the clip that you just placed on the FX 01 track. The Spot dialog box will open.

Figure PR2.11
The Spot dialog box

6. If needed, set the Time Scale to **MIN:SECS**.

7. In the Start field, type **0:13.680** (Min:Sec) and click **OK**. The clip will move to the start time you typed.

8. Click the **SLIP** button to return to Slip mode.

Audition the sound effect:

1. Activate Loop Playback by choosing **OPTIONS > LOOP PLAYBACK**. The Play button will display a looping arrow to indicate Loop Playback mode.

2. With the clip still selected, press the **SPACE BAR** to play back the sound effect with the picture. During playback, you can solo the FX 01 track by clicking the **S** button under the track name.

Tip: Pro Tools also lets you toggle Solo mode on and off for any track containing the Edit cursor by pressing SHIFT+S on the computer's QWERTY keyboard.

3. When you are finished, press the **SPACE BAR** again to stop playback and click the **S** button if necessary to take the track out of Solo mode.

Edit Wind

The wind you've added is a little longer than the scene to which it corresponds. You will use this extra time before and after the scene to create a fade-in and a fade-out effect.

Create a fade-in and a fade-out on the Wind02 clip:

1. If it is not already selected, click on the **A...Z** button in the Edit window to enable Commands Keyboard Focus mode. The **A...Z** button is located above the tracks display area on the right. When selected, the button becomes highlighted in yellow.

Figure PR2.12
Clicking the Commands Keyboard Focus button

Tip: Commands Keyboard Focus mode gives you access to many Pro Tools commands at the touch of a single keystroke. Focus keys are covered throughout the Avid Learning Series courses and are summarized in the Pro Tools 310M and 310P books.

2. Using the **GRABBER** tool, click the Wind02 clip to select it.

3. Press **E** on your keyboard to activate Zoom Toggle. The selected clip will expand to fill the available space in the Edit window.

4. With the SCRUBBER tool, click and drag near the start of the clip.

   Gradually move the mouse back and forth while viewing the Video window. Locate the point where the scene changes to the squire walking. Release the mouse to position the insertion point at this spot.

5. Press **D** on your keyboard to create a fade-in.

6. With the SCRUBBER tool, click and drag near the end of the clip.

   Gradually move the mouse back and forth while viewing the Video window. Locate the point where the squire approaches the stairs before the scene changes to the king's throne room. Release the mouse to position the insertion point at this spot.

7. Press **G** on your keyboard to create a fade-out.

8. Press **E** on your keyboard to deactivate Zoom Toggle, returning the session to the previous view.

Add Drumstick Drop

The next sound effect you need to add is the Drumstick Drop. For this sound effect, you will need to sync the impact point of the sound effect to the point in the movie at which the drumstick hits the plate. To do this, you will use a Sync Point.

Place the Drumstick Drop sound effect on the FX 05 track and identify a Sync Point:

1. Identify the FX 05 track on screen and make sure it is visible.

2. Locate the DRUMSTICK DROP clip in the Clip List and drag it onto any open space of the FX 05 track.

3. With the clip selected, press **E** on your keyboard to activate Zoom Toggle and zoom in on the clip.

4. With the SCRUBBER tool, click and drag across the clip until you hear the sound of the drumstick making impact. Release the mouse to position the insertion point as close as possible to the beginning of the impact.

5. Choose CLIP > IDENTIFY SYNC POINT. A small triangle will appear in the lower part of the clip, under the insertion cursor, signifying a Sync Point at that spot.

6. Press **E** on your keyboard to deactivate Zoom Toggle, returning the session to the previous view.

Having identified a Sync Point in the sound effect clip, you will now need to determine the corresponding point in the movie and spot the sound effect to that point.

Spot the Drumstick Drop sound effect to the movie:

1. With the **Scrubber** tool selected, click and drag on the Video track to locate the point when the drumstick hits the plate. The impact should occur somewhere between 0:13.200 and 0:13.500 (Min:Sec). Take note of the exact time location shown in the Main Counter.

2. Click the **Spot** button in the Edit window to activate Spot mode.

3. With the **Grabber** tool, click on the **Drumstick Drop** clip on the FX 05 track. The Spot dialog box will appear.

4. In the Sync Point field, type the time that you noted in Step 1. Be sure to use the same Time Scale in this dialog box as displayed in the Main Counter (Min:Sec).

5. Click **OK**. The clip's Sync Point will be spotted to the point where the drumstick hits the plate.

6. Click the **Slip** button to return to Slip mode.

Audition the sound effect:

1. Using the **Selector** tool, place the insertion point somewhere around 0:12.000.

2. Press the **space bar** to play back the sound effect with the picture.

3. When finished, press the **space bar** again to stop playback.

4. Press **Enter** (Windows) or **Return** (Mac) to return to the beginning of the Timeline.

Change the Music

Next you will need to replace the existing music for the project to give the soundtrack a different emotional undertone. To do this, you will select from the music that you imported to the Clip List, place the selected music onto the MX New track, and trim the new music to the proper length.

Audition the music in the Clip List:

1. Locate the New Music 1 and New Music 2 clips on the Clip List. If necessary, scroll the Clip List until the New Music clips are visible.

2. **ALT-CLICK** (Windows) or **OPTION-CLICK** (Mac) on the **NEW MUSIC 1** clip in the Clip List. The audio clip will play back as long as you hold down the mouse button.

3. Release the mouse button to stop the audition.

4. Repeat Steps 2 and 3, auditioning the **NEW MUSIC 2** clip.

5. After listening to each music clip, select the clip that you feel is more appropriate for the project. We will refer to this as the Preferred New Music clip for descriptive purposes. (You can use either clip to complete the project.)

Place the selected clip onto the MX New Audio track:

1. Locate the **MX MIX** track and the **MX NEW** track in the Edit window.

2. Using the **GRABBER** tool, click on the **MX_MIX** clip on the MX Mix track. The clip will become highlighted.

3. Hold the **START** key (Windows) or **CONTROL** key (Mac) while dragging the **PREFERRED NEW MUSIC** clip from the Clip List onto the **MX NEW** track. The clip will appear on the track, aligned to the same start time as the MX_Mix clip above it.

Shortcut: Holding the START key (Windows) or CONTROL key (Mac) while dragging a clip from the Clip List constrains its placement to begin at the insertion point or the start time of a selection.

4. Mute the MX Mix track by clicking the **M** button under the track name in the Edit window.

5. Press **ENTER** or **RETURN** to move the insertion point to the beginning of the Timeline, followed by the **SPACE BAR** to play back the session with the new music track.

6. At the end of the clip, press the **SPACE BAR** a second time to stop playback.

Save Work in Progress

You have now completed the editing tasks for your project. You should take this opportunity to save your work.

Save your work:

1. Choose **FILE > SAVE** to save your progress up to this point.

Mixing in Pro Tools

Now that all of the editing is complete, you will use some of the mixing features in Pro Tools to add some real-time processing and blend all of the sound elements together.

Remove the Hum

The Squire 01 clip on the DX 03 track contains a low-frequency hum that you will now need to remove. Using some creative EQ, you can eliminate most of the hum. To do so, you will need to locate and zoom in on the clip, insert an EQ plug-in on the track, and selectively adjust the EQ settings.

Locate and zoom in on the Squire 01 clip:

1. Click on the **Squire 01** clip in the Clip List to select the clip on the Track Playlist. If necessary, scroll the Clip List until the clip is visible (toward the bottom).

Figure PR2.13
Click on the clip in the Clip List to select it

2. Press **E** on your keyboard to activate Zoom Toggle and zoom in. The Squire 01 clip will expand to fill the Edit window.

Insert the EQ III 1-Band on the DX 03 track:

1. Choose **WINDOW > MIX** to activate the Mix window or press **CTRL+=** (Windows) or **COMMAND+=** (Mac).

2. Locate the channel strip for the DX 03 track.

3. Click on **INSERT SELECTOR A** for the track and choose **PLUG-IN > EQ > EQ 3 1-BAND (MONO)** from the pop-up menu. The EQ III 1-band plug-in window will appear.

Figure PR2.14
The EQ III 1-band plug-in window

Adjust the EQ settings to reduce the hum:

1. Solo the DX 03 track by clicking on the **S** button just above the Volume Fader in the Mix window.

2. Press the **SPACE BAR** to initiate playback. With Loop Playback enabled, the clip will loop until playback is stopped.

3. In the EQ III 1-Band plug-in window, activate a Notch filter in the **TYPE** section and drag the gray ball in the graphic display to the left until you hear the hum reduced (around 60 Hz).

4. Press the **SPACE BAR** to stop playback.

5. Close the plug-in window and un-solo the track.

6. Press **CTRL+=** (Windows) or **COMMAND+=** (Mac) to toggle to the Edit window and press **E** on your keyboard to return the session to the previous view.

Add Reverb

Next, you will need to add some reverb to the FX 08 track to help it fit into the rest of the mix. This project includes an Auxiliary Input track that has already been configured with the D-Verb plug-in assigned and the track input assigned to Bus 1-2 (Reverb).

Assign a reverb send on the FX 08 track:

1. Press **CTRL+=** (Windows) or **COMMAND+=** (Mac) to toggle to the Mix window.

2. Locate the **FX 08** channel strip for the Skunk FX.

3. Click on the **SEND SELECTOR A** for the track and choose **BUS > REVERB (STEREO).** The Send A window will appear.

Figure PR2.15
Selecting a send assignment opens the Send window (foreground)

Increase the Send A level on the FX 08 track:

1. Click the **SOLO** button in the Send A window to solo the FX 08 track.

2. Press **CTRL+=** (Windows) or **COMMAND+=** (Mac) to toggle to the Edit window.

3. Using the **SELECTOR** tool, select the audio near the end of the Skunk Group clip group (starting around 0:31.500 and continuing through the end of the clip).

4. With Loop Playback enabled, press the SPACE BAR to begin playback.

5. While listening to the track, raise the level on the send fader to introduce the reverb.

   The reverb will play back while the FX 08 track is soloed because the Reverb track is set to Solo Safe mode. Solo Safe is commonly used on Auxiliary tracks to prevent them from being muted when another track is soloed.

Tip: You can place a track in Solo Safe mode by CTRL-CLICKING (Windows) or COMMAND-CLICKING (Mac) on the Solo button in the Edit or Mix window.

In the Avid Learning Series   More information on Solo Safe mode can be found in the Pro Tools 110 course.

6. When you are satisfied with the results, press the SPACE BAR to stop playback.

7. Press the SOLO button to take the track out of solo mode and close the Send A window.

Enhance the Knock

This project includes a knock sweetener effect that sounds a bit dull. You will need to add some delay and EQ to liven up the sound. You will add delay using an AudioSuite plug-in and add EQ using a 7-Band EQ III plug-in insert.

A Note about AudioSuite Plug-Ins

You will be using the Mod Delay II AudioSuite plug-in to add a delay sound effect. AudioSuite plug-ins behave differently from insert plug-ins in that they are not real-time processors. These plug-ins process and modify audio files on disk, rather than adding the plug-in effect in real time.

In the Avid Learning Series   More information on AudioSuite processing can be found in the Pro Tools 110 course.

Zoom in on the Knock Sweetener clip on the FX 04 track:

1. Select KNOCK SWEETENER in the Clip List to select the clip in the Track Playlist.

2. Press E on your keyboard to activate Zoom Toggle. The Knock Sweetener clip will expand to fill the Edit window.

Use the Mod Delay II to process the Knock Sweetener clip:

1. Choose **AudioSuite > Delay > Delay**. The Mod Delay II plug-in window will appear on screen.

2. Verify that **Use in Playlist** is highlighted. If it isn't, click to highlight it.

3. Adjust the parameter settings to create a long echo effect. Try the following settings as a starting point:

   - **Mix** = 25%

   - **Delay** = 500.00ms

   - **Feedback** = 40%

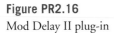

Figure PR2.16
Mod Delay II plug-in

Tip: The Mod Delay II plug-in includes separate parameters for the left and right sides. Since you are using it on a mono track, you only need to set the parameters for the left side.

4. To audition the effect, click **Preview**. During Preview, you may continue to adjust the effect parameters using the sliders, as desired.

5. When you are satisfied with the effect, click **Render** to process the audio clip. A new clip will be generated, combining the source audio with the Delay effect and replacing the selected clip.

6. Close the Delay plug-in window to reduce on-screen clutter.

Add the EQ III 7-Band to Insert A on the FX 04 track:

1. Using the Inserts column in the Edit window, click on INSERT SELECTOR
   A for the FX 04 track and choose PLUG-IN > EQ > EQ 3 7-BAND
   (MONO). The EQ III plug-in window will open.

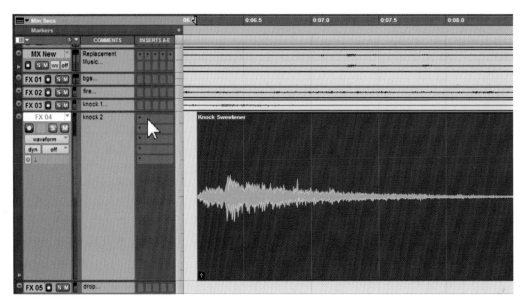

Figure PR2.17
Clicking Insert Selector A in the Edit window

2. With Loop Playback still active, press the SPACE BAR to start playback.
   The Knock Sweetener region will repeat until playback is stopped.

3. Experiment by raising and lowering the colored balls in the graphic display
   of the EQ III plug-in window.

4. When you are satisfied with the results, close the plug-in window and
   press the SPACE BAR to stop playback.

5. Press E on your keyboard to return the session to the previous view.

Save Work in Progress

You have now created a complete mix for your project. You should take this opportunity to save your work.

Save your work:

1. Choose FILE > SAVE to save your progress up to this point.

Listen to the Automated Mix

This portion of the project allows you to experience some of the power that automation offers by activating the preset automation included in the session.

Throughout this project, you have completed your work with all of the track automation modes set to **Auto Off**. Now you will switch the tracks to **Auto Read** mode and play back the session using the previously recorded automation playlists.

In the Avid Learning Series — Automation features are covered in detail throughout the courses in the Avid Learning Series.

Enable Auto Read automation mode for all tracks:

1. Choose **Window > Mix** or press **Ctrl+=** (Windows) or **Command+=** (Mac) to activate the Mix window.

2. **Alt-click** (Windows) or **Option-click** (Mac) on the **Automation Mode selector** for any track and choose **Read**. All of the tracks in the session will switch to Read automation mode.

Figure PR2.18
Selecting Read mode from the Automation Mode selector (Mix window)

3. If needed, choose **View > Narrow Mix** to maximize the number of channel strips being displayed on screen.

Figure PR2.19
Mix window in Narrow Mix view showing all tracks

4. Press **ENTER** (Windows) or **RETURN** (Mac) to move to the beginning of the Timeline, followed by the **SPACE BAR** to play back the session. The Volume Faders and Pan knobs will move automatically to help create a more dynamic mix.

5. When the clip ends, press the **SPACE BAR** a second time to stop playback.

Finishing Your Work

Now that the project is mixed, you will need to create a bounce of the movie to add your version of the soundtrack to the movie file. This will enable the file to be played in a standard movie player application with the soundtrack you've created so that you can share your work with others.

Lastly, you will need to archive your work. Through the process of creating a project you generate many files, not all of which are needed for the completed session. By archiving your work, you are able to preserve your work without taking up excess disk space due to unnecessary files.

Bounce the Movie

You will use the Bounce to Movie command to add your soundtrack mix to the movie file.

Bounce your mix into the movie file:

1. Choose **WINDOW > EDIT** or press **CTRL+=** (Windows) or **COMMAND+=** (Mac) to activate the Edit window.

2. With the **GRABBER** tool, click on the GiftBasket clip on the Video track to select it.

3. Choose **FILE > BOUNCE TO > QUICKTIME MOVIE**. The Bounce dialog box will appear on screen.

4. Click **BOUNCE**. A Save Bounce As dialog box will appear on screen.

5. Select a location for the movie file in the **SAVE IN** section of the dialog box and enter a name for your file in the **FILE NAME** field.

6. Click **SAVE**. You will hear playback begin as Pro Tools creates a QuickTime movie containing your mix and the Video track.

Archive Your Work

Now that your project is complete, you will need to back it up for storage. On a real-world project, you might also need to deliver the session to the client. Because many files are associated with a session, there is a potential that something could get lost if the archival process isn't completed properly. Fortunately, Pro Tools has many features to help ensure that you keep the files you need and remove the files you do not.

In this process, you will complete the following steps:

1. Remove unused audio files and clips that are consuming space on your hard drive.

2. Use the Save Copy In command to "collect" all of the audio and video files and copy them to a new location.

3. Use the Compact Selected command to remove the unused portions of each audio file in the copied session.

Note: The archival process will permanently remove any audio that is not currently being used in the session. This could limit your creative possibilities, should you need to revise some aspect of the session in the future. Perform this process only *after* the project is complete.

Remove Unused Material

To remove unused audio files and clips, complete the following steps:

1. Click on the **CLIP LIST POP-UP** menu and choose **SELECT > UNUSED**. All of the clips that are not included on a Track Playlist will be selected.

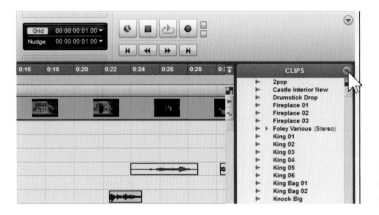

Figure PR2.20
Click the Clip List pop-up menu to select unused clips.

2. Click on the **CLIP LIST POP-UP** menu a second time and choose **CLEAR**. The Clear Clips dialog box will appear on screen.

3. Click **REMOVE** in the Clear Clips dialog box to remove the clips from your session. The audio files will be removed from the session without being deleted from the drive. If you later find that you need an audio file that has been removed, you can re-import it into your session.

Collect Session Files in a New Location

To save a copy of your session and all associated files, do the following:

1. Choose **FILE > SAVE COPY IN**. The Save Session Copy dialog box will appear on screen.

2. In the **ITEMS TO COPY** area, select the following:

   - **AUDIO FILES**
   - **MOVIE/VIDEO FILES**

3. Click the **OK** button. A Save dialog box will appear.

4. Choose a directory to store the session copy and name the copy of the session. If possible, it is best to choose a directory on a drive other than the one used for the current session.

5. Click the **SAVE** button. Pro Tools will begin processing the save, copying the session file along with all of the audio and video files into the directory you chose.

6. Choose **FILE** > **CLOSE SESSION** to close the original session. If you are prompted to save, choose **SAVE** or **OK** to save your changes in the original session. (It will be saved with the unused material removed.)

Compact Your Session

You have one more step to complete your archive: compacting. Most clips in a session reference only a part of a larger audio recording. Because the copied session is now complete, it is safe to compact the session. Compacting is the process of removing the audio from a file that is not used by any clip. Hence, only the used portions of the audio files remain, reducing the amount of disk space being consumed.

To compact your project's audio files, do the following:

1. From the File menu, choose **OPEN SESSION**.

2. Navigate to the copy of your project that you created in the previous section; select the session file and click **OPEN**. A dialog box may appear, indicating that the original disk allocation cannot be used; click **No** to avoid saving a report.

3. When the session opens, click on the **CLIP LIST POP-UP** menu and choose **SELECT** > **ALL**. All of the clips in the Clip List will be selected.

4. Click on the **CLIP LIST POP-UP** menu a second time and choose **COMPACT**. The Compact dialog box will appear on screen with a description of the compacting process.

5. Click **COMPACT** to compact the audio files. Pro Tools will begin modifying the files.

6. When finished, save your work by choosing **FILE** > **SAVE** and close your session by choosing **FILE** > **CLOSE SESSION**.

This concludes the Post Hands-On Project.

Course Completion Information and Appendixes

OVERVIEW

Part IV of the Pro Tools 101 course can be completed in an instructor-led environment at an official Avid Learning Partner location. In this part of the course, you will have the opportunity to work with additional project material, including music sessions by major-label recording artists and post-production sessions for commercial television advertisements and/or movie trailers. Upon completing the coursework, you will be eligible to enroll in the Pro Tools 110 course to continue your Pro Tools training and further your pursuit of Avid Pro Tools certification.

COMPONENTS

Information for Course Completion

Appendix A	Avid Pro Tools Plug-Ins
Appendix B	Creative Collection Plug-Ins

Information for Course Completion

This section provides information for completing the Pro Tools 101 course through an official Avid Learning Partner. Included are instructions for locating an Avid Learning Partner, descriptions of the additional project materials that are available, a description of the course assessment exam, and information on continuing your work toward Pro Tools certification.

Locating an Avid Partner

The Pro Tools 101 course can be completed at any of the 250-plus Avid Learning Partner facilities located in more than 30 countries worldwide. Partner locations offering the Pro Tools 101 course include colleges, technical programs, trade schools, high schools, and other institutions. Depending on the school's training format, Pro Tools courses may span days, weeks, or semesters and may or may not be integrated within a broader educational curriculum.

Avid Learning Partner locations have the ability to deliver exams and certification directly, giving students additional enrollment benefits. With locations in countries such as Australia, Canada, China, France, Germany, Ireland, the Netherlands, Spain, Switzerland, the United Kingdom, the United States, and others, official Pro Tools training is available in most major cities worldwide.

A list of available training centers can be found on the Avid website (go to www.avid.com/US/support/training/find-partner). The web-based partner locator can be used to search for training centers by name or by geographic location.

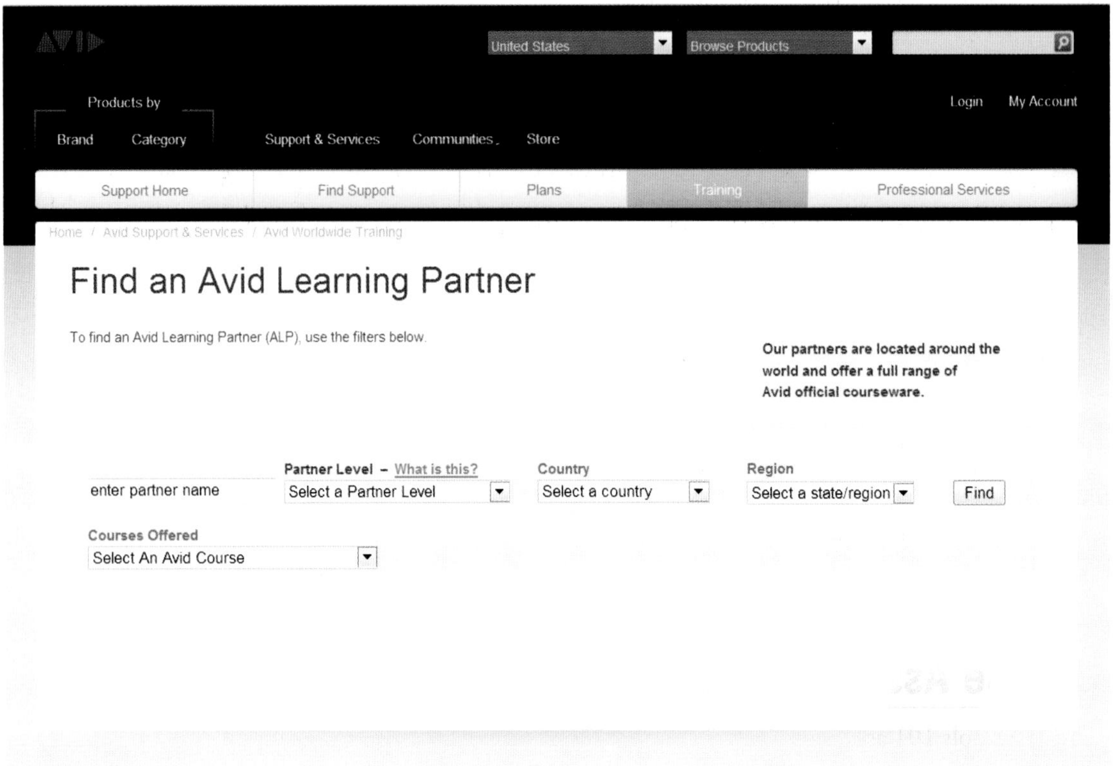

Figure IV.1
Training partner lookup page on the Avid website

Additional Projects

Additional project materials are available at official training partner facilities. As part of your Pro Tools 101 course completion and other Pro Tools courses that you enroll in, you may have the opportunity to work with some of these projects. (Check with the school for completion requirements and project availability.)

Some of the projects that are available include the following:

■ **Black Eyed Peas, "Hey Mama."** This project is a live recording of the band mixed through a VENUE system and recorded as a multi-track session into Pro Tools.

■ *The Time Machine.* This project, a movie trailer for the 2002 movie starring Guy Pearce, Samantha Mumba, Jeremy Irons, and Orlando Jones, features video footage from the movie along with dialogue, music, and sound effects. Session and media files provided courtesy of Dreamworks, SKG.

- **Ugly Duckling.** This television commercial for Ugly Duckling Car Rental is an ideal beginning project for students interested in post-production applications for Pro Tools. Session and media files provided courtesy of Greg Kuehn at Peligro Music & Sound Design.

- *NewsRadio.* In this scene from the U.S. sitcom, one of the characters interviews fellow employees about sharing his apartment. The project contains video footage with audio that lends itself to editing and replacing dialogue. Footage produced by Brillstein/Grey Entertainment; session and media files provided courtesy of BGE.

- Session files of releases by popular recording artists, including:
  - Arcade Fire, "Rococo"
  - Paul Oakenfold, "Bleeder"
  - Romero/Rich Tozzoli, "La Vida Nueva"
  - Westside Connection, "Gangsta Nation"

Course Assessment Exam

The Pro Tools 101 assessment exam consists of 50 multiple-choice questions. The exam is conducted at Avid Learning Partner facilities upon course completion. Students have a specified time limit to answer all questions. A passing score on the assessment exam entitles you to receive a Certificate of Completion for the course.

Certificate of Completion

Upon successful completion of the coursework and assessment exam, you will receive a Certificate of Completion to formally recognize your accomplishment. The Pro Tools 101 completion certificate signifies that you are adequately prepared for the Pro Tools 110 course and continuing progress toward User, Operator, or Expert Certification.

Pro Tools 110

After completing the Pro Tools 101 course, you may enroll in the next course, Pro Tools 110, at any Avid Learning Partner facility, subject to any school prerequisites. Successful completion of the Pro Tools 110 course readies students for the Pro Tools User Certification exam, which is also administered at Avid Learning Partner facilities.

Additional certification options are available at the 200- and 300-level (Operator and Expert Certification, respectively).

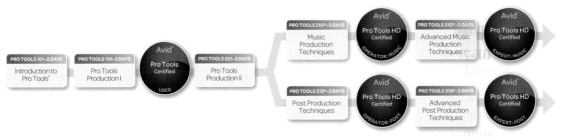

Figure IV.2
Avid audio coursework and certification options

Avid Pro Tools Plug-Ins

The following DSP, Native, and AudioSuite plug-ins are installed with Pro Tools 10:

- **BF-76** (DSP, Native, and AudioSuite). Vintage-style compressor plug-in modeled after the solid-state (transistor) 1176 studio compressor.

- **Channel Strip** (Native). Combines EQ, Dynamics, Filter, and Gain effects processing in a single user interface. The Channel Strip processing algorithms are based on the award-winning Euphonix System 5 console channel strip effects.

- **DigiRack Click** (DSP and Native). Creates an audio click during session playback to serve as a metronome-type tempo reference when performing and recording.

- **Dither** (DSP and Native). Minimizes quantization artifacts when reducing the bit depth of an audio signal.

- **DownMixer** (Native). Provides down-mixing (fold-down) for surround formats (7.1 to stereo, 5.1 to stereo, LCRS to stereo, and LCR to stereo) and stereo-to-mono processing.

- **D-Verb** (DSP, Native, and AudioSuite). Provides studio-quality reverb effects for an audio signal.

- **Dynamics III**: Compressor/Limiter, Expander/Gate, De-Esser (DSP, Native, and AudioSuite). Provides compression/limiting, expansion/gate, and de-esser processing for level control and gain reduction.

- **EQ III**: 7-Band, 2 to 4-Band, 1-Band (DSP, Native, and AudioSuite). Provides three formats for equalization, allowing you to choose the number of bands you need to properly EQ each track.

- **Lo-Fi** (DSP, Native, and AudioSuite). Provides retro and down-processing effects, including bit-rate reduction, sample-rate reduction, soft clipping distortion and saturation, anti-aliasing filter, and a variable amplitude noise generator.

- **DigiRack Mod Delay II** (DSP, Native, and AudioSuite). Provides five different plug-ins for delay (echo) effects of various lengths: Short Delay (up to 43 ms), Slap Delay (up to 171 ms), Medium Delay (up to 341 ms), Long Delay (up to 683 ms), and Extra Long Delay (up to 2.73 seconds).

- **Mod Delay III** (DSP, Native, and AudioSuite). Updated version of the DigiRack Mod Delay II.

- **Maxim** (DSP, Native, and AudioSuite). Provides peak-limiting and sound maximizing for critical mastering applications, as well as standard peak-limiting tasks.

- **DigiRack Pitch** (DSP only). Provides pitch transposition for pitch correction, sound design, and special effects purposes.

- **POW-r Dither** (DSP and Native). An advanced type of dither providing optimal bit-depth reduction for critical mixdown and mastering tasks.

- **Recti-Fi** (DSP, Native, AudioSuite). Provides additive harmonic processing effects through waveform rectification; includes subharmonic synthesizer, full wave rectifier, pre-filter for adjusting effect frequency, and post-filter for smoothing generated waveforms.

- **ReWire** (Native). Provides real-time audio and MIDI streaming between Pro Tools and ReWire client applications, with sample-accurate synchronization and transport control.

- **Sci-Fi** (DSP, Native, AudioSuite). Provides analog synthesizer-type effects, including ring modulation; frequency modulation; variable-frequency; positive and negative resonator; and modulation control by LFO, envelope follower, sample-and-hold, or trigger-and-hold.

- **Signal Generator** (DSP, Native, and AudioSuite). Produces audio test tones in a variety of frequencies, waveforms, and amplitudes, such as reference signals for calibration.

- **DigiRack Signal Tools**: SurroundScope, PhaseScope (DSP and Native). Provides surround metering for multi-channel track types with SurroundScope (Pro Tools HD and Pro Tools with Complete Production Toolkit only) or signal-level and phase information for stereo tracks with PhaseScope.

- **TimeAdjuster** (DSP and Native). Provides compensation for delays due to DSP or Native routing; also provides gain compensation (+/– 24 dB) and phase inversion for correcting out-of-phase signals.

- **Trim** (DSP and Native). Can be used to attenuate an audio signal from –infinity to +6 dB or +12 dB; a multi-mono Trim plug-in provides muting control over individual channels of a multi-channel track.

The following AudioSuite-only plug-ins are installed with Pro Tools 10:

- **DigiRack D-Fx** (Chorus, Flanger, Multi-Tap Delay, Ping-Pong Delay). Adds chorusing (shimmering), flanging (swirling), or delay (echo) effects to a signal, based on the selected plug-in.

- **DigiRack Pitch Shift**. Adjusts the pitch of any source audio file with or without changing its duration.

- **DigiRack Time Compression/Expansion**. Adjusts the duration of selected clips, increasing or decreasing their length without affecting pitch.

- **DigiRack Time Shift**. Provides high-quality time compression and expansion (TCE) algorithms and formant-correct pitch shifting.

- **DC Offset Removal**. Removes DC offset (a type of audio artifact) from audio files to prevent pops and clicks in edited material.

- **Duplicate**. Duplicates the selected audio in place, creating a new, continuous audio file.

- **Gain**. Boosts or lowers a selected clip's amplitude by a specific amount.

- **Invert**. Reverses the polarity of selected audio.

- **Normalize**. Optimizes the volume level of an audio selection to correct low-amplitude signals or inconsistent volume levels.

- **Reverse**. Replaces audio with a reversed version of the selection to create a reverse envelope effect or backward playback of a selection.

- **Vari-Fi**. Provides a pitch-change effect similar to a tape deck or record turntable speeding up from or slowing down to a complete stop.

Creative Collection Plug-Ins

The following Creative Collection effects plug-ins are installed with Pro Tools 10:

- **Chorus.** Applies a short modulated delay to give depth and space to the audio signal.

- **Decimator.** Provides bit-crushing, down-sampling, clipping, rectifying, and mangling effects.

- **Distortion.** Colors the audio signal with various types and amounts of distortion.

- **Dynamic Delay.** Provides a delay (echo) that can synchronize to the Pro Tools session tempo and be modulated by an Envelope follower.

- **Enhancer.** Enhances the low and high broadband frequencies of the audio signal.

- **Ensemble.** Applies fluid, shimmering modulation effects to the audio signal.

- **Filter Gate.** Adds aggressive or subtle rhythmic filtering effects to audio signals.

- **Flanger.** Applies a short modulating delay to the audio signal; the Rate control can be synchronized to the Pro Tools session tempo in various rhythmic patterns.

- **Frequency Shifter.** Changes the pitch of the audio signal.

- **FuzzWah.** Colors the audio signal with various types and amounts of distortion and wah filtering.

- **Kill-EQ.** Zaps out the Low, Mid, or High broadband frequency range from an audio signal for instantaneous "kill switch"–type EQ effects.

- **Multi-Chorus.** Applies a thick, complex Chorus effect to the audio signal, with a user-selectable number of voices (layers).

- **Multi-Tap Delay.** Applies up to six delay lines to the audio signal with selectable rhythmic values, levels, and pan for each.

- **Non-Linear Reverb.** Applies special gated or reversed Reverb effects to the audio signal, creating a synthetic, processed ambience.

- **Phaser.** Applies the classic "whooshy," "squishy" phaser sound to an audio signal; the Rate control can be synchronized to the Pro Tools session tempo in various rhythmic patterns.

- **Reverb.** Applies reverberation to an audio signal to create a sense of room or space.

- **Spring Reverb.** Applies the familiar analog spring reverb sound found in many classic guitar amps and vintage audio gear.

- **Stereo Width.** Creates a wider stereo presence for mono audio signals.

- **Talkbox.** Adds voice-like resonances to audio signals.

- **Vintage Filter.** Applies a modulating, resonant filter to the audio signal.

The following Creative Collection instrument plug-ins are installed with Pro Tools 10:

- **Boom.** A virtual drum machine featuring a broad range of percussion sounds, paired with a simple, drum-machine-style pattern sequencer.

- **DB-33.** A virtual organ with a focus on re-creating the sounds and controllability of classic tonewheel organs and rotating speaker cabinets.

- **Mini Grand.** A virtual piano instrument with seven different acoustic piano sounds to suit a range of styles.

- **Structure Free.** A sample player that brings the world of Structure-compatible sample libraries to Pro Tools.

- **Vacuum.** A virtual analog synthesizer focused on creating rich timbres with a lot of sonic control and employing a new vacuum-tube synthesis method.

- **Xpand².** A virtual workstation synthesizer featuring multi-sampled instruments, FM synthesis, wavetable synthesis, and virtual analog synthesis.

INDEX

License Agreement/Notice of Limited Warranty

By opening the sealed disc container in this book, you agree to the following terms and conditions. If, upon reading the following license agreement and notice of limited warranty, you cannot agree to the terms and conditions set forth, return the unused book with unopened disc to the place where you purchased it for a refund.

License:

The enclosed software is copyrighted by the copyright holder(s) indicated on the software disc. You are licensed to copy the software onto a single computer for use by a single user and to a backup disc. You may not reproduce, make copies, or distribute copies or rent or lease the software in whole or in part, except with written permission of the copyright holder(s). You may transfer the enclosed disc only together with this license, and only if you destroy all other copies of the software and the transferee agrees to the terms of the license. You may not decompile, reverse assemble, or reverse engineer the software.

Notice of Limited Warranty:

The enclosed disc is warranted by Course Technology to be free of physical defects in materials and workmanship for a period of sixty (60) days from end user's purchase of the book/disc combination. During the sixty-day term of the limited warranty, Course Technology will provide a replacement disc upon the return of a defective disc.

Limited Liability:

THE SOLE REMEDY FOR BREACH OF THIS LIMITED WARRANTY SHALL CONSIST ENTIRELY OF REPLACEMENT OF THE DEFECTIVE DISC. IN NO EVENT SHALL COURSE TECHNOLOGY OR THE AUTHOR BE LIABLE FOR ANY OTHER DAMAGES, INCLUDING LOSS OR CORRUPTION OF DATA, CHANGES IN THE FUNCTIONAL CHARACTERISTICS OF THE HARDWARE OR OPERATING SYSTEM, DELETERIOUS INTERACTION WITH OTHER SOFTWARE, OR ANY OTHER SPECIAL, INCIDENTAL, OR CONSEQUENTIAL DAMAGES THAT MAY ARISE, EVEN IF COURSE TECHNOLOGY AND/OR THE AUTHOR HAS PREVIOUSLY BEEN NOTIFIED THAT THE POSSIBILITY OF SUCH DAMAGES EXISTS.

Disclaimer of Warranties:

COURSE TECHNOLOGY AND THE AUTHOR SPECIFICALLY DISCLAIM ANY AND ALL OTHER WARRANTIES, EITHER EXPRESS OR IMPLIED, INCLUDING WARRANTIES OF MERCHANTABILITY, SUITABILITY TO A PARTICULAR TASK OR PURPOSE, OR FREEDOM FROM ERRORS. SOME STATES DO NOT ALLOW FOR EXCLUSION OF IMPLIED WARRANTIES OR LIMITATION OF INCIDENTAL OR CONSEQUENTIAL DAMAGES, SO THESE LIMITATIONS MIGHT NOT APPLY TO YOU.

Other:

This Agreement is governed by the laws of the State of Massachusetts without regard to choice of law principles. The United Convention of Contracts for the International Sale of Goods is specifically disclaimed. This Agreement constitutes the entire agreement between you and Course Technology regarding use of the software.